First World War
and Army of Occupation
War Diary
France, Belgium and Germany

32 DIVISION
Divisional Troops
Machine Gun Corps
32 Battalion
21 February 1918 - 31 October 1919

WO95/2385/5

The Naval & Military Press Ltd
www.nmarchive.com
Published in association with The National Archives

Published by

The Naval & Military Press Ltd

Unit 10 Ridgewood Industrial Park,

Uckfield, East Sussex,

TN22 5QE England

Tel: +44 (0) 1825 749494

www.naval-military-press.com

www.nmarchive.com

This diary has been reprinted in facsimile from the original. Any imperfections are inevitably reproduced and the quality may fall short of modern type and cartographic standards.

© Crown Copyright
Images reproduced by permission of The National Archives, London, England, 2015.

Contents

Document type	Place/Title	Date From	Date To
Heading	WO95/2385 32 Division 32 Btn Machine Gun Corps Feb 21 1918-Oct 1919		
Heading	Lancashire Division (Late 32nd Divn) 32 Bn Machine Gun Corps 1918 Mar-Oct 1919		
Heading	War Diary 32nd Battn Machine Gun No. 1 Period:- February. 21st to February 28th Vol 1		
War Diary	Boesinghe Camp	21/02/1918	25/02/1918
War Diary	Dekort Camp	26/02/1918	26/02/1918
War Diary	Richmond Camp	27/02/1918	28/02/1918
Miscellaneous	14th. M.G. Coy. 32nd. Divn. H.Q. 96th. M.G. Coy. 14th. Bde. H.Q.	24/02/1918	24/02/1918
Operation(al) Order(s)	M.G. Battalion Operation Order No. 1	24/02/1918	24/02/1918
Miscellaneous	Table "A" Issued With M.G. Operation Order No. 1		
Miscellaneous	B.C.34. C.O. "A" Company "B" Company.	28/02/1918	28/02/1918
Miscellaneous	Machine Gun Instructions For Raids of 21th & 30th Brigades	26/02/1918	26/02/1918
Miscellaneous	14th Infantry Brigade Appendix "A"		
Miscellaneous	Appendix "B" for 86th Infantry Brigade		
Miscellaneous	Appendix "B" for 14th Infantry Brigade.		
Miscellaneous	Appendix "C"		
Miscellaneous	Amendment No. 1 to M.G. Instructions for raids of 14th And 96th Infantry Brigades.	26/02/1918	26/02/1918
Miscellaneous	96th Infantry Brigade No. G.42/15/1	27/02/1918	27/02/1918
Miscellaneous	32nd Divisional Machine Gun Battalion Operation Order No. 3	28/02/1918	28/02/1918
Miscellaneous	Appendix "A" Issued With M.G. Operation Order No. 3		
Heading	32nd Divisional M.G.C. 32nd Battalion Machine Gun Corps March 1918 Appendices Attached:- Operation Orders Maps.		
Heading	War Diary of 32nd B Machine Gun Corps from 1st March 1918 to 31st March 1918		
War Diary	Richmond Camp	01/03/1918	25/03/1918
War Diary	Richmond Camp & Wanqueten	26/03/1918	27/03/1918
War Diary	Richmond Camp Ransart	28/03/1918	28/03/1918
War Diary	Richmond Camp Lattre St. Quentin Adinfer	29/03/1918	29/03/1918
War Diary	Lattre St Quentin Adinfer	30/03/1918	30/03/1918
Heading	Appendices 1 To 20		
Miscellaneous	Machine Gun Instructions No. 1 Occupation of Battle Zone (Army Line)	03/03/1918	03/03/1918
Miscellaneous	Machine Gun Instructions No. 2 Anti-Tank Preparations		
Miscellaneous	Appendix "A" issued with M.G. Instructions No. 2		
Miscellaneous	Machine Gun Instructions No. 3 Lines of Fire.	04/03/1918	04/03/1918
Diagram etc	Reference		
Map	Trenches Corrected to 20.12.17		
Miscellaneous	Machine Gun Instructions No. 4. Extending the front.	04/03/1918	04/03/1918
Miscellaneous	Appendix "B" Issued With M.G. Instructions No. 4		
Map			
Miscellaneous	32nd Battalion Machine Gun Corps Operation Order No. 4. Ref. Sheet A.1. 1/10,000		

Map	Appendix "A"		
Miscellaneous	32nd Battalion Machine Gun Corps Operation Order No. 5	03/03/1918	03/03/1918
Miscellaneous	Appendix "A"		
Operation(al) Order(s)	32nd Battalion Machine Gun Corps. Operation Order. No. 6	09/03/1918	09/03/1918
Operation(al) Order(s)	Appendix "A" Issued With M.G. Operation Order No. 6		
Miscellaneous	32nd Battalion Machine Gun Corps Operation Order No. 7	10/03/1918	10/03/1918
Miscellaneous	Appendix "A"		
Miscellaneous	32nd Battalion Machine Gun Corps. instructions No. 5 Renumbering of Guns.	12/03/1918	12/03/1918
Miscellaneous	Appendix "A" Issued With M.G. Insts. No. 3		
Miscellaneous	Instructions		
Miscellaneous	Appendix II. S.O.S. Lines.		
Operation(al) Order(s)	32nd Battalion Machine Gun Corps. Operation Order No. 8 Ref. Sheet. A1.-1/10000	12/03/1918	12/03/1918
Miscellaneous	Table "A" Issued With O.O. No. 8	12/03/1918	12/03/1918
Miscellaneous	Amendment No. 1 to Machine Gun Instructions No. 5 Dated 12/3/1918	12/03/1918	12/03/1918
Miscellaneous	32nd Battalion Machine Gun Corps Operation Order No. 9	16/03/1918	16/03/1918
Miscellaneous	Machine Gun Instructions For Raids of 96th and 97th Infantry Brigades.		
Miscellaneous	Appendix 'A'		
Miscellaneous	Appendix "C"		
Miscellaneous	Amendment No. 1 to M.G. Instructions for raids of 96th and 37th Infantry Brigades Appendix A Issued With Instructions is Cancelled And the Following Substituted.		
Miscellaneous	Appendix B		
Miscellaneous	Amendment No. 2 to Machine Gun Instructions No. 5 Dated 12.3.18	12/03/1918	12/03/1918
Operation(al) Order(s)	32nd Battalion Machine Gun Corps. Operation Order No. 12	22/03/1918	22/03/1918
Operation(al) Order(s)	32nd. Battalion, Machine Gun Corps. Operation Order No. 11	22/03/1918	22/03/1918
Miscellaneous	32nd Battalion Machine Gun Corps Operation Order No. 14		
Operation(al) Order(s)	Operation Order No. 15. Move of 32nd. Battalion Machine Gun Corps By rail, on 28th, March 1918	28/03/1918	28/03/1918
Miscellaneous	Peselhoek Railhead. Proven Railhead.		
Operation(al) Order(s)	32nd. Battalion Machine Gun Corps, Operation Order No. 17	30/03/1918	30/03/1918
Miscellaneous	32nd Bn M.G.Corps Appendix "A" issued With Operation Order No. 17, D/-30.33.18	30/03/1918	30/03/1918
Heading	VI. Corps. Third Army. War Diary 32nd Battalion. Machine Gun Corps. April 1916 Attached: Appendices 1 to 9		
Heading	War Diary of 32nd Bn. Machine Gun Corps. from 1st April, 1918 to 30th April 1918 Vol 3		
War Diary	Humbercamp	01/04/1918	24/04/1918
War Diary	Humbercamp & Saulty	25/04/1918	25/04/1918
War Diary	Saulty	26/04/1918	30/04/1918
Heading	Appendices 1 to 9		

Miscellaneous	32nd Battalion Machine Gun Corps Operation Order No. 18. App 1	01/04/1918	01/04/1918
Miscellaneous	Table "B"		
Miscellaneous	32nd Battalion Machine Gun Corps Instructions No. 6. S.O.S. Arrangements. App.2	07/04/1918	07/04/1918
Miscellaneous	Table "A".		
Miscellaneous	Amendment No. 1 to 32nd Battalion Machine Gun Corps Instructions No. 6	10/04/1918	10/04/1918
Miscellaneous	Table Issued With Machine Gun Instructions No. 6		
Miscellaneous	32nd Battalion Machine Gun Corps Order No. 19 App.3	09/04/1918	09/04/1918
Miscellaneous	Table "A" A.P.3		
Miscellaneous	32nd Battalion Machine Gun Corps Instructions No. 7 Ammunition Supply App.4	09/04/1918	09/04/1918
Miscellaneous	32nd Battalion Machine Gun Corps Instructions No. 8 Defence Scheme. App 5	12/04/1918	12/04/1918
Miscellaneous	32nd Battalion Machine Gun Corps Instructions No. 9 Harassing Fire. App. 6	14/04/1918	14/04/1918
Miscellaneous	List of Harassing Fire Targets.		
Miscellaneous	Reference 32nd Battalion Machine Gun Corps Instructions No. 9	18/04/1918	18/04/1918
Miscellaneous	32nd Battalion Machine Gun Corps Order No. 20 App.7	15/04/1918	15/04/1918
Miscellaneous	Table issued with 32nd Battalion Machine Gun Corps Order No. 20		
Miscellaneous	32nd Battalion Machine Gun Corps Order No. 21 App 8	23/04/1918	23/04/1918
Miscellaneous	Addendum No. 1 to 32nd Battalion Machine Gun Corps Order No. 21	24/04/1918	24/04/1918
Miscellaneous	32nd Battalion Machine Gun Corps Instructions No. 10 Instructions For M.G. Battalion Reserve. App 9	26/04/1918	26/04/1918
Heading	War Diary of 32nd Bn. Machine Gun Corps From 1st May 1918 to 31st May 1918 Vol. 4		
War Diary	Saulty	01/05/1918	11/05/1918
War Diary	Saulty-Bretencourt	12/05/1918	12/05/1918
War Diary	Bretencourt	13/05/1918	22/05/1918
Miscellaneous	Bretencourt & Gastineau	23/05/1918	23/05/1918
War Diary	Gastineau	24/05/1918	31/05/1918
Operation(al) Order(s)	32nd. Battalion Machine Gun Corps. Operation Order No. 22	04/05/1918	04/05/1918
Miscellaneous	Amendment No. 1 And Addendum No. 1 to 32nd Battalion Machine Gun Corps Instructions No. 10	04/05/1918	04/05/1918
Miscellaneous	32nd Battalion Machine Gun Corps Order No. 23	09/05/1918	09/05/1918
Miscellaneous	32nd. Battalion Machine Gun Corps. Operation Order No. 24	17/05/1918	17/05/1918
Miscellaneous	A Form. Messages And Signals.		
Miscellaneous	Table "A" Issued With Order No. 24		
Miscellaneous	32nd. Battalion Machine Gun Corps. Instructions No. 12	17/05/1918	17/05/1918
Miscellaneous	Table A Issued With Instructions No. 11		
Miscellaneous	32nd Battalion Machine Gun Corps Instructions No. 12	17/05/1918	17/05/1918
Miscellaneous	Harassing Fire Targets Appendix 'A'		
Miscellaneous	Appendix "B"		
Miscellaneous	Addendum No. 1 to N.G. Instructions No. 12	18/05/1918	18/05/1918
Miscellaneous	32nd. Battalion Machine Gun Corps. Instructions No. 13	18/05/1918	18/05/1918

Miscellaneous	Appendix "A" issued with Instructions No. 13		
Miscellaneous	32nd. Battalion Machine Gun Corps. M.G. Instructions For Raid of 14th. Infantry Bde.	09/05/1918	09/05/1918
Miscellaneous	Appendix "A"		
Miscellaneous	Appendix "B"		
Miscellaneous	32nd. Battalion Machine Gun Corps. Operation Order No. 25	20/05/1918	20/05/1918
Miscellaneous	32nd Battalion Machine Gun Corps Provisional Defence Scheme.	22/05/1918	22/05/1918
Miscellaneous	List of Appendices and Maps.		
Miscellaneous	Appendix "A". Machine Gun Dispositions.		
Miscellaneous	Appendix "B" S.O.S. Lines.		
Miscellaneous	Appendix "C". Establishment of Ammunition		
Miscellaneous	Appendix "D". Distribution of Armour Piercing S.A.A.		
Miscellaneous	Appendix "E". A.A. Gun Positions.		
Miscellaneous	Appendix "F". Communications.		
Miscellaneous	Map Showing R.A. Defence To Be Superimposed on Sheets 51c S.E. & 51b S.W.		
Map	M.G. Defence		
Map			
Miscellaneous	32nd Battalion Machine Gun Corps Instructions No. 14	27/05/1918	27/05/1918
Miscellaneous	Appendix "A" Issued With M.G. Instructions No. 14		
Map			
Operation(al) Order(s)	32nd Battalion Machine Gun Corps Operation Order No. 86	27/05/1918	27/05/1918
Heading	War Diary of 32nd Bn Machine Gun Corps From 1st Jan 1918 to 30th June 1918		
War Diary	Gastineau	01/06/1918	30/06/1918
Operation(al) Order(s)	32nd Battalion Machine Gun Corps Order No. 27	02/06/1918	02/06/1918
Heading	Appendix "A"		
Miscellaneous	Appendix "B"		
Operation(al) Order(s)	32nd Battalion Machine Gun Corps Order No. 28	03/06/1918	03/06/1918
Operation(al) Order(s)	32nd Battalion Machine Gun Order No. 29	10/06/1918	10/06/1918
Operation(al) Order(s)	32nd Battalion Machine Gun Corps Order No. 30	12/06/1918	12/06/1918
Miscellaneous	Appendix "A"		
Miscellaneous	Appendix "B"		
Operation(al) Order(s)	32nd Battalion Machine Gun Corps Order No. 31	17/06/1918	17/06/1918
Miscellaneous	32nd Battalion Machine Gun Corps Order No. 32	24/06/1918	24/06/1918
Miscellaneous	32nd Battalion Machine Gun Corps Order No. 33	24/06/1918	24/06/1918
Heading	War Diary of 32 Bn M.G.C. From July 1st/18-July 31st/18 Vol. 6		
War Diary	Berle Au Bois W.10.D.0.1	01/07/1918	05/07/1918
Miscellaneous	Berle Au Bois W.10.D.0.1.& V.7.B.5.5 Saulty	06/07/1918	06/07/1918
War Diary	Saulty	06/07/1918	19/07/1918
War Diary	Proven	20/07/1918	31/07/1918
Miscellaneous	32nd Battalion Machine Gun Corps Order No. 34	03/07/1918	03/07/1918
Miscellaneous	Appendix "A" Machine Gun Dispositions.	05/07/1918	05/07/1918
Miscellaneous	Principles Of Defence		
Miscellaneous	Position Of Headquarters.		
Miscellaneous	Table "A" Front Line S.O.S. Yellow.		
Miscellaneous	Appendix "B" S.O.S. Lines		
Miscellaneous	Appendix "D" Distribution of Armour Piercing S.A.A.		
Miscellaneous	Appendix "E" A.A. Gun Positions.		
Heading	Appendix "F" Communications.		
Miscellaneous	32nd Battalion Machine Gun Corps Instructions No. 15 Defence Orders for Battalion Reserve.	08/07/1918	08/07/1918

Miscellaneous	Appendix "A" Positions of Headquarters of Infantry Brigades VI Corps Front.		
Miscellaneous	Herewith Revised Provisional Defence Scheme. Appendix "C" of former Defence Scheme to be Attached.	06/07/1918	06/07/1918
Miscellaneous	32nd. Battalion Machine Gun Corps Defence Scheme.		
Miscellaneous	32nd Battalion Machine Gun Corps Operation Order No. 33	18/07/1918	18/07/1918
Miscellaneous	Entraining Programme		
Heading	War Diary of 32nd Bn Machine Gun Corps From 1st August 1918 to 31st August 1918 Vol 7		
War Diary	Proven F 14 a. O. 3	01/08/1918	01/08/1918
War Diary	Proven	02/08/1918	07/08/1918
War Diary	Hengist	08/08/1918	08/08/1918
War Diary	Gentelle Wood	09/08/1918	09/08/1918
War Diary	D.14.C	10/08/1918	10/08/1918
War Diary	K.15.A	11/08/1918	11/08/1918
War Diary	K 15 a D. 22 a	12/08/1918	12/08/1918
War Diary	D 22 A	13/08/1918	13/08/1918
War Diary	C.2.C.	14/08/1918	17/08/1918
War Diary	C.2.C.& Villers. Brettoneux	18/08/1918	18/08/1918
War Diary	Villers. Brettoneux	19/08/1918	20/08/1918
War Diary	Villers Brettoneux & Q 32 A.2.2	21/08/1918	21/08/1918
War Diary	Q.32.a.2 2	22/08/1918	27/08/1918
War Diary	Q 32 a.2.2. And Quarry X 23 b.	28/08/1918	28/08/1918
War Diary	Quarry X 23 b	29/08/1918	31/08/1918
Miscellaneous	32nd Battalion Machine Gun Corps Order No. 36	06/08/1918	06/08/1918
Miscellaneous	Addendum No. 1 to 32nd Battalion M.G.Corps Order No. 36	19/08/1918	19/08/1918
Miscellaneous	32nd Battalion Machine Gun Corps Order No. 36. (A)	17/08/1918	17/08/1918
Miscellaneous	32nd Battalion Machine Gun Corps Order No. 37	19/08/1918	19/08/1918
Miscellaneous	32nd Battalion Machine Gun Corps Operation Order No. 38	23/08/1918	23/08/1918
Operation(al) Order(s)	32nd Battalion Machine Gun Corps Operation Order No. 39	24/08/1918	24/08/1918
Operation(al) Order(s)	32nd Battalion Machine Gun Corps Operation Order No. 40	29/08/1918	29/08/1918
Operation(al) Order(s)	32nd Battalion Machine Gun Corps Operation Order No. 41	30/08/1918	30/08/1918
Miscellaneous	32nd Battalion Machine Gun Corps Instructions No. 17	21/08/1918	21/08/1918
War Diary	Amendment No. 1 and Addendum No. 1 to 32nd Battalion M.G. Corps Instructions No. 17	22/08/1918	22/08/1918
Miscellaneous	Appendix "A"		
Miscellaneous	Appendix "B".		
Heading	War Diary of 32nd Bn Machine Gun Corps. from 1st September 1918 to 30th September 1918 Vol. 8		
War Diary	S.4.A.10.20 Soyecourt	01/09/1918	03/09/1918
War Diary	V 11 B 77 Montecourt	08/09/1918	10/09/1918
War Diary	V 11.B.77. Montecourt And V 12. C.5.3	11/09/1918	11/09/1918
War Diary	Monchy Lagache		
War Diary	S 4 a 10.20. Soyecourt	04/09/1918	05/09/1918
War Diary	S 4 a 10.20. Soyecourt and T 22.C.4.7. Marchelepot	06/09/1918	06/09/1918
War Diary	T 22 C 4.7 Marchlepot and V 11 G 77 Montecourt	07/09/1918	07/09/1918
War Diary	V.12.C.5.3 Monchy-Lagache	12/09/1918	13/09/1918
War Diary	V.12.C.5.3 Monchy-Lagache and La Neuville	14/09/1918	14/09/1918
War Diary	I.34.d. La Neuville	15/09/1918	24/09/1918

Type	Description	Start	End
War Diary	Q 32.C. Valley Woods	25/09/1918	27/09/1918
War Diary	R. 15. b. Le Verguier Trench.	28/09/1918	29/09/1918
War Diary	H 25 a 92. Magny-La-Fosse	30/09/1918	30/09/1918
Miscellaneous	32nd Battalion Machine Gun Corps Provisional Instructions for Anticipated Active Operations.	03/09/1918	03/09/1918
Miscellaneous	32nd Battalion Machine Gun Corps Instructions No. 18	03/09/1918	03/09/1918
Miscellaneous	Appendix "A"		
Miscellaneous	Report on Operations Carried out by "B" Company, 32nd Battalion M.G. Corps in conjunction with 13th Australian Light Horse 7.9.18	07/09/1918	07/09/1918
Operation(al) Order(s)	32nd Battalion Machine Gun Corps Operation Order No. 42	07/09/1918	07/09/1918
Operation(al) Order(s)	32nd Battalion Machine Gun Corps Preliminary Instructions No. 19	08/09/1918	08/09/1918
Operation(al) Order(s)	32nd Battalion Machine Gun Corps Instructions No. 20	09/09/1918	09/09/1918
Map	32nd Battalion Machine Gun Corps Operation Order No. 42. A	09/09/1918	09/09/1918
Miscellaneous	32nd Battalion Machine Gun Corps Instructions No. 21	10/09/1918	10/09/1918
Map	32nd Battalion Machine Gun Corps Operation Order No. 45	28/09/1918	28/09/1918
Heading	War Diary of 32nd Bn Machine Gun Corps from 1st October 1918 to 31st October 1918 Vol 9		
War Diary	Magny-La-Fosse	01/10/1918	05/10/1918
War Diary	Magny-La-Fosse & Vendelles	06/10/1918	06/10/1918
War Diary	Vendelles & Bouvincourt	07/10/1918	07/10/1918
War Diary	Bouvincourt	08/10/1918	17/10/1918
War Diary	Bouvincourt & Bellenglise	18/10/1918	18/10/1918
War Diary	Bellenglise	19/10/1918	19/10/1918
Miscellaneous	Bellenglise & Bohain	20/10/1918	20/10/1918
War Diary	Bohain (D 15 + D 27)	21/10/1918	30/10/1918
War Diary	Bohain and Bazuel (R 8 A 8.5)	31/10/1918	31/10/1918
Miscellaneous	32nd Battalion Machine Gun Corps Order No. 44	05/10/1918	05/10/1918
Operation(al) Order(s)	32nd Battalion Machine Gun Corps Operation Order No. 44	29/10/1918	29/10/1918
Heading	War Diary of 32nd Bn Machine Gun Corps 1st November, 1918 to 30th November 1918 Vol 10		
War Diary	Bazuel (R 8 A 8.5.)	01/11/1918	04/11/1918
War Diary	Sambreton G 35 G.0.9	05/11/1918	05/11/1918
War Diary	Grand Fayt (I 31 G 3.8)	06/11/1918	06/11/1918
War Diary	Les Ardennes (J 1 9 b 4.8)	07/11/1918	07/11/1918
War Diary	Avesnelles (K 25a 1.6)	08/11/1918	12/11/1918
War Diary	Sains-Du-Nord. (Q 12 A 0.1)	13/11/1918	18/11/1918
War Diary	Sivry	19/11/1918	19/11/1918
War Diary	Fourbechies	20/11/1918	23/11/1918
War Diary	Cerfontaine	24/11/1918	30/11/1918
Miscellaneous	Report on Operations Commencing 06.00 Hours on 2.11.1918. Appendix I	02/11/1918	02/11/1918
Map	To Superimpose on Oise Canal (1/40.000) or Wassigny (1/40.000) Appendix I		
Map	To be superimposed on Messages Map 1/20,000		
Miscellaneous	Appendix II. Times and Rates of Barrage.		
Map	To Superimpose on Messag Map 1:20,000. Appendix III to 32nd M.G.C. O.O. 45		
Operation(al) Order(s)	Amendment No. 1 Appendices I and to Send Battalion Machine Gun Corps Operation Order No. 45	03/11/1918	03/11/1918

Type	Description	From	To
Operation(al) Order(s)	32nd Battalion Machine Gun Corps Operation Order No. 45/1. Appendix II	03/11/1918	03/11/1918
Operation(al) Order(s)	32nd Battalion Machine Gun Corps Operation Order No. 45. In Connection With 32nd Division Order No. 121. Reference Map-Oise Canal-1/40.000. Appendix III	02/11/1918	02/11/1918
Operation(al) Order(s)	32nd Battalion Machine Gun Corps Order No. 46 Appendix IV	04/11/1918	04/11/1918
Operation(al) Order(s)	32nd Battalion Machine Gun Corps Order No. 47 Appendix V	04/11/1918	04/11/1918
War Diary	Cerfontaine	01/12/1918	11/12/1918
War Diary	Florennes	12/12/1918	12/12/1918
War Diary	Riviere	13/12/1918	13/12/1918
War Diary	Durnal	14/12/1918	31/12/1918
Heading	1War Diary of 32nd Bn Machine Gun Corps from 1st Jan. 1st 1919 to 31st Jan 1919 Vol 12		
War Diary	Durnal	01/01/1919	31/01/1919
Heading	War Diary of 32nd Bn Machine Gun Corps from 1st February 1919 to 28th February 1919 Vol 13		
War Diary	Durnal	01/02/1919	05/02/1919
War Diary	Faulx	06/02/1919	06/02/1919
War Diary	Nameche	07/02/1919	08/02/1919
War Diary	Hersel	09/02/1919	28/02/1919
Heading	War Diary of 32nd Bn Machine Gun Corps from 1st March 1919 to 31st March 1919 Vol 14		
War Diary	Hersel	01/03/1919	27/03/1919
War Diary	Buschdorf	28/03/1919	31/03/1919
Heading	War Diary of 32nd Bn Machine Gun Corps from 1st April 1919 to 30th April 1919		
War Diary	Buschdorf	01/04/1919	03/04/1919
War Diary	Dransdorf	04/04/1919	30/04/1919
Heading	War Diary of 32nd Bn Machine Gun Corps from 1st May 1919 to 31st May 1919		
War Diary	Dransdorf	01/05/1919	28/05/1919
War Diary	Villich	29/05/1919	31/05/1919
Heading	War Diary of 32nd Bn Machine Gun Corps from 1st June 1919 to 30th June 1919		
War Diary	Villich (Germany)	01/06/1919	10/06/1919
War Diary	Villich	11/06/1919	18/06/1919
War Diary	Siegburg	19/06/1919	28/06/1919
War Diary	Vilich	29/06/1919	31/07/1919
Miscellaneous	Lancashire Division "A"	03/09/1919	03/09/1919
Heading	War Diary of 32nd Bn Machine Gun Corps From 1st Augt 1919 to 31st Augt 1919		
War Diary	Vilich	01/08/1919	26/08/1919
War Diary	Troisdorf	27/08/1919	31/08/1919
Heading	War Diary of 32nd Bn M.G.Corps from 1st Sept 1919 to 30th Sept 1919		
War Diary	Troisdorf	01/09/1919	31/10/1919

WO95/2385
32 Division
32 Btn MACHINE GUN CORPS

Feb 21 1916 – Oct 1919

LANCASHIRE DIVISION   32 M.G.C.
(LATE 32ND DIVN)   Jan - Oct '19

32 BN MACHINE GUN CORPS
~~32ND MACHINE GUN COY.~~
1918 MAR   ~~JAN~~ - OCT 1919

CONFIDENTIAL.

War Diary.

32nd Battn Machine Gun.

No. 1.

Period :- February. 21st — February. 28th.

32nd Bn: M.G. Bn.

Army Form C. 2118.

WAR DIARY
or
INTELLIGENCE SUMMARY.
(Erase heading not required.)

Instructions regarding War Diaries and Intelligence Summaries are contained in F.S. Regs., Part II. and the Staff Manual respectively. Title pages will be prepared in manuscript.

Place	Date	Hour	Summary of Events and Information	Remarks and references to Appendices
BOESINGHE CAMP.	21/2/1918		Owing to the reorganisation of M.G. Companies into M.G. Battalions, the four M.G. Companies of the 32nd Division were withdrawn from the Infantry Bdes. and formed into the 32nd Battalion, Machine Gun Corps, on from the 21-2-1918; the four said Companies being the 14th, 97th, 96th and 219th M.G. Companies. The following Officers were appointed to Battalion Headquarters and assumed their duties on formation of the unit:- Lieut. Col. J.T.W. REEVE. — Commanding Officer. Major. F.R. HANBURY. (3rd M.G. Company.) — Second-in-Command. Lieut. A.M. HUMBLE. (97th M.G. Company.) — Adjutant. Lieut. W.G. ELIAS. (96th M.G. Company.) — Transport Officer. Hon. Lieut. W.T. RICHARDSON. (10th Norfolk Regt.) — Quartermaster. BOESINGHE CAMP (B.S.d. 6.1.) was allotted to the Battalion and all personnel, animals, transport etc. arrived at	M.G. Bn. Hq. Map. Sheet. 28. 1/40,000.

Army Form C. 2118.

WAR DIARY
or
INTELLIGENCE SUMMARY.
(Erase heading not required.)

Instructions regarding War Diaries and Intelligence Summaries are contained in F. S. Regs., Part II. and the Staff Manual respectively. Title pages will be prepared in manuscript.

Place	Date	Hour	Summary of Events and Information	Remarks and references to Appendices
BOESINGHE CAMP.	22/2/1918		A.S.C: 5.5. and A.S.C: 5.1. were relieved as follows:- 96th Coy. by 10 guns and 14th Coy, first 12 guns in line; 219th Coy. took all remaining guns and took over HOUTHURST FOREST SECTOR; 97 Coy. took over as Battn. H.Q. Strength of Battn:- Officers. 45. Other ranks 367.	Ry. Map. BELGIUM. 28 N.W. 1/20,000.
"	23/2/1918			
"	24/2/1918		General training and instruction of Companies in Battalion.	
"	25/2/1918		Reorganisation of guns in line took place under O.O. No.1. dated 24-2-1918 and M.G. No. C.O.3. dated 24-2-1918.	APPENDICES Nos:- 1 + 2
DEKORT CAMP	26/2/1918	9-30 P.M.	Battalion marched off from BOESINGHE CAMP	

WAR DIARY
or
INTELLIGENCE SUMMARY.
(Erase heading not required.)

Army Form C. 2118.

Place	Date	Hour	Summary of Events and Information	Remarks and references to Appendices
RICHMOND CAMP	27/2/1918		Battalion took over quarters at DEKORT CAMP (B.3.d.25.50) arriving there at 12.0 midday. On this day, Major G.C. SHIPSTER was appointed 2nd in Command of the Battalion vice Major F.R. HANBURY.	Ry. MAP. BELGIUM. 28. N.W.1. 1/10,000.
			Name of DEKORT CAMP officially changed to that of RICHMOND CAMP. Orders received for this Battalion to be drawn upon 32nd Battalion, Machine Gun Corps and to work the 14, 96, 97 and 216 M.G. Coys as normally, 1.3.14 in relation to R.C. 24 dated 28-2-1918. and D Coy returning in turn. Battalion are-operated on the general lines of the Battalions of the Infantry.	APPENDIX No. 3.
			HOUTHULST FORREST on for C.O. No. 2 dated 26-2-1918; 45 Guns were dispatched and 223,000 rounds of S.A.A.	APPENDIX No. 4.
			These operations were carried out in conjunction with the normal defensive harassing fire from the No. 2 Group Machine Gun Corps, the dispositions of which remained unchanged.	

Army Form C. 2118.

WAR DIARY
or
INTELLIGENCE SUMMARY.
(Erase heading not required.)

Instructions regarding War Diaries and Intelligence Summaries are contained in F. S. Regs., Part II. and the Staff Manual respectively. Title pages will be prepared in manuscript.

Place	Date	Hour	Summary of Events and Information	Remarks and references to Appendices
RICHMOND CAMP.	28/2/1918.		Major R. G. PETTLE attached 2nd Command of 5th Battalion vice Major G. C. SHIPSTER. On taking charge of duties of 2nd in command took place on the O.O. No. 3. dated 28-2-1918.	APPENDIX No. 5.

TO.-   M.G.No. C.O.3.

    14th. M.G.Coy.   32nd.Divn.H.Q.)
    96th. " "   14th.Bde.H.Q.)
    97th. " "   96th. " " "   ) For information.
    219. " "   97th. " " "   )

Ref. Map. 1/10,000. Sheet A-1.

(1). In order to increase the strength of the defences in the divisional sector the number of guns is to be raised from 30 (as at present) to 40.

(2). It has been decided to find these as follows:-
   (a) Each Company will find 10 guns permanently in the line.
   (b) Each gun will be manned by 3.O.Rs. and a gun commander with 1 senior N.C.O. per 2 guns.
       There will thus be 45 men in all required to man 10 guns.
   (c) There will be 2 Company H.Qrs. at U.9.C.5.9.(Left sector) and U15.b.05.05. (Right sector).
       The O.C.'Coys., who happen to be in the line, will be left and right group commanders respectively; each having 20 guns under his control.

(3). The remaining 2 Company Headquarters and 6 guns per Company will be in divisional reserve at DEKORT CAMP. and will be prepared to occupy positions in the Army line in case of need.

(4). Companies will relieve the personnel of their guns in the line, completely, every 7 days.
     M.G.Company H.Q. in the line will also be relieved every 7 days.
     All ranks will therefore do 7 days in and 7 days out of the line.

(5). Each Company will be permanently allotted a sub-sector of the line, in depth as follows:-
   (a) <u>219.M.G.Company.</u>   3guns........FAIDHERBE CROSS ROADS.
                                       2 " ....UCKAELD POST.
                                       3 " ....LONELY MILL.
                                    x 1 " ....U.10.d.1.1.

   (b). <u>96th.M.G.Company.</u>   3guns........HILL 20.
                                       2 " ....U.9.d.9.9.
                                       4 " ....U.15.b.4.1.

   (c). <u>14th.M.G.Company.</u>   3guns........MANGELARE.
                                       2 " ....CATINAT.
                                       2 " ....U.9.C.3.4.
                                     3 " ....U.9.C.1.7.

   (d). <u>97th.M.G.Company.</u>   3guns........PAPEGOED Fm.
                                       2 " ....ISLANDS POST.
                                     x 1 " ....VICTORY POST.
                                     x 1 " ....U.8.a.6.5.
                                   x 1 " ....U.7.b.9.6.

x Teams for single guns will be 1 N.C.O. and 4 men.

(6). The construction of new emplacements and shelters in accordance with instructions already issued, verbally to Company commanders will be proceeded with as rapidly as possible and additional guns introduced as soon as possible.

(7). The arrangements of sectors as detailed in para 5. will be modified slightly when the new positions are completed.

                                                            A.M.Humble Lieut. Adjt.
                                                                   for. Lt.Col.
24-2-1918.   Cmdg. 32nd. Divnl. M.G. Battn.

SECRET.　　　　　　　　　　　　　　　　　　　　COPY No. 11

M.G. Battalion Operation Order No 1.

Ref Map 1/10,000 Sheet A.1

1. The re-adjustment of positions detailed in M.G. No. C.O.3. dated 24th inst. will take place in the right brigade sector tomorrow night 25/26th inst.

2. Reliefs will take place in accordance with table "A" attached.

3. O.C. 219th M.G. Coy. will become right group commander for the first 7 days with Headquarters at U.15.c.05.05. Present Headquarters of 96th M.G. Coy at SIGNAL FARM will be abandoned.

4. All other details of reliefs will be arranged direct between Company Commanders concerned.

5. Completion of reliefs will be reported to Battalion Headquarters in code by word "SNUG".

6. All details of work in hand, emplacement stores etc. will be carefully handed over.
   The work in the new positions is not going on fast enough. Officers must "get down" to it. Work on Corps line positions can proceed by day, watch being kept for hostile aeroplanes.

7. All personnel detailed in table "A" will be completely changed after 7 days.

8. Acknowledge.

24.2.18
Issued at 7 pm 24.2.18.
Copies to:-
1. O.C. Battn
2. Adjutant
3. O.C. 114th M.G.Coy
4. " 96th "
5. " 97th "
6. " 219th "
7. " 114th Inf Bde
8. " 96th "
9. " 97th "
10. " 32nd Divn
11.) War Diary
12.)
13. File

A.W. Humble Lt. + Adjt.
for Lt. Col.
O.C. 32nd Divl M.G. Battn.

Table "A" issued with M.G. Operation Order No.1.

Serial No.	No. of guns.	Location.	at present manned by	Relieved by	Instructions
1.	2	FAIDHERBE X ROADS	96	219	1. Teams to consist of 4 O.R. per gun, and 1 senior N.C.O. per 2 guns.
2.	2	UCKAELD POST.	96	219	2. Teams for No.4, 4 O.R. and 1 senior N.C.O.
3.	2	LONELY MILL	96	219	3. Officers will live :—
4.	1	U.10.d.1.1.	96	219	219 at FAIDHERBE. 219 at LONELY MILL. 96 at HILL 20. 96 at U.15.b.1.1.
5.	2	HILL 20.	96	96	4. Guns of 96 at present at MANGELARE will remain until relieved by 14 later.
6.	2	U.9.d.9.0.	219	96	
7.	4	U.15.b.1.1.	219	96	

B.C. 34.

TO:-
C.O.
"A" Company.
"B"   "
"C"   "
"D"   "
Battalion Transport Officer.
14th Infantry Brigade,
96th   "   "
97th   "   "
32nd Division H.Q.
32nd Division Artillery.
32nd Division Signals.
War Diary (2 copies)
File.

1. In accordance with G.H.Q. letter O.B/407. the Machine Gun Companies in the division will be amalgamated into A Battalion and be known as the 32nd Battalion Machine Gun Corps.

2. The Companies will be renumbered forthwith as follows:-
14th Machine Gun Company - "A" Company.
96th   "   "   "   - "B"   "
97th   "   "   "   - "C"   "
218th   "   "   "   - "D"   "

3. The markings allotted to the Battalion which will be worn on the arm beneath the shoulder by all ranks and painted on the transport vehicles will be :-
A RED Square and two Bars.
with colours according to Company.
Bars will be as follows:-
Head Quarters...........2 Black Bars.
"A" Company ....2 Red Bars.
"B"   "   ....2 Green Bars
"C"   "   ....2 Yellow Bars
"D"   "   ....2 Blue Bars.
The transport will conform to its respective Company.

4. Above changes will be effected as soon as possible.

..........................Lieut. & Adjt.
32nd Battalion Machine Gun Corps.

23/2/1918.

SECRET   C.O. No. 2.

MACHINE GUN INSTRUCTIONS FOR RAIDS OF
14th & 96th BRIGADES.

Ref. Sheet 28.1. & A.2.

1. **Information**
   The 14th & 96th Infantry Brigades will shortly carry out raids as follows:-
   A. 14th Brigade   area U.4.a.0.6. and O.34d.
   B. 96th Brigade   MARACHAL FARM O.36 d.1.1.

2. **Objects.**
   A. To kill or capture any Germans found in the area.
   B. To obtain identifications and documents.

3. **Method of Infantry Attack.**
   A. 14th Brigade.
      1. The raiding party will form up in "No Man's/ Land and advance N.E. under a creeping barrage to the edge of ROUTHOULST FOREST from U.4.a.05.95 S.E. to road.
      2. Another party will pass through and raid the CASTLE (O.34 d.88)
      3. A further special party will " mop up" the area round the E of ZEVEKOTEN.
      4. The signal to withdraw will be given from CASTLE dugout at zero plus 45 or later if the mopping up is not complete.
   B. 96th Infantry Brigade
      The Infantry will advance due North under creeping barrage up and on either side of the road as far as 150 yards North of MARSCHAL FARM, blocks being established 150 yards on the road leading East.

4. **Action of Artillery.**
   A. The Field Artillery will provide standing protective barrages round the areas to be attacked by both brigades.
   B. It will also provide a creeping barrage under which the Infantry will advance.
   C. Howitzers and H.A. will concentrate on special areas and avenues of approach to isolate the parts to be attacked as much as possible.

5. **Trench Mortars.**
   Trench Mortars of both Brigades are being employed to reinforce the Artillery, and in case of 96th Brigade to secure their left flank by firing on OWL WOOD.

6. **Action of Machine Guns.**
   A. The Vickers Machine Guns will co-operate in both the raids in accordance with APPENDIX A. attached.
   B. Special instructions for Machine guns are detailed in APPENDIX B. attached.
   C. The importance of personal supervision on the part of Company Commanders and their Section Officers cannot be over estimated.
   D. Company Commanders will submit detailed firing calculations to Battalion Hd. Qrs. by 6 p.m. 20th instant.

7. **Watches.**
   Will be synchronized under arrangements to be made by Battalion Hd. Qrs.- details later.

8. **Reports.**
   Company Commanders (in addition to reports called for in special instructions) will submit a report by 6 p.m. on day following raid bringing forward any points of interest, difficulties encountered
   casualties sustained, etc.

3.

9. Zero day and hour will be notified later.

10. Acknowledge.

26-2-1918.

A.M.Grumble Lt. & Adjt

.............................Lieut. Colonel.
Cmdg. 32nd. Divisional Machine Gun Battalion.

Copies to:-

No.	Copy		No.	Copy	
1.	Copy.	O.C.	8.	"	32nd Divl. Artillery.
2.	"	Adjt.	9.	"	14th. Inf. Bde.
3.	"	14th M.G. Coy.	10.	"	96th. Inf. Bde.
4.	"	96th M.G. Coy.	11.	"	97th. Inf. Bde.
5.	"	97th M.G. Coy.	12.	"	)
6.	"	81th M.G. Coy.	13.	"	) War Diary.
7.	"	32nd Div. H.Q.	14.	"	File.

Appendix "A". 14th Infantry Brigade

Serial No.	M.G. Coy	No. of guns	Present location	Approximate position for raid	Target	Time	Rate of fire
1.	14.	9.	In line	U.2.c. 95.60.	Line O.33.d 55.10. to O.34.c. 55.65.	Z. to Z+90	50 r.p.m.
2.	97.	6.	DEKORT.	U.2.d. 10.25.	as for 1.	as for 1.	as for 1.
3.	97.	6.	DEKORT.	U.8.b. 7.4.	Line O.33.d.9.8 to CHANZY CORNER O.34.a.5.1.	Z to Z+90	50 r.p.m.
4A.	14.	6.)	{ 4 DEKORT 2 PAPEGOED FM.	U.3.c. 00.65.	Dugouts at O.34.d.1.2	Z to Z+20.	120 r.p.m.
4B.	14.	6.)	"	"	as for 1.	Z+60 to Z+90	50 r.p.m.

Traverse to each side of Zero line

Appendix "A" 96th Infantry Brigade

Serial No.	M.G. Coy.	No. of guns	Present location	Approximate position for raid	Target	Time	Rate of fire
5.	96.	9.	In line	LOUVOIS FARM.	Line O.26.b. 40.15. to P.31.c. 15.85.	Z+12 Z+80.	60. R.P.M.
6.	2/9.	5.	In line	U.11.a. 1.0.	Line P.31.c. 15.85. to P.31.c. 25.33.	— do —	— do —
7.	2/9.	4.	DEKORT.	U.11.a. 1.0.	Line P.31.c. 25.33. to 31.a. 36.80.	— do —	— do —

Traverse 1° each side of Zero line or twice distribution angle (whichever is the largest).

APPENDIX "B" for 95th. INFANTRY BRIGADE.

The same special instructions as for raid of 14th Brigade will apply generally.

1. 96 M. G. Coy. will not move their 2 guns on FAIDHERBE CROSS ROADS.

2. Communications.

    96 M.G. Coy. will lay a telephone line from Coy. Hd. Qrs.
    to Batteries at U.11. a.1.
    96 M.G.Coy. will lay a line from there to LOUVOIS FARM.

3. 96th. M.G. Coy. should occupy same position at LOUVOIS FARM as for raid on the 15th instant.

4. All guns will resume their positions in the line at Zero plus 150 and guns from Dekort Camp returning there.

5. Attention is called to APPENDIX "C"; List of Code Signals to be used during raids.

APPENDIX "B" FOR 14th INFANTRY BRIGADE.

1. All guns of 14th M.G. Company in line except gun at MARGELARE and 2 guns at PAPEGOED will form Battery No. 1.

2. The 2 guns at PAPEGOED will form part of Battery No. 2.

3. Battery Commanders will be selected for all 3 Batteries.

    (a) No. 1 Battery should be placed down slope of CONVERSEN VALLEY.
    (b) No. 2 Battery on road between ISLANDS and VICTORY POSTS.
    (c) No. 3 Battery near track South of PAPEGOED FARM.

5. Company Commanders will forthwith reconnoitre and select exact positions.

6. Company Commanders will personally supervise laying out of ZERO lines on "Z" afternoon.
    It is most important that direction should be accurate so as to clear left flank of raiders. Lines must be laid out "T" bases fixed and Zero points put up by daylight.

7. "T" bases will be used by all guns.
    These are being made by C.R.E. and will be drawn tomorrow night, 2/30th.

8. All available clinometers will be brought to use.

9. Screens to hide flash will be used.
    It is important that the screens be brought well round to the North side of each gun, so that no flash will be seen from the high ground there.

10. Slits must be cut in screens so that Zero aiming posts can be seen. Luminous paint for Zero posts can be drawn from 14th Infantry Brigade Headquarters.

11. Directions must be carefully checked after each burst.

12. Ammunition: 20 Belt Boxes per gun, 2 petrol tins of water.

13. A careful record will be kept of number and kind of stoppages encountered and detailed in report.

14. All guns must be in position by Zero – 30 minutes.

15. At Zero plus 120 minutes guns will resume their normal positions in the line as quickly as possible.
    Guns from Dekort Camp will return there.

16. A hot meal must be arranged for the men before zero and an extra ration of rum will be issued as conclusion.
    A hot meal will also be arranged for teams on return to Dekort Camp.

17. Allowance will be made for error of day before commencing firing.

18. Guns should be 10 to 20 yards apart.

19. Fire may be slackened somewhat from zero plus 30 to zero+60 and quickened up again zero plus 60 to zero plus 90.

20. Nos. 1 should be changed round every 15 minutes.

21. **Communications**

    O. C. Signals, 14th Infantry Brigade will arrange for telephonic communication to Nos. 1 and 2 Batteries.
    14th M. G. Company will provide personnel and instruments, arranging direct with O. C. Signals, 14th Infantry Brigade.

22. A Report will be sent in at Zero – 30 minutes that all guns are in position and further reports at Zero plus 30, Zero plus 60 and Zero plus 90 minutes.
    Communications from Battery No.3 at PAPECOUD will be by runner to ISLAND POST and telephone at Battery No.3 under arrangements to be made by 14th M. G. Company.

23. All guns will resume their positions in the line at ZERO plus 120 minutes – guns from Dekort returning there.

24. Attention is called to APPENDIX "C": List of Code Signals to be used during raid.

APPENDIX "C".

Following Code is to be used in sending messages back by visual or phone:-

Assembly completed with no shelling...	succession of A's
" " " little " ...	" " B's.
" " " much " ...	" " C's.
Little M.G. Fire ...	" " F's
Much " " ...	" " G's
All going well ...	" " H's.

Enemy Barrage.

(1) On front posts ...	" " P's.
(2) On Main posts ...	" " Q's.
(3) Between 1 & 2 ...	" " R's.

Followed by Light or Heavy
Light I.   Heavy X.

Casualties Slight ...	" " T's.
" Heavy ...	" " U's.
Casualties ...	" " Z's.
Killed ...	" ZA's.) Foll-
Wounded ...	" ZB's.) owed
Missing ...	" ZC's.) by Nos.

32nd Div. M.G. Battalion. M.G.B.1.
SECRET

AMENDMENT No. 1 to M.G. Instructions
for raids of 14th and 96th
Infantry Brigades.

1. Reference Appendix A.

   All guns for 14th Infantry Brigade raid will open fire at Zero - 2 minutes.

   Reference Appendix A, serial No. 4 (a)

   For "Zero plus 20" read "Zero plus 18"

2. Guns of both raids will re-open fire from Zero plus 3 hours 15 minutes to Zero plus 3 hours 30 minutes on same line.
   Rate 60 per minute. (each gun to fire 4 belts).

   Serial No. 4(a) will again concentrate on dugouts at O.34.d.1.2.

3. Para. 23 of Appendix B. for 14th Infantry Brigade and para. 4 of Appendix B. for 96th Infantry Brigade will be amended to read "Zero plus 3 hours 30 minutes".

4. ACKNOWLEDGE.

26/2/1918.

Reeve
Lieut-Colonel,
Cmdg. 32nd Divl. M.G. Battalion.

Issued to all recipients of Machine Gun
Instructions for Raids of 14th and 96th
Infantry Brigades.

SECRET

96th Infantry Brigade No. G.42/15/1

15th Lancs. Fus.	32nd Division.	C.R.E.
16th Lancs. Fus.	14th Inf. Bde.	A.D.M.S.
2nd Manchester Regt.	97th Inf. Bde.	Div. M.G. Battn.
96th T.M.Bty	105th Inf. Bde.	161st Bde. Group R.F.A.
96th Bde. Signals.	C.R.A.	218th Field Co. R.E.

Reference 96th Infantry Brigade Operation Order No. 429, para. 18 -

ZERO hour will be at 7.52 p.m. to-night.

ACKNOWLEDGE by wire.

Captain,
Brigade Major,
96th Infantry Brigade.

Feb 27th 1918

SECRET.      COPY No. 13

**32nd. Divisional Machine Gun Battalion
Operation Order No.3.**

Ref. sheet. A.1. 1/10000

1. Reliefs in accordance with Appendix "A" attached will take place on Thursday night 28/1st. inst.

2. All details to be settled by Company Commanders concerned.

3. Relief to be complete by 12. p.m. and to be reported to Battalion Headquarters in code by word "TALLY HO."

4. Work in accordance with M.G. No.O.O. 9. will be proceeded with as quickly as possible. O.C. 14th. Machine Gun Company will hand over all details of this to O.C. 97th. Machine Gun Company.

5. All retaliation targets, lines of fire, etc. will be carefully explained to Incoming Unit.

6. ACKNOWLEDGE.

........Reeve........Lieut. Col.
Cmdg. 32nd. Div. M.G. Battalion.

Issued 28/8/18.

Copies to:-
```
    No. 1. Copy to.-  O.C.
         2.           Adjt.
         3.           14th. Machine Gun Company.
         4.           96th.    "     "    "
         5.           97th.    "     "    "
         6.           217th.   "     "    "
         7.           96th. Infantry Brigade.
         8.           97th.   "       "
         9.           14th.   "       "
        10.           32nd. Division Hd. Qrs.
        11.           32nd.    "     "   "
        12.           War Diary.
        13.            "    "
        14.           File.
```

APPENDIX "A" issued with M.G. Operation Order No. 2.

Serial No	M.G. Coy taking over	No. of guns.	Location.	M.G. Coy. relieved.	Instructions
1.	H.Q., 97TH	—	New Post, U.9.c.5.9.	H.Q. 14TH	1. Guns of 96 and 219 will withdraw to RICHMOND CAMP under orders to be issued by O.C. 219 Coy. who will report completion.
2.	14.	2.	MANGELARE.	{ 1 – 14 / 1 – 96. }	
3.	14.	2.	CATINAT.	14.	
4.	14.	1.	U.9.c.55.25.	219	
5.	14.	1.	U.9.c.3.4.	219.	
6.	14.	2.	U.8.c.75.65.	14.	
7.	97	2	PAPEGOED.	14.	
8.	97.	2.	ISLANDE.	14.	
9.	97.	1.	VICTORY.	14.	
10.	97.	1.	U.8.a.55.55.	14	
11.	97.	1.	U.7.b.9.6.	14	

32nd Divisional M.G.C.

32nd BATTALION

MACHINE GUN CORPS

MARCH 1918

Appendices attached :- Operation Orders;
                       Maps.

CONFIDENTIAL

War Diary

of

32nd Bn. Machine Gun Corps

from 1st March 1918 to 31st March 1918.

No 2.
2-4-18.

Army Form C. 2118.

WAR DIARY

INTELLIGENCE SUMMARY.

(Erase heading not required.)

Instructions regarding War Diaries and Intelligence Summaries are contained in F. S. Regs., Part II. and the Staff Manual respectively. Title pages will be prepared in manuscript.

Place	Date	Hour	Summary of Events and Information	Remarks and references to Appendices
RICHMOND CAMP.	1/3/1918		No change in location from WD 28-2-1918. Schedules obeis normal; Action orders during my action between the hours of 7-0 and 7-30 p.m. the following areas being shelled; MANGELARE, ISHARDE, PAPEGOED, and CATINAT POSTS. On this day a large number of rounds of Tracer Ammunition (S.A.A.) were issued to the front line from our own M.G.O. in the 35th Divisional Front. Occasional bursts of fire were heard from the front line of "B" and "D" Coy of previous evening; there were not reported on unusual (R.L.T.) and the attack to be drawn to the manifestation, on the contrary mentioned. Lads were duly notified. Trench Strength of Battalion on this day was: - Officers, 45. Other Ranks, 782.	R.J.M./- A.Z.1/10,000 HOUTHULST FOREST.
"	2/3/1918		Schedules Normal; reports of unusual occurrences received with continued on unkind, out three were informed by U.11.B.20.45 (1), also duplicates at V.11.B.2.6	R.J.M./- A.Z.1/10,000 HOUTHULST FOREST.

D. D. & L., London, E.C. (A6005) Wt. W1771/M2031 750r/c00 5/17 Sch. 52 Forms C2-0/14

Army Form C. 2118.

WAR DIARY
or
INTELLIGENCE SUMMARY.
(Erase heading not required.)

Instructions regarding War Diaries and Intelligence Summaries are contained in F. S. Regs., Part II. and the Staff Manual respectively. Title pages will be prepared in manuscript.

Place	Date	Hour	Summary of Events and Information	Remarks and references to Appendices
RICHMOND CAMP.	3/3/1918		Casualties:- Killed. 1. Other Ranks.	
			Situation normal. M.G. Positions in the Camp have been organised and instructions for the manning of them posted, issued M.G. Instruction No.1. dated 3-3-1918. Anti-Tank Protection was dealt with and Ammn. Pioneer S.A.A. manned as M.G. Instruction No.2 dated 3-3-1918. Major R.G. PETTLE rejoined from 4th Bn. M.G.C. and assumed his duties as 2nd in Command of the Battalion from this date.	APPENDIX No 1 APPENDIX No 2
"	4/3/1918		Situation normal. G.S. installed, minor the forward of the lines was inspected by the Commanding Officer on its Battle Parade Ground by RICHMOND CAMP at 10-30 a.m. One new gun emplacement was drilled at U.S.C.3.7. New M.G. Defence Scheme for the Battalion Sector was then organised and orders accordingly issued Battn. S.W. Defences communicated for Battn. S.W. Defences vide M.G. Instruction. No. 3 dated 4-3-1918. Orders issued for establishing of new Battn. S.W. Defences vide M.G. Instruction No. 4 dated 4-3-1918.	Ry. Map A.2. 1/10,000. APPENDIX No 3 APPENDIX No 4

Army Form C. 2118.

WAR DIARY
INTELLIGENCE SUMMARY.
(Erase heading not required.)

Instructions regarding War Diaries and Intelligence Summaries are contained in F.S. Regs., Part II. and the Staff Manual respectively. Title pages will be prepared in manuscript.

Place	Date	Hour	Summary of Events and Information	Remarks and references to Appendices
RICHMOND CAMP.	5/3/1918		Situation normal. On this day the activity of the enemy M.G.s showed a marked increase, particularly between the hours of 3-30 p.m. and 9-0 p.m; shortbursts during the main barrage. O/C 10-45 a.m. 16 men from "A" Coy and 16 men from "C" Coy. returned to Battn. at the termination of "Decoration" by Capt Cambri; O.C. "A" Coy. in charge of the parade; No. 42162 Serjt. J.N. Ivanoff of "A" Coy. was transferred to Belgium. Croix de Guerre on this parade. Relief in accordance with Operation Order No. 4 dated 3-3-1918 took place.	APPENDIX No. 5.
"	6/3/1918		Situation normal. Lieut Col. Ronneff visited all Guns in the left sub-section. Staff Captain Officer then attended. Relief in accordance with Operation Order. No. 5. dated 5-3-1918. took place.	APPENDIX No. 6.
"	7/3/1918		Situation normal. Work returns were carried on. This day a few slight shots fell in the vicinity of Battn. H.Q.	

Army Form C. 2118.

WAR DIARY
INTELLIGENCE SUMMARY.
(Erase heading not required.)

Place	Date	Hour	Summary of Events and Information	Remarks and references to Appendices
RICHMOND CAMP.	8/3/1918		Situation about normal. At 4-0 a.m. the enemy, under cover of heavy bombardment and with the help of Flammenwerfer, attacked on our front. This attack was repulsed except at posts 13 to 18 of our Right Brigade where our line was forced back. 2 Coys of the Sutho Battalion immediately counter-attacked and recovered the ground from them later. Our casualties were severe. Emplacement at K.12.d.9.0. was destroyed by shell fire, and the Officers Quarters at U.9.d.9.0. were damaged. Simultaneously with the military operations an enemy officer attacked and brought down our Observation Balloon in the vicinity of WOESTEN. Casualties :- 1 O.R. injured. 4 O.R. wounded.	Ref. Map Belgium 2.S.N.W.1
"	9/3/1918		Situation normal. BOESINGHE and ELVERDINGHE were fired on at intervals during the day and night by enemy H.V. Guns. 1 enemy aeroplane from the direction of HOUTHULST FOREST flew over the lines throughout the day.	

Army Form C. 2118.

WAR DIARY
INTELLIGENCE SUMMARY.
(Erase heading not required.)

Instructions regarding War Diaries and Intelligence Summaries are contained in F. S. Regs., Part II. and the Staff Manual respectively. Title pages will be prepared in manuscript.

Place	Date	Hour	Summary of Events and Information	Remarks and references to Appendices
RICHMOND CAMP.	10/3/1918		Situation normal. Church Parade Service was held at WHITE MILL CHURCH ARMY HUT, ELVERDINGHE, at 10-0 a.m. for details at Batt. H.Q. Extracts of Battalion Frontage in the Operation Orders No. 6. dated 9-3-1918 were carried out. Ground was covered by one patrol led by one officer. Aug-ant at 0.9.d. 9.0 constituted.	APPENDIX No. 7 Ref. Map Belgium 20 S.W.4
"	11/3/1918		Situation rather normal. Then dry was extremely heavy & enemy aircraft was noticed, making recce and forced landing of NEW UCKFIELD POST, rifles were appeared coming into mentioned. Our deep shelters good accommodation. Ready in accordance with Operation Order No. 7 dated 10-3-18 Battn. James. Casualties:- Wounded. 1 O.R. Lieut. P.C. Kingsley "C" Coy. reported back from returning. Came to CALAIS.	Ref. Mt. A.2./10,000. HOUTHULST FOREST APPENDIX No. 8
"	12/3/1918		Situation normal. Gas N.C.O. carried out demonstration of ...	

D. D. & L. London, E.C. (A700) Wt. W1771/M2051 750/700 5/17 Sch. 32 Forms C2. 0/14

Army Form C. 2118.

WAR DIARY
or
INTELLIGENCE SUMMARY.
(Erase heading not required.)

Instructions regarding War Diaries and Intelligence Summaries are contained in F.S. Regs., Part II. and the Staff Manual respectively. Title pages will be prepared in manuscript.

Place	Date	Hour	Summary of Events and Information	Remarks and references to Appendices
RICHMOND CAMP.	12/3/1918		M.G. Emplacements B.H.Q. Hrs continued. Huts C.O. J. REEVE transferred over to Camp and Maj. R.G. Ross assumed command of Huts. Rations drawn in advance. Remainder of Camp. Company of 4th Queen's in H.Q. huts took place of M.G. Instructors. No. 5. dated 12-3-19.18. New S.O.S. Line of Fire for M.G. Guns & two in take Lewis were issued. A Appendix No. 10.	APPENDIX No. 9. / APPENDIX No. 10.
"	13/3/1918		Schemes arrived. S.O.S. was observed to go out on the Rifle Gunnery Coast at 7-50 p.m. and one M.G. fired 21,000 rounds on "HELP RIGHT TANGO" which would mean Casualties :- 1 O.R. Wounded.	
"	14/3/1918		Schemes Normal. Were continued until further Orders. No. 8 dated 12-3-18.	APPENDIX No. 11.

Army Form C. 2118.

WAR DIARY
INTELLIGENCE SUMMARY.
(Erase heading not required.)

Place	Date	Hour	Summary of Events and Information	Remarks and references to Appendices
RICHMOND CAMP.	15/3/1918		Situation above normal. Enemy artillery and Machine Gun went very active throughout the day. Our 8-45 to 9 S.O.S. was opened up on the Ruffles Ridge — our answering barrage by the Guns was opened out on S.O.S. lines. 41,000 rounds of our barrage ammunition was fired against enemy M.G.'s and infantry. Enemy casualties unknown. 3 prisoners of different units of enemy were captured. Casualties :- Lieut. G. MASTERS, "C" Coy. O. Ranks. O.R's :- 2 wounded.	
RICHMOND CAMP.	16/3/1918		Casualties :- Nil. Situation normal. Enemy artillery and M.G. on our front rather less active. Our F.G.F. fired 41,000 rounds of S.A.A. in answer to S.O.S. signals during the night. F.O.P's report the enemy was observed carrying material up to the front line trenches. Our infantry intelligence reports the enemy movements were slight.	

WAR DIARY or INTELLIGENCE SUMMARY

Army Form C. 2118.

Place	Date	Hour	Summary of Events and Information	Remarks and references to Appendices
RICHMOND CAMP.	17/3/1918		Situation normal. Churches Outdoor Catering were slightly damaged during fire to our Battery Areas. Our M.G.'s again opened up an impressive programme of harassing fire on enemy M.G.s, front lines & approaches during night. Lewis gunfire also opened a considerable amount of M.G. harassing fire. During the afternoon observed a German aeroplane which was brought down in flames. Two officers were observed to descend. Tents – 13,700 tents were erected and wood was confirmed. Commanding Officer No.1 & No.G. Instructor No.5 were assembled at M.G. Instructors Course School at ELVERDINGHE, at 9-45 a.m.	APPENDIX No. 12
"	18/3/1918		Casualties: 1 O.R. Wounded. Situation normal. Day was very quiet. Our M.G.'s fired 5,000 rounds in retaliation targets. Lieut-Col. J. REEVE returned from leave. Battery positions & 30 line were prepared for particular inspection. Wound testimonial carried on Brigt. Machine Gun Officers Order No. 9 dated 16.3.18 draft force.	APPENDIX No. 13
"	19/3/1918		Situation later remained normal. Machine Gun were issued. 16,500 rounds in retaliation targets.	

Army Form C. 2118.

WAR DIARY
or
INTELLIGENCE SUMMARY.
(Erase heading not required.)

Instructions regarding War Diaries and Intelligence Summaries are contained in F. S. Regs., Part II. and the Staff Manual respectively. Title pages will be prepared in manuscript.

Place	Date	Hour	Summary of Events and Information	Remarks and references to Appendices
RICHMOND CAMP.	20/3/1918		Situation normal. Gas alarm was given at 11.10 p.m. Enemy M.G.s. concentrated their fire on Co.'s in and about line S.W. of HOUTHULST FOREST on tr. M.G. Emplts. for Reliefs of 91st & 97th Inf. Bdes. Ops Nos 12-13 dated 19-3-1918. 56 Gun were engaged and 205,000 rounds of S.A.A. were expended. Gas and fumes well to the front staffeln, and no casualties. Personnel of the Gun Teams on gun-limber side-flaps. One gun of 23 PAPEGOED had its outer casing damaged by enemy intense Machine Gun fire, but remained in action during the day.	APPENDIX. Nil.
RICHMOND CAMP	21/3/1918		Situation normal. Enemy artillery quiet on forward area, a considerable amount of fire was directed on back areas from 5 p.m. GRUYTERSZELE FARM, MONDOVI DUMP & BROMBEEK VALLEY	Ry. Stats. A.i. Y/14/00.

Army Form C. 2118.

WAR DIARY
or
INTELLIGENCE SUMMARY.
(Erase heading not required.)

Instructions regarding War Diaries and Intelligence Summaries are contained in F.S. Regs., Part II. and the Staff Manual respectively. Title pages will be prepared in manuscript.

Place	Date	Hour	Summary of Events and Information	Remarks and references to Appendices
Richmond Camp	21/3/1918 (continued)		were shelled until 7.30 p.m. Our M.G's fired 11,250 rounds on retaliation targets.	Appendix 15.
Richmond Camp	22/3/18.		Casualties:- 1 O.R. Wounded. Situation normal. Between 6 p.m. & 6.30 p.m. Kancier & Korps Ecke shelled. Mondovi shelled at intervals throughout the night. Relief in accordance with O.O. 12 took place on night 22/23. Our M.G's fired 98,000 rounds on special targets between 4 a.m. & 6 a.m. Enemy M.G's very quiet owing to N.E. retaliation.	Appendix 16.
Richmond Camp	23/3/18.		Casualties, 2/Lt. A.J. Wilder "A" Coy wounded & shell on 24 R n.o.t., 1 O.R. killed. Our M.G's co-operated with the 96th Bgde. (88,000 rounds were fired) in a raid on the enemy lines south of Houthulst Forest as per O.O. 11.	Appendix 17.

WAR DIARY
or
INTELLIGENCE SUMMARY.
(Erase heading not required.)

Army Form C. 2118.

Place	Date	Hour	Summary of Events and Information	Remarks and references to Appendices
Richmond Camp	29/3/18		Situation normal. Night quiet. Our M.Gs. fired 15,100 rounds on special targets. 2/Lt. H.J. Dixon reported for duty & posted to B. Coy.	
Richmond Camp	25/3/18		Situation normal. Night quiet. Our M.G. fired 11,600 rounds on suitable targets.	
Richmond Camp & Vanqueter	26/3/18		Situation normal. Night quiet. Our M.G. fired 5,400 rounds on suitable targets. A Coy. went thro' at 4 am. B Coy. 5 guns at C Coy. & 5 guns at D Coy. A Coy. entrained at 11h. north of BLH for another strong train. The 32nd Div. are being relieved by the 4th Belgian Division at d'parture. The relief commenced to-day in accordance with O.O.14. A Coy. entrained at ELVERDINGHE, detrained at AUBIGNY & marched to billets at VANQUETEN.	APPENDIX 18 Ref. ELVERDINGHE LENS II. EDITION 2

Army Form C. 2118.

WAR DIARY
INTELLIGENCE SUMMARY.
(Erase heading not required.)

Instructions regarding War Diaries and Intelligence Summaries are contained in F. S. Regs., Part II. and the Staff Manual respectively. Title pages will be prepared in manuscript.

Place	Date	Hour	Summary of Events and Information	Remarks and references to Appendices
RICHMOND CAMP WANQUETEN	27/3/18		Situation normal. Night quiet. Relief carried out in accordance with O.O. 14. A. Coy in billets at WANQUETEN.	APPENDIX Ref Lens 11 Edition 2
RICHMOND CAMP. RANSART	28/3/18		Battalion HQ & Coys entrained for new area at 0.0.15. First party entrained at 2.40 P.M. On detraining Coys proceeded to LATTRE ST QUENTIN. No billets. A. Coy moved to RANSART. 11.30 AM Coy moved up into Reserve line.	APPENDIX 19 Ref Lens 11 Edition 2
RICHMOND CAMP. LATTRE ST QUENTIN ADINFER	29/3/18		Entrainment completed at 8.40 AM. Battn HQ opened at LATTRE ST QUENTIN. A Coy in reserve at ADINFER.	
LATTRE ST QUENTIN ADINFER	30/3/18		CASUALTIES 2/Lt S.V. SPEARS wounded. 4. O.R. killed. 7. O.R. wounded. A. Coy in reserve at ADINFER. B. Coy moved up to ADINFER. C. Coy, D Coy, & HQ at LATTRE ST QUENTIN	

Army Form C. 2118.

WAR DIARY
or
INTELLIGENCE SUMMARY.

(Erase heading not required.)

Instructions regarding War Diaries and Intelligence Summaries are contained in F. S. Regs., Part II. and the Staff Manual respectively. Title pages will be prepared in manuscript.

Place	Date	Hour	Summary of Events and Information	Remarks and references to Appendices
Inter St Quentin	3/5/18		CASUALTIES 2 OR WOUNDED. The Battn. relieved the 81st M.G. Battn. in the line after 00.17. Battn. HQ. moved to HUMBER CAMP. V.22.a.70.45	APPENDIX 20. Ref. Sheet 51.C.
Humbercamp			O.C. 32 M.G. Bottn took over command of 11 Squadron M.G.C. Cov.	

WAR DIARY OF No. 11 SQUADRON M.G.C. COY.

ENCLOSED

APPENDICES

1 to 20 .

SECRET.

MACHINE GUN INSTRUCTIONS NO. 1.
Occupation of Battle Zone (Army Line)

1. In the event of occupation of the Battle Zone (Army Line) by No. 3 (Reserve) Brigade becoming necessary, all machine guns in reserve at RICHMOND CAMP (24 guns) will also take up their allotted positions in the Battle Zone.

2. Attached map (issued to 4 Coys., C.M.G.C. 38nd Div only) shows the exact location of the guns, their lines of fire and the Coy., finding them.

3. Group Headquarters will be :-
   SAULES FARM (U 25 b 3.2.) - Right group.
   BRISSTIN HOUSE (U 19 a 7 8) - Left group.
   Battalion Headquarters will remain at RICHMOND CAMP.

4. On receipt of the order to "STAND TO" from Divisional Headquarters
   (a) Teams for the necessary fighting and ammunition limbers will be immediately sent from Battalion Transport Lines.
   (b) Personnel for 24 guns (all available Officers, 4 men and 1.N.C.O per gun) will get ready to move at 15 minutes notice.
   (c) Each group commander at RICHMOND CAMP will send an Officer to Battalion Headquarters for orders and will report when he is ready to move at 15 minutes notice.

5. On receipt of the order to "MOVE":-
   (a) Guns will immediately proceed to their allotted positions
   (b) Group commanders will report to G.O.C. No.3. Bde. (H.Q. POST BLEU B 5 a 4 1) when guns are in position.

6. Route from RICHMOND CAMP to the line will be via Road junction T 26 d.7 5 - road junction T 22 a 5 2 - road junction T 22 B 1 c - CHARPENTIER CROSS roads - along track to RUGBY CORNER (for right sector)
   N.B.- The ELVERDINGHE - BOESINGHE ROAD will not be used.

7. The situation may demand changing from limbers to pack (owing to shell-fire and blocked roads) either west or east of the CANAL. Group commanders will exercise their own discretion as to this. Pack saddles will in any event be taken on the horses or mules.

8. Ammunition. 14 belt boxes per gun will be got to each position as quickly as possible.
   Further instructions will be issued later with regard to S.A.A. dumps, from which to refill. In case of emergency the nearest dump should be used.

9. Communications.
   (a) TO No 3 Bde. von Battalion H.Qrs. at BRISSTIN HOUSE and SAULES FARM.
   (b) O.C. Left group will be responsible for laying a line to right group H.Q.
   (c) Communications between group H.Q. and the gun positions will be by runner

10. Position of Officers.
    Section and sub-section officers must be actually with one pair of guns. Positions to be detailed by group commanders.

11. **Lines of fire.**

In addition to close defence lines of fire, group commanders will arrange for all guns to be able to fire on S.O.S. lines on the general line CEMETARY U 23 b 48 -CRAONNE FARM -MONDOVI FARM -GOURDI FARM.

12. **Reconnaissances.**

All officers will reconnoitre their own areas as soon as possible and make themselves acquainted with the exact location of, and the best approch to, the positions allotted to their guns. Coy., commanders and 2nd-in-command will reconnoitre their whole group area, i.e. O'sC and 2nd-in-command D and B Coys will reconnoitre all the right group area. O's C and 2nd-in-command A and C Coys., all the left group area. Coy., commanders will report to Battalion H.Q. when all their officers know the positions allotted to them.

13. It should be the matter of pride and rivalry between all guns to be the first to open in response to a S.O.S. signal.

3/3/18.
Copies to:-
O.C.
Adjutant.
O.C. "A" Coy.
O.C. "B" Coy.
O.C. "C" Coy.
O.C. "D" Coy.
O.C. 14th Inf. Bde.
O.C. 96th "
O.C. 97th "
O.C. 32nd Div.
C.M.G.O.
War Diary.
File.

Lieut.Col.
Cmdg 32nd Divl, M.G. Bn.

SECRET.

MACHINE GUN INSTRUCTIONS NO. 2.

Anti-Tank Preparations.

1. In order to guard against a possible Tank attack, 8000 rounds of Armour Piercing S.A.A. have been drawn and are being issued to Machine guns in the Divisional sector.

2. This ammunition will be distributed as shown in Appendix "A" attached 500 rounds (2 belt boxes) being located at each gun position.

3. To prevent the armour piercing ammunition being used for any other purposes, 32 belt boxes are being painted bright red and the special ammunition will be kept in these.

4. Strict orders will be given to all ranks that the special ammunition is on no account to be used except actually against a Tank attack.

5. The red belt boxes will be kept permanently at the position and handed over with it, but care must be taken to constantly overhaul them and keep them ready for immediate use.

J. Reeve, Lieut. Col.
Commdg. 32nd Divl. M. G. Bn.

Copies to:-
    C.O.
    Adjutant
    O.C. "A" Coy.
    " "B" "
    " "C" "
    " "D" "
    " 14th Inf. Bde.
    " 96th "
    " 97th "
    " 32nd Div.
    War Diary
    File.

Appendix "A" issued with M.G. Instructions No. 2.

Serial No.	Gun Position	Serial No.	Gun Position
1.	UCKFIELD POST (right gun)	7.	MANGELARE (2 guns)
2.	FAIDHERBE CROSS ROADS (2 guns)	8.	PAPEGOED (right gun)
3.	HILL 20 (right gun)	9.	CATINAT (right gun)
4.	LONELY MILL (right gun)	10.	ISLANDE (right gun)
5.	U 10 d 11	11.	U 8 a 55.55
6.	U 9 d. 9.0. (2 guns)	12.	U 9 c 34
		13.	U 9 c 55.30.

SECRET.

C.O. 19.

Copy No... 2...

MACHINE GUN INSTRUCTIONS No. 3.

Lines of Fire.

1. The following system will be introduced in order to enable S.O.S. calls both in our own and neighbouring divisions fronts to be quickly and adequately answered.

2. Each gun will have a number of aiming posts erected, numbered from I to 5 in Roman numerals:-
   No. I post will be for the close defence.
   No. 2 post will be for the S.O.S line.
   No. 3 post will be for retaliation target.
   No. 4 post will be for "Help Right".
   No. 5 post will be for "Help Left".

3. A new pattern post is being issued painted BLACK with a one inch diameter bulls eye of luminous paint and a number (from I to 5) also in luminous paint.

4. Company commanders will personally and carefully supervise the erecting of these posts so that fire may be brought to bear in accordance with Appendices I to 5 attached (to 4 M.G. Coys. 32nd Div. and C.M.G.O. only).

5. In many cases guns will not have all 5 posts (i.e. many guns could not "help right" and some of the front line guns have no S.O.S. line etc.) but in every case the number of the post will stand for the target as detailed in para. 2.

6. The attached map shows the exact present locations of all guns on the divisional front and their close defence lines and the areas permanently occupied by each M. G. Coy. in the line.
   It also shows:-
      (a) The S.O.S. lines   in YELLOW
      (b) The present retaliation targets   in RED
      (c) The "help right" area   in BLUE
      (d) The "help left" area   in GREEN.
   Guns with A.T. in fire cone are Anti-Tank guns with armour piercing ammunition.

7. Rates of fire will be as detailed in Appendices I to 5.

8. Whenever a gun position is changed etc., group commanders will forward its new pin point location to Battalion Headquarters immediately and new lines of fire will be issued for the gun.

9. All guns will be normally laid on their S.O.S. lines and section officers must constantly check them to see that they are correctly laid. Guns that have no S.O.S. lines will be laid on their close defence line.

10. No zero aiming post is to be touched without orders from the group commander. If one is destroyed or knocked down, the group commander will be responsible for seeing it is correctly replaced as soon as possible.

11. A copy of the meaning of the numbers (as in para. 2) on the zero posts will be posted up in all emplacements and men will be frequently questioned until they thoroughly understand them. The detailed calculations from which the zero posts are set up will be entered up in the log books.

12. Group commanders will see that the bull eyes on the posts and the numbers are re-painted from time to time so that they remain luminous.
    A supply of paint for the purpose is being indented for and will be kept at group Headquarters.

13. It is hoped shortly to improve the signalling communications to many of the guns so that fire can be instantly opened on any target.

14. Whenever fire is opened on any target as detailed in Appendices 1-5, the time, number of rounds, behaviour of gun etc., will be entered up in the log book and history sheet.

15. A C K N O W L E D G E.

                              J Reeve
                              Lieut-Col.
            Commdg. 32nd Divl. M.G. Bn.

4/3/18.

Issued at
Copies to:-
1. C.O.
2. Adjutant
3. O.C. "A" Coy.
4. " "B" "
5. " "C" "
6. " "D" "
7. H.Q. 32nd Div.
8. O.C. 32nd Div. Signals
9. C.M.G.O.
10. H.Q., 14th Inf. Bde.
11. " 96th " "
12. " 97th " "
13. " 35th Div.
14. " 4th Belgian Div.
15. War Diary.
16. File.
17. C.R.A., 32nd Div.

REFERENCE.

▭ Area occupied by "A" Coy.

▭ Area occupied by "B" Coy.

▭ Area occupied by "C" Coy.

▭ Area occupied by "D" Coy.

◁ Gun positions and close defence lines.   ◁ Guns of 35th Div.

◁ AT "Anti-tank guns.   ◁ Guns of 4th Belgian Div.

● S.O.S. lines.

● Help Right lines

● Help Left lines

● Retaliation targets.

The black dots show the exact aiming points of guns.

SECRET.

C.O. 22
Copy. No............ 13

MACHINE GUN INSTRUCTIONS NO. 4.

Extending the front.

1. In the event of the Corps being ordered to send a Division away, the 35th Division on our right will be taken out and the gap thus caused will be filled by the 1st Division extending to its left and by our extending to the right.

2. The new boundary would in this case be as shown on attached map.

3. The new M.G. positions to be taken over would be as shown in Appendix "A" attached.

4. The total number of guns in the Divisional area would be 40 (10 per Coy.) and would be manned by Coys., as shown on the attached map - "D" Coy. taking over the whole of the new area and the other 3 Coys. adjusting themselves to take over the whole of the present Divisional front.

5. Positions which would be held by each Coy. after re-adjustment would be as detailed in Appendix "B" attached.

6. Group Headquarters will remain in present positions.

7. Close defence lines in the area taken over will be as shown on the attached map - further instructions as to S.O.S. lines will be issued.

8. Anti-Tank armour piercing ammunition as detailed in M.G. Instructions No. 2 Appendix "A" will be re-distributed as follows under arrangements to be made by group commanders:-

From.	To.
U 9 d 9.0 (L)	NAMUR CROSSING (L)
U 9 c 55.30	VEE BEND (R)
FAIDHERBE CROSS ROADS (R)	LES 5 CHEMINS
MANGELARE (L)	EGYPT HOUSE
U 10 d 1.1	GRUYTERSZALE FM. (L).

9. Officers commanding right group will establish close liaison with the 35th Battalion M.G.C. with a view to reconnoitring the positions in the new area.

10. A C K N O W L E D G E.

J Reeve
Lieut.-Col.,
Commdg., 32nd Battalion M.G.C.

4/3/18.

Issued at:-
Copies to:-
1. O.C.
2. Adjutant
3. O.C., "A" Coy.
4. " "B" "
5. " "C" "
6. " "D" "
7. H.Q., 14th Inf.Bde.
8. " 96th "
9. " 97th "
10. " 32nd Div.
11. O.C., 32nd Div. Artillery
12. H.Q., 35th Div.

Appendix "B" Issued with M.G. Instructions No. 4.

"C" COY.

1. PAPEGOED (2 guns)
2. BOUCHARD (1 gun)
3. CATINAT (2 guns)
4. ISLANDS (2 guns)
5. U 2 c 75. 70 (1 gun)
6. U 8 a 55. 55 (1 gun)
7. U 7B 9.6 (1 gun)

"A" COY.

1. MAMGELARE (2 guns)
2. HILL 20 (2 guns)
3. U 9 d 8.0 (1 gun)
4. U 9 c 35. 40 (1 gun)
5. U 8 a 75. 65 (2 guns)
6. U 15 b 1.1 (2 guns)

"B" COY.

1. UXBRIDGE (2 guns)
2. FATHER'S CROSS ROADS (2 guns)
3. LONEY MILL (2 guns)
4. X c & 2.1 (1 gun)
5. U 9 d 95.00 (1 gun)
6. GRAGNIE M. (2 guns)

"D" COY.

1. LES 5 CHEMINS (1 gun)
2. EGYPT HOUSE (1 gun)
3. RAILWAY CROSSING U 12 d 85.95 (1 gun)
4. VEE BEND (2 guns)
5. HAMER CROSSING (2 guns)
6. GRUYTERZALE M. (2 guns)
7. U 17 c 35.65 (1 gun)

U16 b 7.8 } 2
U17 a 0.8 }

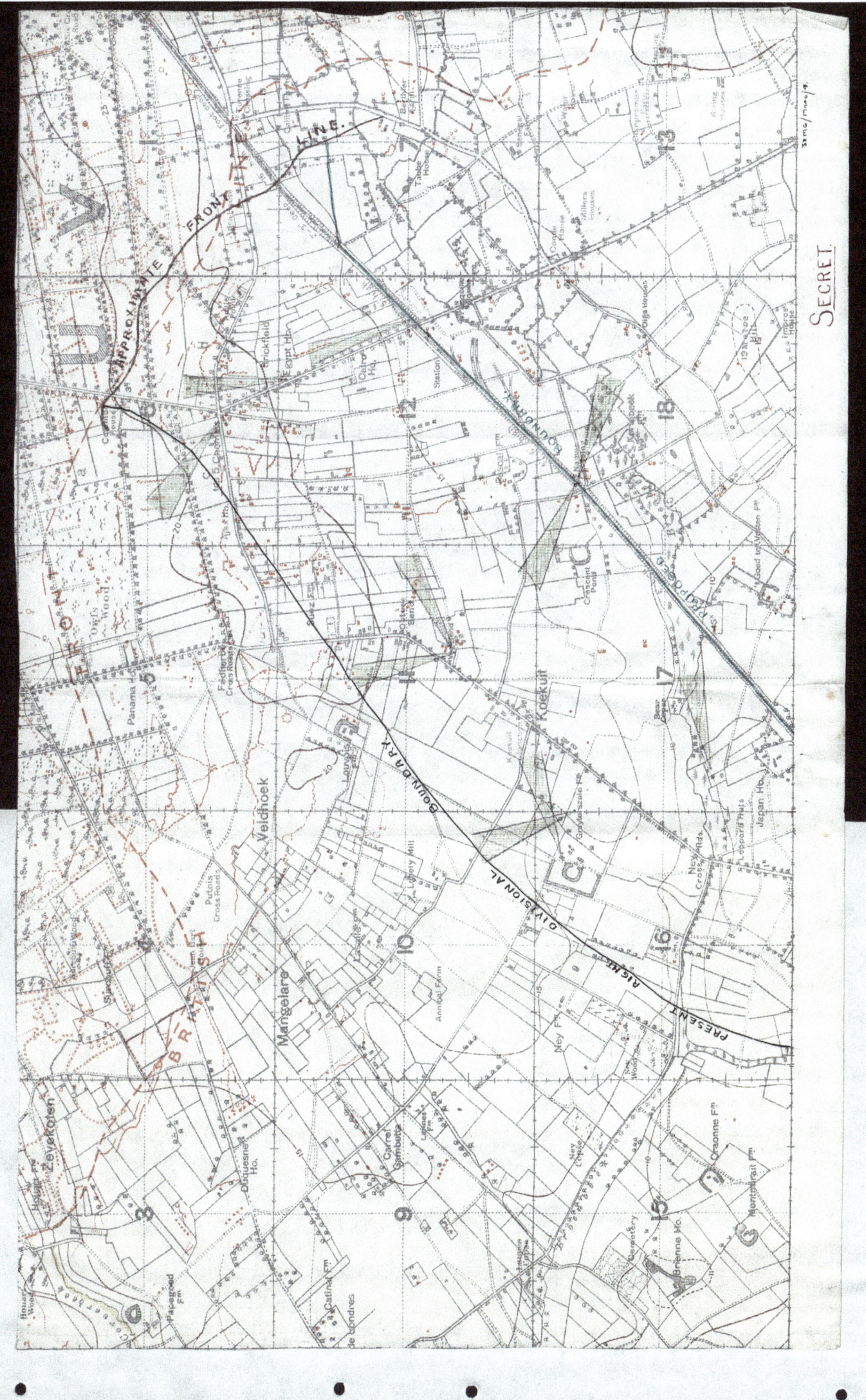

SECRET   COPY. No. 12

32nd BATTALION MACHINE GUN CORPS

OPERATION ORDER No.4.

Ref. Sheet A.1. 1/10,000

1. Reliefs in accordance with Appendix "A" will take on Monday night 4/5th instant.

2. All details to be settled by Company Commanders concerned.

3. Reliefs to be complete by 10 p.m. and to be reported to Battalion Headquarters in code by word CHEERI-OH.

4. Each Company will take up three guns and three tripods, and 6 boxes of ammunition will be exchanged at each position. *for exchange*

5. All personnel at each gun position will be completely relieved.

6. Work in accordance with instructions which have been issued will be proceeded with as soon as possible. O.C. "D" Company will hand over all details of this to O.C. "B" Company.

7. All retaliation targets, lines of fire, ect. will be carefully explained to in-coming companies.

8. ACKNOWLEDGE.

...................Lieut. Col.
Cmdg, 32nd Battalion Machine Gun Corps.

Issued at

Copies to :-
    No.1. O.C.
       2. Adjutant,
       3. O.C. "A" Company,
       4. O.C. "B"   "
       5. O.C. "C"   "
       6. O.C. "D"   "
       7. 96th Infantry Brigade.
       8. 97th   "   "
       9. 14th   "   "
     10. 32nd Div. H.Q.
     11.   "   "   "
     12. War Diary,
     13.   "   "
     14. File.

APPENDIX A.

Serial No.	No. of Guns.	Location.	At Present Manned By.	Relieved By
1.	2	Taillerbe Cross Roads.	D.	D.
2.	2	Uchfield Post.	D.	D.
3.	2	Lonely Mill.	D.	D.
4.	1	U.15.d.1.1.	D.	D.
5.	2	Hill 70.	B.	B.
6.	2	U.9.d.9.0.	B.	B.
7.	4	U.13.A.4.	B.	B.

SECRET   Copy No. 14

                    32nd Battalion Machine Gun Corps.
                    Operation Order No. 5.

Ref Sheet A_1 1/10000 .

(1)   Reliefs in accordance with Appendix "A" will take place
        on Wednesday night 6/7th inst.

(2)   All details to be settled by Company Commanders concerned.

(3)   Relief to be complet- by 10p.m. and to be reported to
        Battalion Headquarters by word:_"XXXXXXX " HULLO"

(4)   Guns and tripods will be exchanged at 6 of the positions
        each company taking up 3 guns and 3 tripods for this
        purpose.

(5)   Each gun team will take up 6 Belt Boxes for exchange and
        the outgoing teams will bring back the same number.

(6)   All personnel at each gun position will be completely
        relieved.

(7)   Work in accordance with instructions which have been
        issued will be proceeded with as soon as possible
        O.C. "C" Company will hand over all details of this to
        O.C. "A" Company .

(8)   All retaliation targets lines of fire etc will be
        carefully explained to the incoming teams.

(9)   Acknowledge.
                                            A.M.Hamble. Lieut.
                                                for Lieut. Col.
6/3/18
                                    Cmdg 32nd Battalion Machine Gun Corps.

Copies issued to:
(1) O.C.
(2) Adjutant.
(3) Transport Officer.
(4) O.C. "A" Coy.
(5) O.C. "B" Coy.
(6) O.C. "C" Coy.
(7) O.C. "D" Coy.
(8) 96th Infantry Brigade
(9) 97th   "   "
(10) 98th   "   "
(11) 32nd Div. Headquarters
(12) "   "   "
(13) War Diary
✓(14) "   "
(15) File.

APPENDIX "A"

Serial No.	No. of Guns.	Location.	At Present Manned By.	Relieved By.
1.	2	Mangalore	A.	A.
2.	2	Catinat	A.	A.
3.	2	U.9.c.3.4.	A.	A.
4.	2	U.9.c.1.4.	A.	A.
5.	2	Pate Goed Fm.	C.	C.
6.	2	Island Post	C.	C.
7.	1	Victory Post	C.	C.
8.	1	U.8.a.6.5.	C.	C.
9.	1	U.9.b.9.6.	C.	C.

SECRET. Ref Sheet. A1. 1/10000   Copy No...15...
28. N.W.

32nd BATTALION MACHINE GUN CORPS, OPERATION ORDER, No. 6.

1. The 35th Division will be withdrawn from the line tonight, 9/10th March and the gap thus caused will be filled in by the 1st Division extending to its left and the 32nd Division extending to its right.

2. The new inter-divisional boundary will be the YPRES-STADEN Railway as far as U 17 a 6 9 and thence to U 13 a 3 9 to U 12 b 9 0 to U 7 a 9 4

3. The 32nd Battn Machine Gun Corps will relieve the guns of the 35th Battn Machine Gun Corps in the sector to be taken over on the night 10/11th March.

4. "D" Company will take over all the new positions and the other three companies will simultaneously extend to their right so as to take over the area at present held by all four companies.

5. The new positions to be taken over and position of all guns in the divisional area on completion of relief are shown in Appendix "A" attached.(This modifies the positions as detailed in M.G.Instructions No 4 dated 3/3/18.

6. Group Head Quarters will remain in their present positions

7. All details of relief will be made direct between Company commanders concerned.

8. Completion of reliefs will be reported to Battn H.Q. in code by word "SHUFFLE".
Reliefs to be complete by 9 p.m.

9. Guns of the 35th Battn to be relieved are found as follows :-
"A" Coy.(guns in forward system) with Head Qrs. at IRON CROSS C 3 a 5 4
"D" Coy.(guns in corps line) with Head Qrs. at MORTELDJE ESTAMINE C 15 C 9 5.

10. Great care must be taken that all details of positions are very carefully taken over. Guns relieved will not withdraw till incoming gun has completely taken over.
"D" Coy., will take over the existing lines of close defense and S.O.S from 35th Battn: fresh instructions in regard to these will be issued later.

11. No guns or tripods will be taken over from the 55th Battn. Belt boxes will be taken over and receipts given for them, a copy being forwarded to Battn. H.Q. 55th Battn. will arrange to collect a similar number of belt boxes from Battn. H.Q.

12. Acknowledge.

                                                       Lieut & Adjt.
                                32nd Battalion Machine Gun Corps.

9/3/18.
Copies to:-
O.C.
Adjt.
4th Inf. Bde.
6th "   "
7th "   "
O.C. "A" Coy.
 "   "B" "
 "   "C" "
 "   "D" "
2nd Division.
 "   "
1st   "
5th   "
R.A 32nd Division.
War Diary.
File.

APPENDIX "A" ISSUED WITH M.G. OPERATION ORDER No 1.

"C" Company.	"A" Company.	"B" Company.	"D" Company.
FREEHOLD (2).	MANGELAKE (2).	FAIRHEAD CROSS ROADS. (2).	Le SCHERIES. (1)
INDY HAKS (1) (DUQUESNE Mo)	HILL 20. (2).		EGYPT. HO. (1)
CATINAT. (2)	U.9.d.90. (2)	U.11.L.1.6. (2).	TRANQUOIS Ho. } (1) RAILWAY CROSSING
ISLANDE (2).	U.9.c.6.3. (1).	LONELY MILL (2)	U.12.d.65.95 (1)
U.2.C.15.40 (1).	U.9.C.35.40. (1).	U.9.d.1500 (2)	VEE BEND. (2)
U.8.a.52.55 (1)	U.8.d.45.65 (2).	U.15.L.11. (2).	NAMUR CROSSING (1)
U.4.d.9.£ (1)			U.10.c.2.1. (1)
			GUNTERZAAL. (2)
			U.14.C.25.65. (1)

ALL SINGLE GUNS MUST HAVE A GOOD N.C.O. IN CHARGE.

SECRET. Copy No...15...

32nd BATTALION MACHINE GUN CORPS OPERATION ORDER NO. 7.

Reference Sheet :- A1-1/10000.

1. Reliefs in accordance with attached table "A" will take place on Monday night 11/12th inst.

2. All details to be settled by Company Commanders concerned.

3. Relief to be complete by 10p.m. and to be reported to Battalion H.Q. by word :- "CUDDLE".

4. Guns and tripods will be exchanged at six of the positions and each company will take up three guns and three tripods for this purpose.

5. Each company will take up six belt boxes per gun and the outgoing teams will bring back the same number.

6. All personnel at each gun position will be completely relieved.

7. Work in accordance with instructions C.O.32. will be proceeded with as soon as possible.

8. All retaliation targets lines of fire etc., will be carefully explained to incoming teams.

9. Acknowledge.

..................Lieut & Adjt.
32nd Battalion Machine Gun Corps.

10/3/18.
Issued to :-
No. 1. O.C.
2. Adjt.
3. Transport Officer
4. O.C. "A" Coy.
5. " "B" "
6. " "C" "
7. " "D" "
8. 14th Inf Bde.
9. 96th " "
10. 97th " "
11. 32nd Division.
12. " "
13. " " Artillery.
14. War Diary,
15. " "
16. File.

APPENDIX "A"

Gun No.	No. of Guns	Location	At Present Manned By	Relieved
1.	2.	Tirlemont Cross Roads.	B.	B.
2.	2.	U.11.b.1.6. Lonely Mill.	B.	B.
3.	2.	U.9.d.95.03.	B.	B.
4.	2.	U.15.b.1.1	B.	B.
5.	2.	Le Chemins.	B.	B.
6.	1.	Egypt House.	D.	D.
7.	1.	Tranquille House Railway Crossing.	D.	D.
8.	6.	Vee Bend.	D.	D.
9.	2.	Namur Crossing.	A.	A.
10.	1.	U.10.d.2.4.	A.	A.
11.	1.	Gruyterzale.	A.	A.
12.	2.	U.4.c.25.65.	A.	A.
13.	1.		A.	A.

SECRET.

32nd BATTALION MACHINE GUN CORPS. INSTRUCTIONS NO.6.
RENUMBERING OF GUNS.

1. To avoid confusion the guns in the divisional sector will be renumbered as soon as possible, in accordance with the following plan.

2. Guns in the front line posts will be allotted the letter "W"
   " " " second " " " " " " " " "X"
   " " " corps " " " "Y"
   " " south of the BROEN BEEK " " "Z"
   All guns will be numbered in succession from the right of their line.

3. Each position will be provided with a notice board showing the number of the gun and the exact location on the map.
   i.e. M.G.X.7.   or M.G.Y.9.
        U.19 b 30.00   U 9 d 29.42

4. Gun positions will also be known by the nearest name on the map, i.e. Y4 to Y47 will be called the NEY COPSE BATTERY.

5. All guns in batteries will be provided with Zero line posts of the same pattern as already issued with the letter "Z" in luminous paint. These posts will be placed on grid north line.

6. Fighting maps will be issued for all battery positions so that, in conjunction with the Zero posts, fire can be switched on to any target at a moments notice. Battalion Intelligence Officer will issue these.

7. Appendix "A" attached shows the number allotted, exact map location and name of every gun in the divisional sector. Alternative gun emplacements will be called Y6a Y6b etc.

P. Acknowledge.

12/5/18.
Copies to:-
O.C. "A" Coy.   Adjt.
 "   "B" "   War Diary
 "   "C" "   "   "
 "   "D" "   File.
14th Inf. Bde.
96th "   "
97th "   "
32nd Div.
 "   "
 "   " C.R.A.
 "   " C.R.E
1st   "
C.O.

Humble Lieut + Adjt
.... Lieut Col.
Cmdg. 32nd Battalion Machine Gun Corps.

APPENDIX "A" — Issued with N.G. Instr. No. 3

Line	Map Location	Number Allotted	Name	Line	Map Location	Number Allotted	Name
Front Line of Posts	U.12.d.65.95	W.1	Tranquille House	Support Line of Posts	U.18.a.04.42	X.1	Namur Crossing
"	U.12.b.20.85	W.2	Egypt House	"	U.11.d.38.54	X.2	} Vee Bend
"	U.6.c.85.40	W.3	Les Cinq Chemins	"	U.11.d.36.65	X.3	}
"	U.5.d.66.62	W.4	} Faidherbe Cross Roads	"	U.11.b.04.56	X.4	} Louvois Farm
"	U.5.d.44.41	W.5	}	"	U.11.b.00.56	X.5	}
"	U.5.c.38.20	W.6	} Hill 20	"	U.10.b.37.05	X.6	} Lonely Mill
"	U.5.c.30.20	W.7	}	"	U.10.b.30.00	X.7	}
"	U.10.a.50.60	W.8	} Mangelaere	"	U.9.a.99.43	X.8	} Catinat
"	U.10.a.45.65	W.9	}	"	U.9.a.92.40	X.9	}
"	U.3.d.18.41	W.10	Duquesne House	"	U.8.b.44.44	X.10	} Islande
"	U.3.c.40.80	W.11	}	"	U.8.b.36.80	X.11	}
"	U.3.c.32.82	W.12	} Papegoed	"	U.2.c.45.90	X.12	Victory

APPENDIX "A" (Contd).

LINE	MAP LOCATION	NUMBER ALLOTTED	NAME	LINE	MAP LOCATION	NUMBER ALLOTTED	NAME
Subsidiary	J.14.b.5.41.	Y.1.	GRUFFERSOLE FARM BATTERY.	South of RAILWAY	J.19.c.32.53.	Z.1.	15 PINE HOUSE.
	J.14.b.50.87.	Y.2.			J.18.d.18.17.	Z.2.	RIGHT COMPANY HD. QRS.
	J.14.d.5.84.	Y.3.			J.18.d.42.16.	Z.3.	
	J.14.c.05.00.	Y.4.	NEY COPSE BATTERY.		J.19.c.80.87.	Z.4.	RUINED FARM
	J.8.d.9.97.	Y.5.					
	J.14.b.90.07.	Y.6.					
	J.8.b.92.25.	Y.7.					
	J.9.c.30.47.	Y.8.	LATINES COPSE BATTERY.				
	J.14.a.07.43.	Y.9.					
	J.8.d.39.58.	Y.10.					
	J.8.d.97.61.	Y.11.					
	J.8.a.50.55.	Y.12.	GOURD FARM				

INSTRUCTIONS.

1. All guns detailed in this Appendix will be normally kept/laid day and night as detailed ready to open fire immediately.

2. Rates of fire - 250 per minute for 5 minutes and 120 per minute for next 10 minutes except when S.O.S. signals are still being sent up when maximum rates will be maintained.

3. Traverse 1° each way.

4. Careful allowance must be made for error of the day.

5. The new "T" shaped aiming mark will normally be put up close behind the S.O.S. post to allow of accurate traversing. It should be 9½ yds. from the gun.

6. The necessity of sentries being absolutely alert so that fire can be opened at once must be constantly impressed on all ranks.

APPENDIX II. — S.O.S. LINES.

No. I Posts.

Gun No.	Gun Positions	Range yds.	Grid Bearing	V.I.	Q.E.
X 1	NAMUR CROSSING	2125	24	+7	5°8'
X 2	VEE BEND R	2100	48	+2	4°52'
X 3	VEE BEND L	2075	47	+2	4°44'
X 4	LOUVOIS FM. R	1875	58	-1	3°38'
X 5	LOUVOIS FM. L	1575	308	-5	2°18'
W 7	HILL 20 L	1525	302	-8	2°
W 9	MANGELARE L	1300	340	-5	1°27'
X 7	LONELY MILL L	1675	332	-7	2°37'
X 9	CATINAT L	2050	355	+3	4°38'
X 10	ISLANDS R	1600	50½	-	2°34'

No. II Posts.

Gun No.	Gun Position	Range yds.	Grid Bearing	V.A.	Q.E.
X 11	ISLANDS L	1925	17	+6	4°5'
X 12	VICTORY	1725	74	+5	3°74
Z 2	RIGHT COY. H.Q. R.	2275	14	+4	6°
Z 3	RIGHT COY. H.Q. L.	2275	14	+4	6°
Y 10	LANNES COPSE	1925	53	-2	3°50'
Y 11	"	1925	33	-2	3°50'
Y 8	"	1950	17½	-1	3°59
Y 9	2	1950	20	-1	3°59
Y 12	COURH FM.	2150	63	+6	5°15'
Z 4	RUINED FM.	2250	55	+6	5°50'

No. 11 Posts.

APPENDIX II — D.O.B. LINES.

No. 11 Posts.

Gun No.	Gun Position	Range yds.	Grid Bearing	V.I.	Q.E.
W 6	MILL 20 R	1250	35	- 4	13°1'
W 8	BACCLARE R	2075	49½	- 1	10°30'
X 6	CAYEAU R	2580	58	+ 2	7°22'
Y 4	SNY COPSE R	2650	22½ 38½	—	8°15'
Y 5	"	2550	36 west	—	7°54'
Y 6	"	2550	37½	—	7°36'
Y 7	" L	2450	47 37	—	7°4'
Y 2	GRUTHERSTAL R	2485	50½	—	6°53'
Y 3	"	2375	24½	+ 2	10°9'
Y 9	" L	2325	29	+ 1	11°1'

SECRET.   Copy No......

32nd BATTALION MACHINE GUN CORPS.
OPERATION ORDER NO.3.

Ref. Sheet. A1.-1/10000.

1. Reliefs in accordance with attached table "A" will take place on the night 14/15th inst.

2. All details to be settled by Company Commanders concerned.

3. Relief to be complete by 10p.m. and to be reported to Battalion H.Q. by code word:-"SQUEEZE"

4. Guns and tripods will be exchanged at six of the positions, and each Company will take up three guns and three tripods for this purpose.

5. Each Company will take up six belt boxes per gun, and the outcoming teams will bring back the same number.

6. All personnel at each gun position will be completely relieved.

7. Work in accordance with instructions C.O. 32.will be proceeded with as soon as possible.

8. All retaliation targets lines of fire, etc will be carefully explained to the incoming teams.

9. Acknowledge.

[signature] Lt. & Adjt.

............Lieut. Col.
Cmdg. 32nd Battalion Machine Gun Corps.

12/3/18.
Issued to :-
No. 1.   O.C.
    2   Adjt.
    3   Transport Officer
    4.   O.C. "A" Coy.
    5   B
    6   C
    7   D.
    8   14th Inf Bde.
    9   96th "   "
    10. 97th "   "
    11. 32nd Division.
    12.   "   "
    13.   "   "   Artillery.
 ✓14.   War Diary.
    15.   B   "
    16. File.

TABLE "A"

Issued with O.O. Nº 8.

Serial Nº	Nº of Guns	Location	At present manned by	Relieved by
1	2	PAPEGOED	C	C
2	1	HOUCHARD	C	C
3	2	CATINAT	C	C
4	2	ISLANDE	C	C
5	1	U2c 75.70.	C	C
6	1	U8a 55.55	C	C
7	1	U7b 9.6.	C	C
8	2	MANGELARE	A	A
9	2	HILL 20	A	A
10	2	U9d 9.0	A	A
11	1	U9c 6.3.	A	A
12	1	U9c 35.40	A	A
13	2	U8d 75.65.	A	A

12th MARCH 18

SECRET.

AMENDMENT NO.I. TO MACHINE GUN INSTRUCTIONS NO.6.
dated 13/3/1918.

Four map locations.

M.8.	U.9.c.30.27.	read	U.9.c.29.43.
Y.9.	U.9.c.29.43.	"	U.9.c.26.44
Y.10.	U.8.c.83.88.	"	U.9.c.20.43.
Y.11.	U.8.d.74.61.	"	U.9.c.30.43.

W. Harrison Capt
.... Lieut. Col.
Cmdg. 33rd Battalion Machine Gun Corps.

17/3/18.
Copies to :-
C.C.
O.C.A. Coy.
  B
  C
  D
14th Inf Bde.
96th " "
97th " "
32nd Division.
 "   "
 "   " C.R.A.
 "   " C.R.E
1st   "
War Diary.
 "   "
File.

Copy No. 13

32nd BATTALION MACHINE GUN CORPS OPERATION ORDER NO. 3.

An inter-company relief will take place on the right sector on night 13/14th inst.

All details will be arranged between Company Commanders concerned.

ACKNOWLEDGE.

.... Lieut. & Adjt.
for Commanding 32nd Battalion M.G. Corps.

16/4/1918.
Copies to :-
1. O.O.
2. Adjutant.
3. O.C. "A" Coy.
4. O.C. "B" "
5. O.C. "C" "
6. O.C. "D" "
7. 14th Infantry Brigade.
8. 96th Infantry Brigade.
9. 97th Infantry Brigade.
10.) Headquarters 32nd Division.
11.)
12. 32nd Div. Artillery.
13.) War Diary.
14.)
15. File.

Aff. 13.

SECRET.   MACHINE GUN INSTRUCTIONS FOR   Copy No... 12 ....
RAIDS OF 96th and 97th INFANTRY BRIGADES.

Ref Sheets. A.1. & A.2. 1/10,000.

1. **INFORMATION.**
   The 96th and 97th Infantry Brigades will shortly carry out raids as follows:-
   (a) 96th Infantry Brigade area enclosed by a line drawn through the following points:-
   U.5.a.45.70. - O.35.c.30.60. - O.34.c.75.20. - U.4.b.35.15.

   (b) 97th Infantry Brigade area V.1.a. and c.

2. **OBJECTS.**
   (1) To locate position of enemy's main line of resistance.
   (2) To capture all enemy found in the area raided.
   (3) To obtain identifications, and bring back documents, maps, samples of food, clothing, and gas masks.
   (4) To secure Machine Guns, Trench Mortars, and other material and booty.

3. **ARTILLERY.**
   The raids on the areas will take place under cover of an Artillery barrage, supplemented by Machine Guns and Trench Mortars.

4. **MACHINE GUNS.**
   (a) Vickers Machine Guns will co-operate in both raids in Accordance with Appendix "A" & "B" attached.
   Appendix "B" will be forwarded later.
   (b) Special instructions for Machine Guns are detailed in Appendix "C" attached.
   (c) The importance of personal supervision on the part of Company Commanders and their Section Officers cannot be over-estimated.
   (d) Group Commanders will submit detailed firing calculations to Battalion Headquarters by 6.p.m. 19th instant.

5. **REPORTS.**
   Group Commanders (in addition to reports called for in special instructions) will submit a report by 6.p.m. on the day following raid, bringing forward any points of interest, difficulties, encountered, casualties sustained, etc.

6. **WATCHES.**
   Watches will be synchronized under arrangements to be made by Battalion Headquarters. (Details later).

7. Group Commanders will be prepared to repeat the firing exactly, the following night.

8. **ZERO.**
   Zero day and hour will be notified later.

9. **ACKNOWLEDGE.**

W. Harrison, Capt
for Lieut Col,
Cmdg, 32nd Divisional Machine Gun Battalion.

/Copies.

Appendix 'A'.

Serial No.	M.G. Coy	No. of Guns	Present Location.	Approximate Position for Raid.	Target.	Time.	Rate of Fire.
1.	C	6	Papegoed (2) Islande (2) Victory (1) Goldfish Fm. (1)	U.3.c. 25.90.	Dug-outs O.34.d.2.1.	Z to Z+20	120 rounds per minute
2.	Do.	Do.	Do.	Do.	Line O.34.c.1.7. to O.34.a.7.4.	Z+40 to Z+90.	50 rounds per minute
3.	A	10	U.9.c. (6) Richmond Camp (4)	U.2.c. 80.50.	Line O.34.c.9.0. to O.35.c.5.5.	Z to Z+30	50 rounds per minute
4.	Do.	Do.	Do.	Do.	Line O.34.c.7.4. to O.35.a.25.15	Z+60 to Z+90	50 rounds per minute
5.	B and D	8	Lancet Hill (3) Ney Hoop. (3) Graoinnefm (2) Gruttersfale (2)	U.10.d. 90.25.	Line 44.a.6.5. to O.34.c.4.3.	Z to Z+90	50 rounds per minute
6.	D	6	Veebend (2) Richmond Camp (4)	U.11.d.	Line O.35.c.95.60. to O.35.a.5.3.	Z to Z+90	50 rounds per minute

APPENDIX "C".

1. Guns will be found and targets engaged in accordance with Appendix "A" & "B".

2. All guns must be in position ready to open fire at Zero - 30 minutes.

3. "T" or "Y" bases will be used by all guns.

4. All available clinometers will be brought into use.

5. Directions must be carefully checked after each burst.

6. Ammunition, 20 belt boxes per gun, 2 petrol tins of water.

7. A careful record will be kept of number and kind of stoppages encountered and detailed in report.

8. At Zero plus 120 minutes guns will resume their normal positions in the line as quickly as possible.
Guns from RICHMOND CAMP will return there.

9. A hot meal must be arranged for the men before Zero and an extra ration of rum will be issued at conclusion.
A hot meal will also be arranged for teams on return to RICHMOND CAMP.

10. Allowances will be made for error of the day before commencing firing.

11. Fire may be slackened somewhat from Zero plus 30 to Zero plus 60 and quickened up again Zero plus 60 to Zero plus 90.

12. Nos. 1 should be changed round every 15 minutes.

13. Group Commanders will arrange their own communications.
Telephones and personnel for same will be provided by Battalion Headquarters.
Further instructions will be issued later.

14. Screens to hide flash will be used.
It is important that the screens be brought well round to the North side of each gun, so that no flash will be seen from the high ground there.

15. Slits must be cut in screens so that Zero aiming posts can be seen.

Amendment No. 1 to M.G. Instructions for raids of 96th and 97th Infantry Brigades

Appendix A issued with Instructions is cancelled and the following substituted.

Serial No.	M.G. Coy.	No. of Guns	Present Location	Approximate position for raid	Target	Time	Rate of fire.
1	C	6	PAPEGOED (2) ISLANDE (2) VICTORY (1) GOURBI (1)	U 3 c 25.30	CASTLE DUG-OUTS O 34 d 2.1.	Z to Z plus 20	120 rds. per min.
2	"	"	"	"	Line O.34 c 2.5 to O 3.4 b 8.2	Z plus 40 to Z plus 90	50 rds. per min.
3	A	10	LANNES COPSE (4) NEY Copse (2) RICHMOND CAMP (4)	U 2 c 8.5	Line O 34 c 9.0 to O 35 a.3.5.	Z to Z plus 30	60 rds. per min.
4.	"	"	"	"	as in No. 2	Z plus 40 to Z plus 90	"
5	B & D	8	LONELY MILL(2) NEY COPSE (2) RT. GrOUP H.Q.(2) GRUYTERSZALE FM	U 10 b 90 20	Line U 4 a. 6.5 to O 34 c 25.30	Z plus 90 Z to Z plus 50 90	" "
6	D	6	VEE BEND (2) RICHMOND CAMP (4)	U 11 d	Line O 35 c 85.80 to O 35 a 3.4.	Z to Z plus 90	50 "

APPENDIX B

Serial No.	M.G. Coy.	No. of Guns	Present Location	Location during raid	Target	Time	Rate.
7	B	4	RICHMOND CAMP	NAMUR CROSSING	V 1 d 44 Z to V 1 a Z plus 95.10 50		90 rds. per min.
8	D	2	1 NAMUR CROSSING 1 JAPAN HO.	" "	CROSS ROADS P 31 d 60. 15.		100 rds. per min. in bursts
9	B	2	LOUVOIS FM.	LOUVOIS FM.	ROAD JUNCTION O 36 b 40.15		"
10	A	2	HILL 20	U 5 c 4.f.	ROAD JUNCTION O 36 d 25.10		"

O.H.15.

SECRET. AMENDMENT NO.1. TO MACHINE GUN INSTRUCTIONS NO.6. dated 18.3.18.

For Map Locations:-

Y.1.   U.16.b.67.71.   read   U.16.b.72.82.
Y.2.   U.16.b.62.87.   "   U.16.b.68.88.
Y.3.   U.16.d.15.04.   "   U.16.b.63.90.

21st March, 1918.

Copies to:-

C.C.   2nd Division (3)
O.C. "A" Co.   C.R.A.
     "B" "   C.R.E.
     "C" "   1st Division
     "D" "   War Diary (2).
14th Inf.Bde.   File.
 2nd " "
 3rd " "

Annandale
Capt. & Adjt:
for O.C., 2nd. Bn. Machine Gun Corps.

COPY NO. 14

62nd. Battalion Machine Gun Corps,

Operation Order No. 12.

An Inter-Company relief will take place in the Left Sector, on night 22/23rd. March.

All details will be arranged between Commanders concerned.

ACKNOWLEDGE.

22/3/1918.

Capt. & Adjt.
62nd. Battalion Machine Gun Corps.

ISSUED TO:-

1. C.O.
2. Adjt.
3. O.C. "A" Company.
4. O.C. "B"
5. O.C. "C"
6. O.C. "D"
7. 185th. Infantry Brigade.
8. 186th.
9. 187th. Infantry Brigade.
10.) H.Q. 62nd. Division.
11.)
12. 62nd. Div. Artillery
13.) War Diary.
14.)
15. File.

SECRET.

Copy No............

23RD. BATTALION, MACHINE GUN CORPS.

OPERATION ORDER NO. 11.

1. Operations in accordance with M.G.Instructions for 8th Infantry Brigade said will be repeated on night 2nd/3rd. instant.

2. This only affects the guns at VICTORY, FAYBOND, LONELY HILL, and THE ELMS. Lines of fire and times of fire will be the same as before.

3. Batteries will be prepared to fire for a longer period than once now laid down to 4600 plus on orders from C.O., 8th Infantry Brigade.

4. Zero hour will be notified later.

5. Acknowledge.

Ounna....
Capt. & Adjt.,
23rd.Bn., Machine Gun Corps.

Issued, 22nd. March, 1918.

Copies to :-

No. 1	....	Adjt.
2	....	1 Coy.
3	....	2 "
4	....	3 "
5	....	4 "
6	....	4th Inf.Bde.
7	....	8th "
8	....	17th "
9	....	Capt.Division.
10	....	Hqr Diary.
11	....	File.
12	....	C.R.A.

SECRET.

Copy No.........

32nd. Battalion Machine Gun Corps

Operation Order No. 1.

1. The 32nd. Division is being relieved in the Left Sector of the IInd. Corps front, by the 4th. Belgian Division d'Infanterie. The relief is commencing to-day, 26th. March and will be completed (less artillery) by 6-a.m. on 28th inst.

2. (a). The 18th. Belgian Regt. will relieve the 14th. Infantry Brigade in the Right Brigade Sector.
   (b). The 10th. Belgian Regt. will relieve the 96th. Infantry Brigade in the Left Sector.
   (c). The 8th. Belgian Regt. will be the Reserve Regt. on completion of relief.

3. The organization of the Belgians is as follows:-

   Each Regt. = 3 Battalions.
   Each Battalion = 3 Companies and 1 Machine Gun Company.
   Each Machine Gun Company = 6 guns.

4. The guns of the 32nd. Battalion Machine Gun Corps, in the line will be withdrawn on night March 27/28th., completion of withdrawal being reported by each Company to Battalion H.Qrs.

5. The withdrawal will not commence till 8-p.m. on night 27/28th. inst. at which hour the Belgian Machine Guns will become responsible for the Machine Gun defence of the line.

6. The 5th. Belgian Machine Gun Company Commanders are proceeding to the line to-day, 26th. inst., and the Belgian machine gunners go into the line to-night, 26/27th., mounting their guns close alongside our own.

7. The suggested 8 additional positions to be taken over by the Belgians are as follows :-

   RIGHT SECTOR :- HILL 20.......1 gun.
                   Japan House...1 gun.
                   CRAONNE Fm....2 guns.

   LEFT SECTOR :- MONDOVI WOOD..1 gun.
                   GOUEBI Fm.....1 gun.
                   U.8.c.3-5.....2 guns.

8. All details of the incoming of the Belgians will be arranged direct with Company Commanders as follows :-

   M.G.Companies of 18th. Belgian Regt. with Os.C. "B" & "D" Coys.
   M.G.Companies of 10th.   "   "   "   O.C. "C" Coy.

9. Completion of the entry of Belgian M.Gs. will be reported, in code, to Battalion H.Qrs., by the word "SARDINE".

10. (a). During the 24 hours that the Belgian guns are with our own, Company Commanders will be responsible for carefully handing over all details of position, "T" and "V" bases, firing calculations for guns, meaning of all numbered posts, maps, work in hand or projected, signalling communications etc.
    (b). Great care will be taken to see that the incoming Belgians thoroughly understand all details.
    (c). Receipts for everything handed over will be made out in triplicate, 2 copies being forwarded to Battalion H.Qrs.
    (D). All our guns, tripods, spare parts, belt-boxes and 1 petrol tin per gun will be brought out.
    (e). Every emplacement and dug-out must be scrupulously clean, before being handed over.

11. "A" Company are proceeding — by rail (less some transport, by road) to-day to another Army area.
    Remaining Companies will entrain on afternoon of 28th. inst. under orders to be issued later.

12. Great care will be taken to see that the camp and horse lines are left in a thoroughly clean condition before entraining.

13. ACKNOWLEDGE.

                                            Lieut. Col.
                                Comdg. 32nd. Battalion Machine Gun Corps.

- 2 -

Copies to :-

1- Adjt.
2- Bn. Transport Officer.
3- O.C. "A" Company.
4- O.C. "B" "
5- O.C. "C" "
6- O.C. "D" "
7- 14th. Infantry Bde.
8- 36th. "
9- Belgian H.Q. 2nd. Division.
10- 5th. Belgian Regt.
11- 10th. " "
12- 8th. " "
13- 7th. Belgian Div. d'Infanterie.
14- Area Comdt. WORSTEN.
15-) War Diary.
16-)
17- File.

SECRET.   **Operation Order No. 15.**   Copy No:- 9

Move of 2nd. Battalion Machine Gun Corps.

By rail, on 28th. March 1918.

ENTRAINMENT.

1- Attached programme shows the composition and order of march of trains.

2- The hour at which train No. 1 of each series will depart will be wired as soon as known. Succeeding trains of each series will follow at 3 hour intervals from each entraining station.

3- Entraining Stations :-
          1. PESALHOEK.
          2. PROVEN.

  Detraining Stations :-
          1. SAVY BERLETTE.
          2. TINQUES.

4- Units will entrain with their first and second line transports complete.

5- Transports will arrive complete 3 hours before the departure of the trains.

6- All trains will consist of one officers' carriage, 17 flat trucks and 30 covered trucks.
Each flat truck will take an average of 4 axles.
Each covered truck will take 8 H.D.horses, 9 L.D. horses or 40 men.

7- No personnel or stores will be allowed in the brake vans at each end of the train or on the roof of the trucks.

8- Strong advance parties will accompany transport of each unit to the entraining station to assist in loading.

9- Small billeting parties, limited to 2 men per unit, with bicycles will proceed in the first train of each series.

10- A complete marching out state, showing the number of men , horses , G.S., limbered G.S., and two wheeled wagons and bicycles, will be sent down with the transport of each unit so that accomodation in the train can be checked by the R.T.O. at the beginning of the entrainment.

11- Supply and baggage wagons will accompany their own units in every case.

12- The entrainment of all units must be completed half an hour before the time of departure of trains.

13- Transit ropes for horse trucks must be provided by the Units themselves ; ropes for lashing vehicles on the flat trucks will be provided by the railway.

14- SUPPLIES. All units will entrain with the following rations.-
    (1). Iron ration.
    (2). Unexpended portion of the days ration.
    (3). The next day's ration.

15- ACKNOWLEDGE.

27th. March 1918.   *[signature]* Adjt.
                                          2nd. Battalion Machine Gun Corps.

Copies to:-
1- Commanding Officer.
2- Adjutant.
3- O.C. "A" Company.
4- O.C. "C" "
5- O.C. "D" "
6- Transport Officer.
7- R.S.M.
8- R.Q.M.S.
9- War Diary.
10-)
11-) H.Q. Comdt. Division.
12- File.

PESELHOEK Railhead.	PROVEN RAILHEAD.

PESELHOEK Railhead.

1st Train.
    Divisional H.Q.
    No.1 Signal Section.
    H.Q., R.E.

2nd Train.
    215th Field Coy. R.E.
    Pioneer Coy,
    1 Coy. Pioneer Bn. Cooker &
        Team.
    H.Q., Divl. Train.
    Mobile Vet. Section.

3rd Train.
    Pioneer Bn., less 1 Coy.
        Cooker & Team.

4th Train.
    90th Field Ambulance.
    1 Coy. 15th H.L.I. Cooker
        & Team.
    Employment Coy.
    Salvage Coy.

5th Train.
    14th Bde. H.Q.
    Bde. Signal Section.
    "C" Coy. M.G. Battalion.
    T.M. Battery.
    1 Coy. Cooker & Team, 5/6th
        R.Scots.

6th Train.
    5/6th Royal Scots, less 1 Coy
        Cooker & Team.

7th Train.
    1st Dorset Regt., less 1 Coy.
        Cooker & Team.

8th Train.
    15th H.L.I. less 1 Coy, Cooker
        & Team.

9th Train.
    206th Field Coy. R.E.
    No. 2 Coy. Divl. Train.
    1 Coy. 1st Dorset Regt. Cooker
        & Team.
    Pioneer Coy.

PROVEN RAILHEAD.

1st Train.
    96th Brigade H.Q.
    Bde. Signal Section.
    "B" Coy., M.G. Battalion.
    1 T.M. Battery.
    1 Coy., 15th Lanc.Fus. Cooker
        & Team.

2nd Train.
    15th Lanc. Fus., less 1 Coy.
        Cooker & Team.

3rd Train.
    16th Lanc.Fus., less 1 Coy.
        Cooker & Team.

4th Train.
    2nd Manchester Regt., less 1 Coy.
        Cooker & Team.

5th Train.
    218th Field Coy. R.E.
    No. 3. Coy. Divl. Train.
    1 Coy. 16th Lanc.Fus. Cooker
        & Team.
    Pioneer Coy.

6th Train.
    "D" Coy. M.G. Battalion.
    91st Field Ambulance.
    1 Coy., 2nd Manchester Regt.
        Cooker & Team.

7th Train.
    S.A.A. Section, D.A.C.
    H.Q., M.G.Battalion.

8th Train.
    S.A.A. Section, D.A.C.

SECRET. 32nd. BATTALION MACHINE GUN CORPS, Copy No. 16

OPERATION ORDER No. 17.

1. The 32nd. Division is relieving the 31st. Division, in the right Divisional sector, of the VI.Corps front.
    It will have the 42nd. Division on the right and the Guards Division on the left.

2. Machine gun reliefs, which in front of the PURPLE line, take place the night after Infantry reliefs, will be in accordance with attached Appendix "A".

3. In all reliefs in front of the PURPLE LINE one man per team and one Officer per Company H.Qrs. will be sent into the line 24 hours in advance of times stated in Appendix "A".

4. Transport will accompany Companies to ADINFER, off-load there and proceed to lines at BIENVILLERS. (M.2.)

5. 14/boxes per gun will be taken into the line. Belt boxes are not being handed over by the 31st.Division. Belt

6. Battalion H.Qrs. will be at HUMBER CAMP, where it will move on afternoon of 31st. inst.

7. Command of M.G. defences in the Divisional sector will pass on completion of relief of PURPLE LINE on 31st. inst.

8. Completion of all reliefs will be reported, in code, to Battalion H.Qrs., as follows:-

    Relief complete   = KISS ME.
    Quiet.   = QUICK.
    A lot of shelling. = SLOW.

9. The 11th. M.G.Squadron will remain in its present position, in the PURPLE LINE (QUESNOY Fm., inc. - ESSARTS, inc.) and will come under orders of O.C. 32nd. Battalion, on Command passing.

10. Special instructions to Companies are as in Appendix "B" attached, (to Companies and 11th. M.G.Squadron only).

11. All other details of relief will be arranged by Company Commanders concerned.

12. ACKNOWLEDGE.

                                        A.M.Humble, Capt. & Adjt.
30-3-1918.
                                        for. Lieut. Col.
                                        Comdg. 32nd. Battalion Machine Gun Corps

Copies to:-

    1- O.C.
    2- Adjt.
    3- C.O. "A" Company.
    4- C.O. "B"   "
    5- C.O. "C"   "
    6- C.O. "D"   "
    7- H.Q. 14th. Infantry Bde.
    8- H.Q. 95th.   "   "
    9- H.Q. 97th.   "   "
    10- H.Q. 31st. Division.
    11- O.C. 31st. Battalion M.G.Corps.
    12- H.Q. 32nd. Division.
    13- H.Q.
    14- Transport Officer.
    15- Signals Officer.
    16-) War Diary.
    17-)
    18- File.
    19- 11th. M.G.Squadron. (C/O. 31st. Division).

2nd By M.G Corp.

APPENDIX "A" issued with Operation Order No. 17, d/- 30.3.18.

Serial No.	Date.	M.G. Coy.	From	To	Parties of 31st Bn. M.G.C.	Guides at	Time.	Route.
1.	30/3/18	"B"	LATTRE ST. QUENTIN.	ADINFER.				WANQUETIN — BEAUMETZ — RIVIERE — RANSART — ADINFER.
2.	31/3/18. to 1/4/18.	"A"	ADINFER	Front Line Left.	8 guns "A" 8 guns "B"	E. corner of ADINFER WOOD X.27.b.7.0.	7 p.m.	
3.	31/3/18. to 1/4/18.	"D"	LATTRE ST. QUENTIN.	PURPLE LINE. (right sector)	"C"	S.W. corner of ADINFER WOOD F.3.a.9.1.	5 p.m.	
4.	31/3/18. to 1/4/18.	"C"	LATTRE ST. QUENTIN.	PURPLE LINE. (left sector)	8 guns "A" 8 guns "B"	as for 2.	5 p.m.	
5.	About 1/4/1918	"B"	ADINFER.	Front Line Right.	"D"	as for 3	7 p.m.	

Instructions.

1. If roads are narrow movement will be in file.
2. After RANSART movement by sections at 100ᵗ intervals.

VI.Corps.
Third Army.

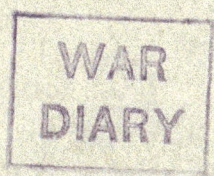

32nd BATTALION, MACHINE GUN CORPS.

A P R I L

1 9 1 8

Attached:

Appendices 1 to 9.

CONFIDENTIAL.

Vol 3

War Diary

of

32ⁿᵈ Bⁿ Machine Gun Corps

from 1ˢᵗ April 1918 to 30ᵗʰ April 1918.

R. Carville Major
for Lieut. Col. Commanding
32ⁿᵈ Bn M.G.C.

Nº 3

Army Form C. 2118.

WAR DIARY
or
INTELLIGENCE SUMMARY.

(Erase heading not required.)

Instructions regarding War Diaries and Intelligence Summaries are contained in F.S. Regs., Part II. and the Staff Manual respectively. Title pages will be prepared in manuscript.

Place	Date	Hour	Summary of Events and Information	Remarks and references to Appendices
Humbercamp	1/4/17		CASUALTIES. 2. O.R. WOUNDED. SITUATION NORMAL. NIGHT QUIET. SLIGHT INCREASE IN THE SHELLING OF THE FORWARD EDGE OF ADINFER WOOD.	REF SHEET 51c S.E.
Humbercamp	2/4/17		CASUALTIES. 1. O.R. WOUNDED. 1. O.R. WOUNDED AT DUTY. SITUATION NORMAL. NIGHT QUIET. REORGANIZATION OF M.Gs IN ACCORDANCE WITH O.O. 18 COMMENCED.	APPENDIX 1.
Humbercamp	3/4/17		CASUALTIES. LT. T. M. LAMONT. WOUNDED. 3. O.R. WOUNDED. At 2.AM OUR M.Gs CO-OPERATED WITH ARTILLERY IN SUPPORT OF INFANTRY. IN THE CAPTURE OF AYETTE. ROUNDS FIRED 31,000. 250 ROUNDS FIRED AT ENEMY AIRCRAFT ACTING ON INFORMATION FROM ARTILLERY O.P. ONE OF OUR M.Gs FIRED AT A PARTY OF BOSCHE (15) PRESUMABLY A STAFF RECONNAISSANCE IN FRONT OF AYETTE AERODROME. THE PARTY WAS SCATTERED + CASUALTIES INFLICTED. ROUNDS FIRED 500. TIME 4 PM. At 9-30 PM. IN RESPONSE TO GREEN LIGHTS OUR M.Gs OPENED FIRE IN SUPPORT OF INFANTRY HOLDING AYETTE.	REF SHEET 57d N.E.
Humbercamp	4/4/17		CASUALTIES. 5. O.R. WOUNDED. SITUATION NORMAL. NIGHT QUIET. 500 ROUNDS FIRED AT ENEMY AIRCRAFT	

Army Form C. 2118.

WAR DIARY
or
INTELLIGENCE SUMMARY.
(Erase heading not required.)

Instructions regarding War Diaries and Intelligence Summaries are contained in F. S. Regs., Part II. and the Staff Manual respectively. Title pages will be prepared in manuscript.

Place	Date	Hour	Summary of Events and Information	Remarks and references to Appendices
Humbercamp	5/4/17		CASUALTIES 1.O.R. KILLED 8.O.R. WOUNDED Whole Sector Heavily Shelled From 5am. Until Noon. Enemy M.G.s Fired Into Ayette. Sweeping The Streets. Our M.Gs Fired 15,500 Rounds In Support Of Operation By 2nd Manchester Regt. 500 Rounds Were Fired At Enemy Aircraft.	Ref. Sheet 57.N.E.
Humbercamp	6/4/17		CASUALTIES 2.O.R. KILLED 7.O.R. WOUNDED Situation Normal. Enemy Artillery Active On Area. Edge Of Adinfer Wood Our M.Gs Fired 1850 Rounds At Enemy Aircraft.	Ref Sheet 51.S.E
Humbercamp	7/4/17		CASUALTIES 3.O.R. WOUNDED Situation Normal. Enemy Artillery Active On S.W. Corner Of Adinfer Wood & Adinfer Village. Monchy Was Shelled Between 10 P.M. & Midnight Our M.Gs Fired 5,500 Rounds At Enemy Aircraft. S.O.S. Arrangements Carried Out As Per M.G. Instructions No. 6.	Ref. Sheet 51C.S.E 57.N.29 Appendix 2.

Army Form C. 2118.

WAR DIARY
or
INTELLIGENCE SUMMARY.
(Erase heading not required)

Instructions regarding War Diaries and Intelligence Summaries are contained in F.S. Regs., Part II. and the Staff Manual respectively. Title pages will be prepared in manuscript.

Place	Date	Hour	Summary of Events and Information	Remarks and references to Appendices
Hunqarcamp	6/4/18		CASUALTIES. 3 O.R WOUNDED. 1 O.R S.I.W. 3 O.R HOSPITAL N.Y.D GAS. SITUATION NORMAL. NIGHT QUIET. 4AM-7AM BONKER WOOD HEAVILY SHELLED WITH H.E. AND GAS. ENEMY M.G's FIRED AT INTERVALS DURING NIGHT. OUR M.G's FIRED 500 ROUNDS HARASSING FIRE.	REF SHEET 51 & 5.E. APPENDIX 3.
Hungarcamp	9/4/18		CASUALTIES. Lt. T.H. ELDER. GASSED. 2/Lt E.G LORD GASSED. 14. O.R. GASSED. 1 O.R. S.I.W. (AT DUTY) (MISSING) SITUATION NORMAL. NIGHT QUIET. 11. MACHINE GUN SQUADRON WITHDRAWN FROM LINE & MACHINE GUN DEFENCE RE-ADJUSTED AS PER S.O.P. CHAIN OF AMMUNITION SUPPLY ESTABLISHED AS PER INSTRUCTIONS No. 7. OUR M.G's FIRED 1250 ROUNDS HARASSING FIRE.	APPENDIX 4.
Hungarcamp	10/4/18		CASUALTIES 3. O.R. WOUNDED SITUATION NORMAL. NIGHT QUIET. ENEMY M.G's SWEPT OUR LINES INTERMITTENTLY DURING THE NIGHT. OUR M.G's FIRED 1500 ROUNDS HARASSING FIRE AND 250 ROUNDS AT ENEMY AIRCRAFT.	

Army Form C. 2118.

WAR DIARY
or
INTELLIGENCE SUMMARY.

(Erase heading not required.)

Instructions regarding War Diaries and Intelligence Summaries are contained in F.S. Regs., Part II. and the Staff Manual respectively. Title pages will be prepared in manuscript.

Place	Date	Hour	Summary of Events and Information	Remarks and references to Appendices
Humbercamp	11/4/18		CASUALTIES. 2.O.R. WOUNDED. Situation Normal. Night Quiet. Ayette, Douchy, Quesnoy Farm, Adinfer Wood & Adinfer Village Shelled At Intervals. E.A. Active Throughout The Day. Our M.Gs Fired 8750 Rounds At Enemy Aircraft + 450 Rounds Harassing Fire.	Ref. Sheets 57.D.N.E. 51.C.S.E.
Humbercamp	12/4/18		CASUALTIES. 1.O.R. WOUNDED. Situation Normal. Night Quiet. Enemy Artillery Active On Adinfer Wood & Region Of Quesnoy Farm. Our M.Gs Fired 4450 Rounds At Enemy Aircraft. M.G. Defence For This Sector Laid Down In Instructions No. 8.	Ref. D N.E. 51.C.S.E. 57.D.N.E. A.P.5.
Humbercamp	13/4/18		CASUALTIES. 1.O.R. KILLED. Situation Normal. Night Quiet. Enemy Artillery Below Normal. Our M.Gs Fired 10,000 Rounds Harassing Fire.	
Humbercamp	14/4/18		CASUALTIES. 2/Lt J. Griffin. Wounded. At Duty. 1/Lt W. Sharrock. Gassed. 8.O.R. Gassed. Situation Normal. Night Quiet. Enemy Artillery Active With Gas Shells In Valleys Behind Quesnoy Farm. Our M.Gs Fired 6,000 Rounds Harassing Fire. Programmes For Harassing Fire Issued In Instructions No. 9	A.P.G.

Army Form C. 2118.

WAR DIARY
or
INTELLIGENCE SUMMARY.

(Erase heading not required.)

Instructions regarding War Diaries and Intelligence Summaries are contained in F. S. Regs., Part II. and the Staff Manual respectively. Title pages will be prepared in manuscript.

Place	Date	Hour	Summary of Events and Information	Remarks and references to Appendices
HUMBERCAMP	15/6/18		Casualties. 3.O.R. Gassed. Situation Normal. Night Quiet. Numerous small parties of Enemy seen during day. Our M.Gs Fired 6,000 Rounds of Harassing Fire. Guns moved in Accordance with O.O 20	App. 2.
HUMBERCAMP	16/6/18		Casualties. 4.O.R. Killed. 6 O.R. Wounded. 1.O.R. Wounded at Duty. 1.O.R. Gassed. Note of these casualties 2.O.R Killed occurred 5 O.R Wounded preparatory to move of transport. Situation Normal, Night Quiet. Enemy Artillery Normal. Vicinity of Quesnoy Farm being shelled between 10 & 11 P.M. Our M.Gs. Fired 13,000 Rounds on Special Targets. Transport lines moved from Bienvillers au Bois to Pommier	Ref Sheet 57° N.E.
HUMBERCAMP	17/6/18		Casualties. 1 O.R Gassed Situation Normal. Night Quiet. Enemy Artillery Below Normal. Pommier Wood & Neighbourhood shelled at intervals during Day & Night during afternoon. Artillery active in vicinity of Douchy. Enemy M.Gs Displayed Little activity Our M.Gs Fired 9,000 Rounds on Special Targets	Ref Sheet 51° S.S.E

WAR DIARY
or
INTELLIGENCE SUMMARY.

(Erase heading not required.)

Army Form C. 2118.

Instructions regarding War Diaries and Intelligence Summaries are contained in F. S. Regs., Part II. and the Staff Manual respectively. Title pages will be prepared in manuscript.

Place	Date	Hour	Summary of Events and Information	Remarks and references to Appendices
Humbercamp	18/4/18		CASUALTIES 10.OR Gassed. Situation Normal. Night Quiet. Artillery Active on Forward Areas. Little Farm, Pommier Wood + Purple Line Shelled at Intervals. Our M.Gs Fired 12,650 Rounds. Harassing Fire on Special Targets. Lt C.E. Duggan + 2/Lt H.V. Murray Reported for Duty + Posted to B. Coy.	Ref Sheet 57P.N.E.
Humbercamp	19/4/18		CASUALTIES 4.OR Wounded 5.OR Gassed. Situation Normal. Night Quiet. Artillery Activity Above Normal. Ayette, Douchy and Pommier Wood were Shelled at Intervals. Our M.Gs Fired 14,000 Rounds. On Special Targets. Also 50 Rounds Anti-Aircraft. At Hoppy Aran Seen At A.2.C.1030 Was Killed by one of our M.Gs. Lt W.E. Sandom, M.G.C. Reported for Duty + Posted to B.Coy.	Ref Sheets 57P.N.E. 57C.N.W.
Humbercamp	20/4/18		CASUALTIES 1.OR Gassed 2.OR Wounded. Situation Normal. Night Quiet. Artillery Anve. Our M.Gs Fired 14,700 Rounds On Special Targets + 50 Rounds A.A. Hon. Captain + Q.M.R. A Barker Joined For Duty.	

Army Form C. 2118.

WAR DIARY
or
INTELLIGENCE SUMMARY

(Erase heading not required.)

Instructions regarding War Diaries and Intelligence Summaries are contained in F. S. Regs., Part II. and the Staff Manual respectively. Title Pages will be prepared in manuscript.

Place	Date	Hour	Summary of Events and Information	Remarks and references to Appendices
Humbercamp	2/4/18		Casualties Nil. Situation Normal. Night Quiet. Enemy Artillery Active. At 2:30AM. Vicinity of Quesnoy Farm was Heavily Shelled For An Hour. Little Farm. Cosuel Valley. Were Shelled. Our MG's Fired 14,000 Rounds Harrassing Fire On Special Targets & 2400 Rounds At Enemy Aircraft.	Ref Sheet 57°.N.E.
Humbercamp	22/4/18		Casualties Nil. Situation Normal. Night Quiet. From 4PM to 6PM Quesnoy Farm Area was Shelled. 6PM Little Farm was Shelled With G.S. Enemy M.G. Retaliated To Our M.G Fire. Our M.G's Fired 13,400 Rounds Harrassing Fire On Special Targets. Also 1,000 Rounds At Enemy Aircraft.	Ref Sheet 57°.N.E.
Humbercamp	23/4/18		Casualties Nil. Situation Normal. Night Quiet. Enemy Artillery Active On Usual Targets Ayette Douchy Coseul Valley Adinfer Quesnoy Farm. Enemy MG's Active During Night & Early Morning. Our MG's Fired 14,800 Harrassing Fire & 1,000 At E.A. Relief Orders Issued. M.G.O.O 21.	Ref Sheet 51°.SE 57°.NE A.P.S

WAR DIARY
or
INTELLIGENCE SUMMARY

Army Form C. 2118.

Place	Date	Hour	Summary of Events and Information	Remarks and references to Appendices
Humbercamp	24/4/18		Casualties 2/Lt. J.I. Hamilton Wounded. I.O.R. Gassed. I.O.R. Wounded at Duty. Situation Normal Night Quiet. Enemy Artillery Below Normal During Day. From Dusk to Midnight Tracks & Roads were Harrassed. Monfer Wood Purple Line, Ayette, Coteul Valley and Quesnoy Farm Received Considerable Shelling. Bienvillers was Shelled During Early Evening. Enemy M.G's Active from the Direction of Ablainzville. Our M.G's Fired 14,000 Rounds Harrassing Fire 7250 at Enemy Aircraft.	Ref Sheets 51c S.E. 57º N.E.
Humbercamp Saulty	25/4/18		Casualties 2/Lt. E.H. Dallas. Admitted Hospital. Diag. Wounded Gas. I.O.R. Wounded. Situation, Normal, Night Quiet. Our M.G's Fired 6000 Rounds Harrassing Fire on Special Targets. Battalion Hq. Closed at Humbercamp at 5pm & Reopened on Arrival at Saulty. V.7b 50.50 A + D Coys were Relieved as per O.O. 21 & Stayed the Night in the Caves at Monchy Au Bois.	Ref Sheet 51c S.E. 57º N.E. A.P.8.
Saulty	26/4/18		Casualties. I.O.R Wounded. A + D. Coys. Marched to Billets in Saulty arriving at 10am. B. & C. Coys. were Relieved on Night of 26/27. As per O.O. 21 on Relief Coys. Marched to Billets in Bienvillers. Au. Bois. M.G. Instructions. No. 10. For M.G. Batt. in Reserve, issued to Coys.	Ref Sheet 51c S.E. 57º N.E. A.P.8. A.P.9.

Army Form C. 2118.

WAR DIARY
or
INTELLIGENCE SUMMARY

(Erase heading not required.)

Instructions regarding War Diaries and Intelligence Summaries are contained in F.S. Regs., Part II. and the Staff Manual respectively. Title Pages will be prepared in manuscript.

Place	Date	Hour	Summary of Events and Information	Remarks and references to Appendices
Saulty	27/4/18		Battalion Spent Day In Cleaning Equipment + Clothes.	
Saulty	28/4/18		Church Parade. Draft Of 80 Men Arrived From Base. 2/Lt. J.A. Bridgewater Taken on Strength + Posted To A Coy.	
Saulty	29/4/18		A + D Coys Spent Day Bathing. B+C Coys Carried Out Training.	
Saulty	30/4/18		Training Carried Out.	

APPENDICES

1 to 9.

SECRET. *War diary*   Copy No. 15

32nd BATTALION MACHINE GUN CORPS OPERATION ORDER NO. 18.

1. The Divisional front is being reorganised on a three brigade front on night 1/2nd April.
   Each brigade will have 2 battalions for defence of ground in its sector in advance of PURPLE LINE and 1 battalion for defence of PURPLE LINE in its sector.

2. The M.G. Companys will also be reorganised in depth on 2nd April and night 2/3rd in accordance with attached map "A".

3. Each brigade will have its attached M.G. Company covering approximately the brigade front, each Coy. having 8 guns for defence of forward area and 8 guns for defence of ground between forward area and PURPLE LINE.

4. As regards the front line guns, the attached map is only meant to serve as a guide to placing the guns, the exact positions being decided by the Coy. Commander concerned in consultation with the G.Os.C. Brigades. Whenever possible Machine Guns should be placed behind the front line firing through gaps between posts and not _in_ the front line trench.

5. The 11th M.G. Squadron will remain in its present position on the right flank and "D" Coy. will be disposed laterally behind the PURPLE LINE to add depth to the whole defences.

6. The above reorganisation will take place in accordance with attached table "B".

7. Coy. Headquarters will be located as follows:-

   "A" and "C" at   ADINFER
   "B" and M.G. Squadron at   QUESNOY FARM.
   "D" at   MONCHY.

8. The signalling Officer will arrange for telephonic communication between Coy. Headquarters and their respective Brigades. "D" Coy. will be connected with both 96th and 14th Brigades. Visual communication will also be arranged from section Headquarters in the front line back to QUESNOY FARM and ADINFER.

9. In siting all guns, concealment is the first thing to aim at. Newly dug trenches should be avoided and old German trenches, pits etc, made use of whenever possible.

10. Attention is called to the instructions contained in Appendix "B" of 32nd Batt. M.G.C. O. No. 17.

11. Section Officers and N.C.O's. in charge of guns must realise that their guns are not necessarily meant to fire in one direction only; many guns can be reversed and made to fire either flank at will with very little if any movement.
    The more guns that can be brought to bear on the attacking troops the better.

12. Coy. Commanders will send in a map to Battalion Headquarters as soon as possible after the reorganisation showing the exact positions they have taken up in accordance with these instructions.

13. All details of moves to be arranged between Coy. Commanders. Belt boxes will be handed over whenever possible.

14. After the reorganisation, if the situation is quiet, teams will be reduced to 5 men per team, the remainder being brought back to BIENVILLERS or HUMBERCAMP so as to admit of a partial relief in the line taking place.

/15.

15.   Completion of reorganisation will be reported by Companys to Battalion Headquarters by word "ORGAN".

16.   ACKNOWLEDGE.

                                          J. Reeve
                                                    Lt.-Col.
                                    Commanding 32nd Battalion M.G. Corps.

1/4/1918.

Issued at:-

Copies to:-
1. C.O.
2. Adjutant.
3. O.C. "A" Coy.
4. O.C. "B" Coy.
5. O.C. "C" Coy.
6. O.C. "D" Coy.
7. Transport Officer.
8. Signal Officer.
9. Headquarters, 14th Infantry Brigade.
10.   "   96th   "
11.   "   97th   "
12/13.   "   32nd Division.
14. O.M.G.O.
15. War Diary.
16. File.
17. 11th M.G. Squadron.

TABLE "B"

Serial No.	No. of guns	M.G. Coy.	Approx. Location	Move to	In relief of	No of guns	Remarks.
1	(4 (4	C C	F.5.a.7.5. F.4.d.9.9.?	X.29.d.91.	A	4	Move to new positions on left of Bde. Sector.
2.	(4 (4	A A	X.29.d.9.1. F.5.b.	F.5.d.4.5. (quarry)	B	4	
3.	4	B	F.5.d.4.5.	F.10.b.7.4 (2) F.3.c.7.1 (2) F.10.d.5.4.	C C	2)) 4)	These 6 guns are in F.10.a
4.	6	C	F.10.a.	F.29.c.4.2. (4) F.28.a.94. (2)			To replace those moved in Serial No. 1.

INSTRUCTIONS.

1. Above reliefs to take place starting at 7.p.m. on night 2/3rd April.

2. "D" Coy, and 11th M.G. Squadron will assume new positions during Tuesday 2nd April.

3. Guns that are being relieved in the same position by guns of another company will not move until their relief arrives and has taken over completely.

4. Above table only deals with front line guns, other guns not detailed will move from present positions, without waiting for relief. Some of these movements can be carried out by day at discretion of Company Commander.

SECRET. Copy No. 12

32nd BATTALION MACHINE GUN CORPS INSTRUCTIONS NO. 6.
S.O.S. Arrangements.

1. Company Commanders will submit detailed calculations to bring fire to bear in accordance with attached table "A".

2. Care must be taken to see that the fire cone clears the crest in some cases.

3. D. Coy. will not fire on their line by night and only by day when it is clear that the enemy has broken through our front line and is in the valley.

4. Fire at usual S.O.S. rates.

5. T and V bases will be employed. Companies will submit their requirements for them to Battalion Headquarters.

6. Guns detailed will be normally kept laid on their S.O.S. lines ready to open fire at a moment's notice.

7. It is essential that sentries should be absolutely on the alert so that fire can be instantaneously opened.

7th April 1918.

J. Reeve, Lt. Col.
Commanding 32nd Battalion M.G.C.

Copies to:-
1. O.C.
2. Adjutant.
3. O.C. "A" Coy.
4. O.C. "B" Coy.
5. O.C. "C" Coy.
6. O.C. "D" Coy.
7. 11th M.G. Squadron.
8. 14th Infantry Brigade.
9. 96th Infantry Brigade.
10. 97th Infantry Brigade.
11. Headquarters, 32nd Division.
12. War Diary.
13. File.

TABLE "A".

1. D. Coy. guns 1 to 12 -

    line F.15 central - F.10.d.00.

2. 11th M.G. Squadron.

    4 guns at F.14.d.6.3.) F.17.c.9.9.
    2 guns at F.15.d.4.0.) to F.23.a.7.7.

3. B. Coy. 2 guns at F.9.c.1.6.) F.17.c.9.9.
           2 guns at F.10.c.48.)   to
           2 guns at F.10.a.5.2.) F.12.c.0.0.

4. A. Coy. 2 guns at F.9.a.7.8.) F.12.c.0.0.
           4 guns at F.4.d.1.5.)   to
           2 guns at F.4.a.0.7.) A.1.d.0.0.
           2 guns at X.28.c.33.)

5. B. Coy. 2 guns at F.16 central) A.1.d.00.
           4 guns at F.10.d.6.5.)   to
                                   A.1.b.00.

6. A. Coy. 2 guns at F.10.b.8.2. (A.1.b.00.
                                  (to
                                  (A.1.b.4.2.

7. C. Coy. 2 guns at X.29.c.0.7. (A.1.b.4.2.
                                  (to
                                  (A.2.a.0.4.

8. C. Coy. 4 guns at X.29.c.9.3.) A.2.b.0.5.
           2 guns at F.5.b.9.9.)   to
                                   S.27.c.3.2.

SECRET.

Amendment No. 1 to 32nd Battalion Machine Gun Corps Instructions No. 6.

1. Table "A" issued with 32nd Battalion Machine Gun Corps Instructions No. 6 is cancelled and the attached substituted.

2. Company Commanders will submit their detailed calculations in accordance with these instructions and will report as soon as their guns are laid on these lines.

3. It is essential that the gun position on the map should be located as accurately as possible.

Lt. Col.,
Commanding 32nd Battalion M. G. C.

Issued to all recipients of Instructions No. 6.

10th April 1918.

Table issued with Machine Gun Instructions No. 6.

Serial No.	No. of Guns	Coy.	Location	Target	Serial No.	No. of Guns	Coy.	Location	Target
1.	2	B	F.10.d.5.4.	F.23.a.72.72.	13.	2	B	F.10.d.6.5.	A.1.d.90.77
2.	2	A	F.10.c.1.9.	F.23.a.73.78.	14.	2	A	F.10.b.8.3	A.1.d.81.74
				F.23.a.75.84.					A.1.d.72.72
3.	4	B	F.14.d.6.2.	F.23.a.76.91.	15.	2	A	X.28.c.4.4	A.1.d.63.70
				F.23.a.77.98.					{A.1.d.54.67
				F.17.c.78.03.					{A.1.d.45.64
				F.17.c.79.10.					A.1.d.35.61
4.	2	B	F.15.d.3.1.	F.17.c.80.18.	16.	2	C	X.28.a.9.4.	A.1.d.25.58
				F.17.c.81.25.	17.	1	B	F.15.d.3.9	A.1.d.16.55
				F.17.c.83.30.	18.	2	C	S.25.b.9.2.	F.12.a.10.15
5.	2	A	F.4.d.1.5.	F.17.c.84.37.	19.	10	D		F.15. central
				F.17.c.85.43.					to
6.	2	B	F.9.c.1.6.	F.17.c.89.62.					F.16.a.8.9.
				F.17.c.90.69.					
7.	2	A	F.3.c.7.0.	F.17.c.91.75.					
				F.17.c.92.81.					
8.	1	C	F.5.D.8.7.	F.17.c.93.87.					
9.	2	C	X.29.d.0.4.	F.17.c.94.92.					
				F.17.a.95.00.					
10.	2	C	X.29.c.8.1.	A.2.c.42.90.					
				A.2.c.35.88.					
11.	2	A	F.10.a.5.2.	A.2.c.25.85.					
				A.2.c.18.83.					
12.	2	A	F.4.d.1.6.	A.2.c.09.82.					
				A.2.c.00.80.					

SECRET

32nd Battalion Machine Gun Corps Order No. 19.

Copy No.

1. The 11th Machine Gun Squadron will be withdrawn from the line to-night 9/10th inst. and withdrawn to FROHEN-LE-GRAND under separate instructions already issued.

2. The Machine Gun defence will be re-adjusted in accordance with Table 'A' attached.

3. Detailed arrangements will be made by Company Commanders concerned.

4. Completion of moves will be reported to Battalion Headquarters in code by word "SHUFFLE".

5. Guns of 11th Machine Gun Squadron will not withdraw until properly relieved. All details of position, lines of fire, work in hand, etc. will be carefully handed over.

6. Maps will be returned to Battalion Headquarters.

7. ACKNOWLEDGE.

9th April 1918.

J Reeve
Lieut-Colonel,
Commanding 32nd Battn, M.G.Corps.

Copies to:- O.C.
Adjutant.
'A' Company.
'B' Company.
'C' Company.
'D' Company.
11th M.G. Squadron.
14th Inf. Brigade.
96th Inf. Brigade.
97th Inf. Brigade.
32nd Division.

P.T.O.

TABLE 'A'.

Serial No.	No. of guns.	M.G. Coy.	Location.	Relieve No. of guns.	M.G. Coy.	Map location.
1.	2.	D.	F.2.c.8.7.	2	B.	F.8.b.4.2.
2.	2	D.	F.13.c.9.9.	4	11th M.G. Sqdn.	F.19.b.95.60.
3.	2	B.	Front line F.16.d.8.9.	2	do.	F.15.d.4.1.
4.	2	B.	F.8.b.4.2.	2	do.	F.14.b.2.4.
5.	6	B.	F.10.a.& c.	4	do.	F.14.d.6.2.
6.	2	A.	F.11.b.1.1. F.11.c.9.6.	2	B.	F.10.c.2.9.
7.	2	A.	F.5.b.5.2.	2	B.	F.10.a.5.2.
8.	2	C.	Front line F.6.a.	2	A.	F.5.b.5.2.

SECRET.

Copy No......15...

Off. 4

32nd BATTALION MACHINE GUN CORPS INSTRUCTIONS No. 7.

Ammunition Supply.

The following chain of ammunition supply will be established in order to ensure an adequate flow of filled belt boxes to the Machine guns in all circumstances :-

1. Each gun in the line will maintain a minimum of 14 filled belt boxes and all except the front line guns, 10 boxes of S.A.A. in addition - the special M.G. bundle packed ammunition being used whenever possible.

2. Each Coy. will keep one 4 horse (or mule) limber on the western outskirts of MONCHY, each containing 64 filled belt boxes, and all the animals being provided with pack saddles and panniers.
Coys. will detail their own men to look after these limbers and their teams, but O.C. B. Coy. will be responsible for looking after and supervising all of them.

3. Each Coy. will similarly keep one limber at the transport lines BERVILLERS containing 64 filled belt boxes. These boxes will be always kept ready in the limbers and will not be used for any other purpose.

Action in case of attack.

1. In the case of front line guns it is considered their establishment of belt boxes is sufficient to enable them to beat back the attack if it is not overwhelming or for the attack to have over-run them if made in sufficient force.

2. Os. C. Coys. will be responsible for sending down to their limber at MONCHY as early as possible in the event of a serious attack and directing it where to come to. Part of it can then be dumped to form a central reserve and the remainder taken as close up to the guns as possible by pack, the animals returning with empty belt boxes.

3. In the event of limbers at MONCHY moving forward, the limbers at BY BVILLERS will be prepared to move forward and take their place or as directed by Battalion Headquarters.

If operations should assume a semi-open character the M.G. Battalion will deal direct with the S.A.A. section of the D.A.C. for its supplies of ammunition. The D.A.C. will be responsible for delivering the ammunition up to the place fixed by Battalion Headquarters for its reserve and Battalion sending it forward from there to Coys. one limber per Coy. or more if necessary being drawn from the Coys. for this purpose.

In the event of a Company being attached to an Infantry Brigade, that company will draw on the Infantry Brigade Reserve for its supply of ammunition under arrangements to be made by the Coy. Commander with the G.O.C. Brigade concerned.

Every empty or partly empty belt should always be refilled as quickly as possible. It must be impressed on all ranks that in a big attack a very large part will be played by the Machine Guns, that their consumption of ammunition will be enormous and that the supply of filled belts a very vital factor. Every team should make it a point of honour to see that their gun has always belts ready to fire however much it may consume.

Coys. will indent on Battalion Headquarters for the

number of belt boxes they require to bring them up to the establishment as detailed in these instructions.

G. Rawe
Lt. Col.
Commanding 32nd Battalion M.G.C.

9/4/1918.

Copies to :-

1. O.C.
2. Adjutant.
3. Transport Officer.
4. O.C. "A" Coy.
5. O.C. "B" Coy.
6. O.C. "C" Coy.
7. O.C. "D" Coy.
8. 11th M.G. Squadron.
9. 14th Infantry Brigade.
10. 96th Infantry Brigade.
11. 97th Infantry Brigade.
12/13. Headquarters, 32nd Division.
14. D.A.C. 32nd Division.
15. War Diary.
16. File.

SECRET.   Copy No...13....

32ND BATTALION MACHINE GUN CORPS INSTRUCTIONS NO. 8.

Defence Scheme.

1. **Boundaries.**
    The front held by 32nd Division extends from F.22.b.8.7. to S.27.a.00., with the 62nd Division on our right and the Guards Division on our left.
    The boundaries are shown on maps already issued to all concerned.

2. **Organizations.**
    The Machine Guns are organized in depth mutually supporting and crossing their fire with one another, the scheme being based on the plan of having as much of the Divisional area to a depth of 3000 to 4000 yards as possible under direct fire, special attention being paid to the valleys.

3. **Dispositions.**
    A. The guns are disposed as shown on map already issued each Brigade being covered by its old Brigade Company.
    B. The fourth Coy. (the old Divisional Coy.) is disposed laterally behind the PURPLE LINE, special attention being paid to the right flank.
    C. One Section (4 guns) of Vickers guns and 3 Sections of German light Machine guns will be kept in reserve at the caves in MONCHY. In case of attack they will be prepared to move at once on receipt of orders from Battalion Headquarters under the command of O.C. D. Coy.

4. **Lines of fire.**
    A. All guns are sited primarily for direct fire. The nature of the terrain, open grassy belts and well defined valleys is peculiarly suited for direct M.G. fire and enables the guns not only to fire on the normal lines as indicated on the map but also in case of necessity to switch their fire round in the opposite direction without change of position.
    B. Nearly all guns have, in addition, an indirect line which will bring their fire down on 2 selected areas on the S.O.S. signal being made.
    C. Guns in the PURPLE SUPPORT line and ADINFER SWITCH which cannot reach the front line, can bring down a barrage in the COJEUL VALLEY in case of need, special arrangements with regard to this are being made.

5. **Principles of defence.**
    A. All machine gunners must be imbued with the determination to "hang on" and "stick it out" in the position where they are even if absolutely outflanked.
    B. The duties of the Machine Guns are :-

    1. To kill as many Germans as possible.
    2. To protect the infantry.
    3. In case the infantry are forced back by weight of numbers to gain time for them to re-form and for the counter-attack to develop.
    4. Should a withdrawal be ordered by the higher command, to cover it by their fire and finally to mutually cover their own withdrawal.

/C

2.

C.　　　The Machine guns will best carry out their duties
(B.1 - 3 above) by holding their ground and firing to the
last, knowing that they by so doing, are carrying out their
job in the best possible way. There will be no withdrawal
from any position without direct orders from the G.O.C.
Brigade concerned.

6. **Action if a gun is disabled.**

　　　It is the duty of any team whose gun is put
totally out of action and is beyond repair to join the nearest
gun to them which is in action, taking with them all available
full belt boxes, spare parts etc.

　　　The action taken will be reported to Coy. Headquarters as quickly as possible.

7. **Ammunition supply.**

　　　Instructions on the chain of ammunition supply
from the rear forward have already been issued. All ranks must
realize that the supply of ammunition is a most vital factor.
All empty belts must be re-filled as quickly as possible.

8. **Gun Numbers.**

　　　Only Nos. 1 and 2 will be actually at the gun whilst
firing, other numbers will remain under cover to a flank re-
filling empty belts etc.

9. **Reconnaissance.**

　　　All officers and especially officers and N.C.Os.
of guns in reserve will reconnoitre all approaches and ground
within the Divisional area up to the PURPLE RESERVE line,
special attention being paid to the ground N.W. of ESSARTS.

10. **Communications.**

　A.　　　All Coy. Headquarters are in communication with
their respective Brigades by telephone, and also with
Battalion Headquarters.
　B.　　　Communication from section to Coy. Headquarters is
by runner.
　C.　　　Visual stations in the forward area back to Coy.
Headquarters are being arranged.
　D.　　　The transport lines at BIENVILLERS are connected
by telephone to Battalion Headquarters.
　E.　　　Officers must realize the importance of keeping their
superiors informed of the situation. Without this, control
is impossible.

11. **Position of Headquarters.**

　　　Battalion Headquarters is at HUMBERCAMP U.29.a.8.4.
　　　Transport lines are at BIENVILLERS E.2.c.
　　　A.Coy. Headquarters)
　　　B.Coy.　　"　　　) In caves at MONCHY
　　　D.Coy.　　"　　　) E.5.a.9.7.
　　　A and C Coys. are moving forward to bank about
　　　X.28.a.0.4. when accommodation has been constructed.
　　　B. Coy. near QUESNOY FARM - F.13.d.3.9.

12. ACKNOWLEDGE.

　　　　　　　　　　　　　　　　　　J Reeve
　　　　　　　　　　　　　　　　　　　　　　Lt. Col.
12.4.1918.　　　　　　　　Commanding 32nd Battalion M. G. C.

Distribution of 32nd Battalion Machine Gun Corps Instructions No. 8.

1. O.C.
2. Adjutant.
3. Transport Officer.
4. O.C. "A" Coy.
5. O.C. "B" Coy.
6. O.C. "C" Coy.
7. O.C. "D" Coy.
8. 14th Inf. Bde.
9. 96th Inf. Bde.
10. 97th Inf. Bde.
11/12. Headquarters, 32nd Division.
13/14. War Diary.
15. File.

SECRET.

Copy No. 14

32ND BATTALION MACHINE GUN CORPS INSTRUCTIONS NO.9.

Harassing Fire.

1. The machine guns will carry out a policy of harassing fire with the object of inflicting casualties and causing the enemy as much annoyance and inconvenience as possible.

2. The following limitations will be observed:-

    A. No gun that is under direct observation will fire i.e. all firing will be indirect.

    B. Not more than 7000 rounds per 24 hours will be fired on any one Brigade front.

    C. No regular sequence either in times of firing or targets engaged will be followed.

3. It is essential that the positions of our M.Gs. should not be disclosed. If there is any doubt as to whether a gun is under observation or not, the gun will remain silent.

4. All belts expended must be refilled as quickly as possible.

5. A list of suitable targets is attached. These will be supplemented at discretion of G.O.C. Brigades on information received from their O.Ps. etc.

6. Coy. Commanders will work out calculations for firing on such of the targets as their respective guns can reach. Traversing and searching will be freely employed.

7. A C K N O W L E D G E.

14th April 1918.

J. Reeve
Lt. Col.
Commanding 32nd Battalion M.G.C.

Copies to:-

   1. C.O.
   2. Adjutant.
   3. Intelligence Officer.
   4. O.C. "A" Coy.
   5. O.C. "B" Coy.
   6. O.C. "C" Coy.
   7. O.C. "D" Coy.
   8. 14th Inf. Bde.
   9. 96th Inf. Bde.
   10. 97th Inf. Bde.
11/12. Headquarters, 32nd Division.
13/14. War Diary.
   15. File.

List of Harassing Fire Targets.

Serial No.	Nature of target	Location
1.	Suspected Headquarters	F.18.a.05.60.
2.	Short length of trench and shelters	F.18.a.0.3. and surrounding area.
3.	Aerodrome	A.7.d.6.1.
4.	Hutments and dug-outs in sunken road	F.17.d.2.6.
5.	Embankment running N.E. with dug-outs	F.17.d.5.1. to F.17.d.85.25.
6.	CROSS ROADS	A.14.a.4.5.
7.	Movement and shelters	A.14.a.4.5. to N.E. along road.
8.	Centre of movement and work	A.14.c.
9.	Movement on track	A.1.a.4.6. to E.N.E.
10.	Short length of trench	A.2.c.8.7. to A.2.d.2.9.
11.	Trench	A.2.a.4.5. to A.3.c.0.7.
12.	Huts	A.3.c.50.45.

Reference 32nd Battalion Machine Gun Corps Instructions No. 9.

1. Machine Guns so situated, that when firing as detailed in M.G. Instructions No. 9, their cone only just clears the rear crest thereby endangering anyone walking on the crest, will not fire unless asked to do so by the O.C. Battalion in whose sub-sector they are.

2. In the event of fire being called for, the O.C. Battalion will be responsible for posting sentries to keep men away from the dangerous zone.

3. The above does not apply to an S.O.S. signal, all guns having an S.O.S. line in advance of our front line will automatically open fire on the S.O.S. being sent up.

Reeve
Lt. Col.,
Commanding 32nd Battalion M.G.C.

18th April 1918.

Issued to all recipients of M.G. Instructions No. 9.

SECRET.   Copy No. 13

32ND BATTALION MACHINE GUN CORPS ORDER NO. 20.

1. Moves in accordance with attached table will take place tomorrow 16th inst.

2. Completion of move will be reported to Battalion Headquarters.

3. Positions selected for D. Coy. in the PURPLE RESERVE line will be reconnoitred and marked but not occupied.

4. One Section of D. Coy. will remain in reserve at MONCHY caves.

5. ACKNOWLEDGE.

                                                     Lt. Col.
                                    Commanding 32nd Battalion M.G.C.

15th April 1918.

Copies to :-
   1. O.C.
   2. Adjutant.
   3. O.C. "A" Coy.
   4. O.C. "B" Coy.
   5. O.C. "C" Coy.
   6. O.C. "D" Coy.
   7. 14th Infantry Brigade.
   8. 96th Infantry Brigade.
   9. 97th Infantry Brigade.
10/11. Headquarters, 32nd Division.
12/13. War Diary.
   14. File.

Table issued with 32nd Battalion Machine Gun Corps Order No. 20.

Serial No.	No. of guns	M.G. Coy.	Location.	Move to.
1.	2	A	F.4.d.1.5.	F.5.c.40.45.
2.	2	A	F.4.d.85.25	F.4.d.85.95.

SECRET.

Copy No. 21

att. 8

32nd Battalion Machine Gun Corps Order No. 21.

1. (a) The Guards Division (less Artillery) will relieve the 32nd Division (less Artillery) in the Right Sector of the VI Corps front on 24th and 25th inst. as follows:-

   April 24th and)   1st Guards Brigade relieves 14th Infantry Brigade
   night 24/25th)   in centre sector.

   April 25th and)   3rd Guards Brigade will relieve 96th Infantry
   night 25/26th)   Brigade in the Right sector.

                   2nd Guards Brigade will relieve 97th Infantry
                   Brigade in the Left sector.

   (b) On relief, 32nd Division will move into the COUTURELLE area and be in Third Army Reserve.

2. The Guards Machine Gun Battalion will relieve the 32nd Battalion Machine Gun Corps as follows:-

   Night April 25/26th - No. 3 Coy. Guards Battn. will relieve "A" Coy. in centre sector.
                           No. 1 Coy. Guards Battn. will relieve "D" Coy. in PURPLE system.

   Night April 26/27th - No. 2 Coy. Guards Battn. will relieve "B" Coy. in right sector.
                           No. 4 Coy. Guards Battn. will relieve "C" Coy. in left sector.

3. Command of the Machine Gun defence will pass to O.C. Guards M.G. Battn. on completion of reliefs on night 25/26th.

4. Completion of reliefs on both nights will be reported in code to Battalion Headquarters as follows :-

          Relief complete   ...   LEAVE
          Little shelling   ...   OPEN
          Much shelling   ...   CLOSED.

5. Officers commanding Companies in Guards Battalion will visit their opposite numbers on 24th inst. and mutually arrange all details of relief except as herein specified.

6. All trench stores, maps, lines of fire, bases, T aiming marks, work in hand etc. will be carefully handed over and receipts in duplicate obtained, a copy being forwarded to Battalion Headquarters.

   Great care will be taken that all possible information about the defences is given to relieving units.

7. Ten belt boxes per gun will be handed over, all other belts, boxes anti-tank S.A.A. and German S.A.A. will be brought out.

8./

2.

8. Relieving units will not go forward of the PURPLE Line before 8 a.m.

9. (a) For billeting purposes the battalion is grouped with the 14th Brigade group.

   (b) Details of billeting arrangements and move to rear area will be issued later.

   (c) Probable dispositions will be -

   Headquarters "A" and "D" Coys. - SAULTY.
   "B" and "C" Coys. - BIENVILLERS.

   (d) "A" and "D" Coys. on relief from the line will stage at BIENVILLERS under arrangements to be detailed.

   (e) Moves of transport will be issued later.

10. In the event of 2 Coys. remaining at BIENVILLERS, the Signalling Officer will arrange for telephonic communication between them and Battalion Headquarters.

11. Battalion Headquarters will close at HUMBERCAMPS and re-open at SAULTY at an hour to be notified later.

12. ACKNOWLEDGE.

JReeve.
Lt. Col.,
Commanding 32nd Battalion M. G. C.

23/4/1918.

Issued to :-

1. O.C.
2. Adjutant.
3. O.C. "A" Coy.
4. O.C. "B" Coy.
5. O.C. "C" Coy.
6. O.C. "D" Coy.
7. Transport Officer.
8. Signal Officer.
9. Quartermaster.
10. O.C. Guards M.G. Battn.
11. 14th Infantry Brigade.
12. 96th Infantry Brigade.
13. 97th Infantry Brigade.
14.) Headquarters, 32nd Division.
15.)
16. 174th Tunnelling Coy.
17. Town Major, BIENVILLERS.
18.   "   SAULTY.
19.   "   POMMIER.
20. 32nd Div. Train.
21.) War Diary.
22.)
23. File.

SECRET.

ADDENDUM No. 1 to 32nd Battalion Machine Gun Corps Order No.21.

Reference para. 9 (b).

Coy. Commanders will arrange to send on advance parties to take over their new billets.

Dispositions will be as detailed in para. 9 (c).

Reference para. 9 (d) "A" and "D" Coys. will stage at MONCHY caves on night 25/26th and Not BIENVILLERS.

"A" and "D" Coys. will march to SAULTY independently on 26th starting any time before 9.a.m.
Route – E.4.b. thence track "A" to HUMBERCAMPS – road junction V.15.d.9.0. – cross roads U.14.a.4.0. – SAULTY. Heavily loaded limbers will move all the way by road and not on the track.
As much use as possible will be made of the tracks. An amended map of these is issued herewith (to Coys. and Transport Officer only).

The strictest march dicipline will be observed. 25 yards interval will be maintained between sections of both men and vehicles.
100 yards interval between a Coy. and its transport when together on the road.

Reference para. 9 (d).

The moves of the transport will be arranged direct between the Battalion Transport Officers concerned.

Transport of "B" and "C" Coys. will clear POMMIER by 4.p.m. on 26th.

Reference para. 11.

Battalion Headquarters will close at HUMBERCAMPS at 5.p.m. 25th and re-open at SAULTY on arrival.

Personnel and Transport of Battalion Headquarters will be clear of HUMBERCAMPS by 4.p.m. on 25th.

The O.C. 32nd Battalion M.G.C. will remain at HUMBERCAMPS till 9.a.m. 26th.

Reference para. 6.

A.A. sights and mountings will not be handed over. 5 Gas rattles per Coy. will be brought out as unit equipment, the remainder being handed over.

24/4/1918.
J. Reeve
Lt. Col.,
Commanding 32nd Battalion M.G.C.

Issued to all recipients of 32nd Battn. M.G.C. Order No. 21.

SECRET.

Copy No. 20

32nd Battalion Machine Gun Corps Instructions No.10.

Instructions for M.G. Battalion in Reserve.

Ref. sheets 51 c) 1/40,000 and special map (to Coys., Transport Officer
       57 d)   and Signal Officer only).

1. Position of our own troops.

(a) The VI Corps front is held as follows:-

        Right sector ... Guards Division.
        Centre sector ... 2nd Division.
        Left sector ... 2nd Canadian Division.
    Division in Third Army Reserve (at disposal of VI Corps in case
        of attack) ... ... 32nd Division.

(b) The 129th French Division has) one battalion at BIENVILLERS.
) one battalion at BERLES-AU-BOIS.

    In case of attack these battalions will occupy the RED line from its junction with MONCHY SWITCH (E.4.c.00.) to Point 147 (inc.) about W.17.a.0.0. with posts pushed out along the MONCHY SWITCH to MONCHY (inc.) and thence N. to Point 147 in selected portions of the old British and German lines.

    Each French Battalion has a M.G. Coy. attached to it.

2. Role of Reserve Division.

The 32nd Division will be prepared:-

(a) To counter-attack to regain the PURPLE system if penetrated on any part of the VI Corps front as far N. as ADINFER VILLAGE spur.

(b) To occupy if required:-

    (i) The front line of the RED system from the BIENVILLERS-AU-BOIS - FONQUEVILLERS Road to its junction with the MONCHY SWITCH.

    (ii) The old British line from E.16.d.3.0. to the MONCHY SWITCH (E.5.c.).

    (iii) The old German trenches in E.12.c. and a.

    (iv) The MONCHY SWITCH from its junction with any of the above indicated lines to their junction with the PURPLE RESERVE line in X.25.b.

    (v) The PURPLE RESERVE line from HAMEAU FARM to MILL in X.8.d.

    (vi) The RED line from BASSEUX northwards to the Corps boundary in R.9. central.

3./

3. **Important Tactical points.** With reference to para. 2 (a).

The most important tactical points which must be regained by counter-attack if lost are:-

(i) SAUSAGE RISE and QUESNOY FARM.

(ii) The old British trenches in E.16.d. and E.11.c. and a.

(iii) The old German trenches in E.12.c. and a. and E.11.b.

(iv) MONCHY SWITCH in E.6.c. and a. W.30.d. and X.25.c.

(v) HAMEAU FARM plateau.

(vi) ADINFER VILLAGE spur.

4. **RENDEZVOUS in case of attack.**

Brigades will be prepared to move at once on receipt of orders from Divisional Headquarters to:-

A. 97th Inf. Bde. - Valley S.W. of BERLES-AU-BOIS in W.26.b.
(Right Bde.) Brigade Headquarters - HUMBERCAMPS.

B. 14th Inf. Bde. - Valley N.E. of BERLES-AU-BOIS in W.10.c.& d.
(Centre Bde.) Brigade Headquarters - BAILLEULMONT.

C. 96th Inf. Bde. - Valley S.W. of MONCHIET in Q.26.c.
(Left Bde.) Brigade Headquarters - GOUY Chateau.

The above rendezvous will be known by the letters A. B. and C. respectively.

5. **Movements of 97th Inf. Bde.**

The 97th Inf. Bde. will be prepared to move as follows on receipt of orders from Divisional Headquarters:-

(a) Two Coys. from LA COUCHIE or BAZEQUE direct to outpost positions as under:-

One Coy. to old British line E.16.d. and E.17.a.

One Coy. to old German line E.12.a. and c. and MONCHY SWITCH in E.6.c.

(b) 97th Inf. Bde. (less 2 Coys.) from Rendezvous A. to:-

(i) Occupy front line of RED line from BIENVILLERS-AU-BOIS - FONQUEVILLERS Road to its junction with the MONCHY SWITCH and the MONCHY SWITCH to its junction with the QUESNOY-MONCHY Road.

(ii) The old British line from E.16.d.3.0. to the MONCHY SWITCH and the MONCHY SWITCH to its junction with the QUESNOY-MONCHY Road.

(iii) The old German trenches in E.12.c. and d. and the MONCHY SWITCH as above.

(vi)/

(vi) Not less than one battalion will be kept in Reserve near BIENVILLERS in case of a threat against the right flank of the Brigade.

6. **Movements of 14th Inf. Bde.**

The 14th Inf. Bde. will be prepared to move as follows on receipt of orders from Divisional Headquarters:-

(a) Two Coys. direct to outpost positions in the MONCHY SWITCH from the MONCHY-QUESNOY Road to its junction with the PURPLE RESERVE in X.25.b.

(b) 14th Inf. Bde. (less 2 Coys.) from Rendezvous B. to:-

(i) The valley in W.23.a. and W.17.d.

(ii) Occupy the MONCHY SWITCH from its junction with the QUESNOY-MONCHY Road to its junction with the PURPLE RESERVE and the PURPLE RESERVE northwards to the MILL in X.8.d.

7. **Movements of 96th Inf. Bde.**

The 96th Inf. Bde. will be prepared to move from Rendezvous C. as follows on receipt of orders from Divisional Headquarters:-

(a) To occupy the RED line from BASSEUX northwards to VI Corps boundary in R.9.central.

(b) To move South in Reserve to the other two Brigades.

8. **Role of 32nd Battn. M.G.C.**

On receipt of orders from Battalion Headquarters -

(a) "C" Coy. at BIENVILLERS will come under orders of G.O.C. 97th Inf. Bde.

(b) "A" Coy. at SAULTY will move to rendezvous B. and come under orders of G.O.C. 14th Inf. Bde.

(c) "D" Coy. at SAULTY will move to rendezvous C. and come under orders of G.O.C. 96th Inf. Bde.

(d) "B" Coy. at BIENVILLERS will remain in its vicinity in Divisional reserve.

(e) O's.C. "C" and "A" Coys. will be prepared to detail at least one section each to proceed with the outpost Coys. (para. 5 a and 6 a).

9. **Reconnaissance.**

(a) "C", "A" and "B" Coys. will reconnoitre the area FONQUEVILLER - ESSARTS - western edge of ADINFER WOOD - BERLES-AU-BOIS.

Special /

Special attention will be paid to the contingency of a counter-attack being necessary to regain the QUESNOY - ESSARTS ridge.

    (i) With ESSARTS still in our possession.

    (ii) With ESSARTS in enemy's hands.

    (iii) For contingency (ii) the counter attack would probably be on a large scale in conjunction with a Division of IV Corps.

(b) "D" Coy. will reconnoitre:-

    (i) The RED line from BASSEUX northwards to the Corps boundary with a view to holding the spurs in Q.29 and 30 R.19 and 25 and R.14. and 15.

    (ii) The MONCHY SWITCH, the old British line in E.16.d. and E.17.c. and the old German line in E.12.a. and c.

(c) All Coys. will reconnoitre routes and cross-country tracks to their Rendezvous and thence to the various lines of defence. A new track map will shortly be issued.

(d) All these reconnaissances will be carried out as soon as possibl

(e) The possibility of a counter-attack to retake the QUESNOY ridge is of special importance and will receive the closest consideration of Coy. Commanders.

10. Lines of fire.

(a) In selecting positions to carry out the tasks indicated, guns will be so sited as to:-

    (i) Bring direct overhead fire at medium ranges to cover troops in front who may be forced back.

    (ii) Sweep all approaches to the lines they are protecting with direct fire, especially the valleys.

    (iii) Enfilade the wire of the various trench and switch lines.

    (iv) The importance of depth in all M.G. defences must never be overlooked.

    (v) Guns will be kept in batteries of 4 as far as possible. Pairs will only be detailed for special purposes.

(b) Coy. Commanders will actually site their positions to fulfil their allotted tasks and see that their section officers know them and the best routes to them.

11. Ammunition supply. (see Instructions No.7).

(a) Coys. being affiliated to brigades will draw from the Brigade ammunition reserve under arrangements to be made by the Staff Captain concerned.

(b) "B" Coy. will be affiliated to 97th Inf. Bde. for ammunition supply.

(c) /

(c) Ammunition limbers will be kept ready packed at BIENVILLERS and SAULTY respectively.

(d) Pack transport will be used when necessary to get ammunition right up to the guns.

12. **Position of Headquarters.**

   (a) Battalion Headquarters will remain at SAULTY.

      O.C. M.G. Battalion will be at Divisional Headquarters, BAVINCOURT CHATEAU.

   (b) Coy. Headquarters will be -

      "C" and "B" Coys. ... BIENVILLERS.

      "A" Coy. ... ... BERLES-AU-BOIS.

      "D" Coy. ... ... BASSEUX.

   unless otherwise ordered by G.O.C. Brigade concerned.

13. **Communications.**

The Signal Officer will arrange for communications by every possible means between Battalion Headquarters and Coy. Headquarters, and between Coy. Headquarters and their respective Brigades.

14. **Degree of Readiness.**

While in Third Army Reserve the units of the Battalion will be at one hour's notice to move from 8.a.m. till 12 noon and $2\frac{1}{2}$ hours' notice from 12 noon to 8.a.m.

15. ACKNOWLEDGE.

                                                    Reeve Lt. Col.,
Commanding 32nd Battalion M. G. C.

26/4/1918.

Copies to :-

1. O.C.
2. Adjutant.
3. O.C. "A" Coy.
4. O.C. "B" Coy.
5. O.C. "C" Coy.
6. O.C. "D" Coy.
7. Transport Officer.
8. Signal Officer.
9. Medical Officer.
10. Quartermaster.
11. 14th Inf.Bde.
12. 96th Inf.Bde.
13. 97th Inf.Bde.
14. 32nd Division.
15. O.C. Guards M.G. Battn.
16. O.C. 37th M.G. Battn.
17. O.C. 2nd M.G. Battn.
18. O.C. 2nd Canadian M.G. Battn.
19. C.M.G.O. (VI Corps).
20.)
21.) War Diary.
22. File.

CONFIDENTIAL.

No 4

WAR DIARY

OF

32ND BN. MACHINE GUN CORPS.

From 1st May 1918 to 31st May 1918.

[signature]
Lieut-Col.
Comdg. 32nd Bn. M.G. Corps.

No 4.

Army Form C. 2118.

WAR DIARY
or
INTELLIGENCE SUMMARY.
(Erase heading not required.)

Instructions regarding War Diaries and Intelligence Summaries are contained in F.S. Regs., Part II. and the Staff Manual respectively. Title pages will be prepared in manuscript.

Place	Date	Hour	Summary of Events and Information	Remarks and references to Appendices
SAULTY	1/5/18		Draft of 60 Men arrived from Base. Training carried out by Coys.	Ref SS158 / YD.000
SAULTY	2/5/18		Training carried out by Coys. Conference of Coy Commdrs held by Commanding Officer. A.D. & H.Q. Coys. Transport inspected by CO.	
SAULTY	3/5/18		Training carried out by Coys. B/Order of VI Corps. All Battle Training to be carried out in Steel Helmets.	
SAULTY	4/5/18		Training carried out by Coys. M.G. 00. 22. issued to Coys. Appendix No. 1. & Appendix No. 1. to M.G. Instructions No. 10 issued to Coys. The following officers reported from Base & were posted to Coys. As under Lt. W.H. Clark to A Coy. 2/Lt. Torre W.J. to B Coy. 2/Lt. Williams T.O. to A Coy. 2/Lt. Wall W.J. to D. Coy.	Appendix No. 1 Appendix No 2
SAULTY	5/5/18		Church Parade.	
SAULTY	6/5/18		Move carried out as per M.G. 00 22 already issued to Coys. 4/Sgt Sims G.Coy. A.P.1. & 4/Sgt Sievewright A Coy were presented with the Military Medal by the Corps. Commander.	

Army Form C. 2118.

WAR DIARY
or
INTELLIGENCE SUMMARY.
(Erase heading not required.)

Instructions regarding War Diaries and Intelligence Summaries are contained in F. S. Regs., Part II. and the Staff Manual respectively. Title pages will be prepared in manuscript.

Place	Date	Hour	Summary of Events and Information	Remarks and references to Appendices
SAULTY	7/5/18		TRAINING CARRIED OUT BY COYS. AS PER PROGRAMME.	
SAULTY	8/5/18		TRAINING CARRIED OUT BY COYS AS PER PROGRAMME.	
SAULTY	9/5/18		TRAINING CARRIED OUT BY COYS. AS PER PROGRAMME. COY COMDRS. RECONNOITRED THEIR RESPECTIVE AREAS IN THE CENTRE SECTOR OF VI CORPS FRONT. M.G. OO. 23 ISSUED.	
SAULTY	10/5/18		TRAINING CARRIED OUT BY COYS AS PER PROGRAMME. BOXING TOURNAMENT HELD IN AFTERNOON.	
SAULTY	11/5/18		TRAINING CARRIED OUT BY COYS AS PER PROGRAMME. 2/Lt. WOODOWSON R.J. POSTED TO B.C.Y. 2/Lt. SMITH O.B POSTED TO A.Y.	9P3
SAULTY + BRETENCOURT	12/5/18		CHURCH PARADE A + D COYS RELIEVED C + A COYS OF 2ND BN. IN THE CENTRE SECTOR OF REF. SHEET. 51.SE. LT's.F. MOAT. RE. 12/13 BATT. HQ MOVED TO BRETEN COURT. ATTACHED FROM RES. VI CORPS. ON NIGHT 12/13.	
BRETENCOURT	13/5/18		SITUATION NORMAL. NIGHT QUIET. B + C COYS RELIEVED D + B COYS OF 2ND BN IN THE CENTRE SECTOR OF VI CORPS ON THE NIGHT 13/14.	

WAR DIARY
or
INTELLIGENCE SUMMARY.
(Erase heading not required.)

Army Form C. 2118.

Place	Date	Hour	Summary of Events and Information	Remarks and references to Appendices
BRETENCOURT.	14/5/18		Situation Normal. Night Quiet. Enemy Artillery Active on Hendecourt & Adinfer from 5.30 PM to 9 PM. Considerable Counter Battery Work. Carried out by Enemy. Enemy A.A Guns Very Active. Enemy M.G'S Active during night. Our M.Gs Fired 2,700 Rounds at Enemy Aircraft.	Ref Sheet. 51.C.S.E.
BRETENCOURT.	15/5/18		Situation Normal. Night Quiet from 5PM. To 7.30PM Hendecourt - Boisleux Au Mont Rd. Shelled by 5.9S. Enemy T.MS. Active at Stand To. Night & Morning. Our M.G's Fired 17,500 Harassing Fire & 1650 Rounds at E.A.	51.C.S.E. 51 S.W.
			Casualties 1 O.R. Killed. 2 O.R. Wounded. 2 O.R. Wounded at Dury.	
BRETENCOURT	16/5/18		Situation Normal. Night Quiet. Enemy Artillery Active on Valleys in Neighbourhood of Blairville At 10PM. Heavy Barrage Put Down on Front Line. Our S.O.S Went up at 10.25PM From Right Bn. of Right Bde. All Quiet By 11 PM. Our M.Gs Fired 11,250 Rounds on S.O.S Lines. 12,000 Rounds Harassing Fire. 1,600 AA Fire.	Ref Sheet 51.C.S.E.

WAR DIARY
or
INTELLIGENCE SUMMARY.

(Erase heading not required.)

Army Form C. 2118.

Place	Date	Hour	Summary of Events and Information	Remarks and references to Appendices
Bretencourt	17/5/18		CASUALTIES. 1.O.R. Killed 1.O.R. Wounded 1.O.R. S.W. Situation Normal. Night Quiet. Enemy Artillery Active on Blairville, Hendecourt + Boinfer. Our M.G's Fired 15000 Rounds on Special Target 4750 Rounds @ A.T.E.A. O.O.24. Issued M.G. Instructions No.11. S.O.S. lines. Issued M.G Instructions No.12 Harassing Fire. Issued.	Ref Sheet 51c.S.E A.P.4. A.P.5. A.P.6.
Bretencourt	18/5/18		Situation Normal. Night Quiet. Enemy Artillery Below Normal. Purple line + Sugar Factory Shelled. Our MG's Fired 15000 Rounds on Special Target. 4.350 Rounds fired M.G. Instruction No.13. Liaison Issued.	Ref Sheet 51c.S.E A.P.7.
Bretencourt	19/5/18		CASUALTIES 1.O.R. Wounded Situation Normal. Night Quiet. Our MG's Fired 20000 Rounds on Special Targets + 1750 Rounds A.A. M.G. Instructions for Raid Issued.	A.P.8

Army Form C. 2118.

WAR DIARY
or
INTELLIGENCE SUMMARY.

(Erase heading not required.)

Instructions regarding War Diaries and Intelligence Summaries are contained in F. S. Regs., Part II. and the Staff Manual respectively. Title pages will be prepared in manuscript.

Place	Date	Hour	Summary of Events and Information	Remarks and references to Appendices
BRETENCOURT	20/5/18		SITUATION NORMAL. NIGHT QUIET. ARTILLERY ACTIVE ON RANSART BLAIRVILLE MERCOURT POMPER. RAID CARRIED OUT BY 1ST DOMERS. OUR MGS FIRED 52000 ROUNDS IN SUPPORT OF RAID. O.O. 25 ISSUED 2/LT. R.B. TICHENER ARRIVED AT DEPOT BN. ON 12/5/18	FROM SHEET 51.S.E. A.P.9 2/LT. R.B. TICHENER
BRETENCOURT	21/5/18		SITUATION NORMAL. NIGHT QUIET. ARTILLERY ACTIVE CARRIED OUT HARASSING + COUNTER BATTERY WORK. OUR MGS FIRED 14,700 ROUNDS ON SPECIAL TARGET. 4,500 ROUNDS AT E.A.	
BRETENCOURT	22/5/18		SITUATION NORMAL. NIGHT QUIET. ARTILLERY ACTIVITY BELOW NORMAL DURING ACTIVE AT NIGHT. RANSART JOINEER BOIRY ST MARTIN. OUR MG' 1700 ROUNDS ON SPECIAL TARGETS. 3,700 ROUNDS AT E.A.	51.S.E. 51.S.W.
BRETENCOURT + GASTINEAU	23/5/18		SITUATION NORMAL. NIGHT QUIET. ENEMY ARTILLERY NORMAL. ENEMY MG' FIRED 18,000 ROUNDS ON RETALIATED TO OUR FIRE. OUR MGS FIRED 18,000 ROUNDS ON SPECIAL TARGETS + 3250 ROUNDS AT E.A. BN. HQ MOVED TO GASTINEAU	51.S.E.

Army Form C. 2118.

WAR DIARY
or
INTELLIGENCE SUMMARY.
(Erase heading not required.)

Instructions regarding War Diaries and Intelligence Summaries are contained in F. S. Regs., Part II. and the Staff Manual respectively. Title pages will be prepared in manuscript.

Place	Date	Hour	Summary of Events and Information	Remarks and references to Appendices
GATINEAU	24/5/18		CASUALTIES. 2.O.R. WOUNDED. SITUATION. NORMAL. NIGHT QUIET. ENEMY ARTILLERY FIRED CONCENTRATIONS ON WINDMILL FARM, HAMEAU FARM, PURPLE LINE. OUR M.GS. FIRED 12,000 ROUNDS ON SPECIAL TARGETS.	REF. SHEET. 51.C.SE. 51.B.S.W.
GATINEAU	25/5/18		SITUATION NORMAL. NIGHT FAIRLY QUIET. ARTILLERY ABOVE NORMAL. BOIRY ST MARTIN POINTER SHELLED AT INTERVALS. OUR M.G.S. FIRED 9000 ROUNDS. SPECIAL TARGETS 4250 AT E.A.	51.B.S.W.
GATINEAU	26/5/18		CASUALTIES 2.O.R. KILLED. 6 O.R WOUNDED. SITUATION NORMAL. NIGHT QUIET. ENEMY ARTILLERY ABOVE NORMAL. ROADS + TRACKS IN VICINITY OF HENDECOURT SHELLED. BOIRY POINTER SHELLED. OUR M.GS FIRED 6,200 ROUNDS HARASSING FIRE. 9.00 ROUNDS AT E.A.	51.C.SE. 51.B.S.W.
GATINEAU	27/5/18		CASUALTIES 1 O.R. ACCIDENTALLY WOUNDED. SITUATION NORMAL. NIGHT QUIET. ENEMY ARTILLERY ABOVE NORMAL. COUNTER BATTERY WORK + HARASSING BACK AREAS. HENDECOURT, BOIRY, CEMETERY, WINDMILL FARM SHELLED. OUR M.GS FIRED 10,000 ROUNDS HARASSING FIRE + 1,800 ROUNDS AT E.A. PROVISIONAL DEFENCE SCHEME ISSUED. M.G. INSTRUCTIONS No 19 $\frac{F}{S}$ + 20 O ISSUED 9200 + 12	51.C.SE. M.S.B.15 AP.10 11.- 12.

WAR DIARY
or
INTELLIGENCE SUMMARY.

(Erase heading not required.)

Army Form C. 2118.

Place	Date	Hour	Summary of Events and Information	Remarks and references to Appendices
Gastineau.	28/5/18		CASUALTIES. 5 O.R. GAS. N.Y.D. Situation Normal. Night Quiet. Enemy Artillery Very Active on Roads in Forward Area. Our MGs Fired 11,500 Rounds on Special Targets. 2,500 Rounds at E.A.	
Gastineau.	29/5/18		Situation Normal. Night Quiet. Enemy Artillery Active on Back Areas 51°S.E. During Early Morning & on Forward Areas During Afternoon. Pomfer Hendecourt. Shelled Frequently. Our MGs Fired 7000 Rounds on Special Targets. 2,250 Rounds at E.A. CASUALTIES 1 O.R. KILLED. 2 O.R. WOUNDED.	
Gastineau.	30/5/18		Situation Normal. Night Quiet. Enemy Artillery Active on Back Areas 51°S.E. & Counter Battery Work. Boisleux & Windmill Farm Shelled Our 51B.S.W. MGs Fired 16,000 Rounds on Special Targets. 1450 Rounds on E.A. CASUALTIES NIL	
Gastineau.	31/5/18		Situation Normal. Night Quiet. Enemy Artillery Active on Support System. Our MGs Fired 9000 Rounds on Special Targets. 2300 Rounds at E.A. Lt Hendrie MG Reported for Duty & Posted to B.Coy. Lt Rowe S. Reported for Duty & Posted to A.Coy.	

SECRET.   32nd. BATTALION MACHINE GUN CORPS.   Copy No........

OPERATION ORDER No. 22.

1. The following moves will take place on Monday, 6th. inst.

    "A" and "D" Companies to BIENVILLERS.
    "B" and "C" Companies to SAULTY.

2. "A" Company will take over billets etc., from "C" Company and "D" Company from "B" Company.

3. Details of moves to be arranged direct between Company Commanders. Moves to be completed by 12, noon.

4. The strictest march discipline will be observed. Companies will move by Sections at 25 yards interval; 100 yards between a Company and its Transport.

5. On the arrival of "A" and "D" Companies at BIENVILLERS, the following modifications in para.8 of M.G.Instructions No.10 will come into force:-

    (a). "A" Company at BIENVILLERS will come under orders of 97th.Inf.Bde.
    (b). "C" Company at SAULTY will come under orders of 14th.Inf.Bde.
    (c). "B" Company at SAULTY will come under orders of 96th.Inf.Bde.
    (d). "D" Company at BIENVILLERS will remain in its vicinty in Divisional Reserve.
    (e). As before.
    (f). In the event of the Battalion of the 97th.Inf.Bde., now at BERLES-AU-BOIS, being ordered to occupy the whole outpost position (para.5(a) and 6(a)), "A" Company will be prepared to detail 2 Sections to proceed direct to the outpost line covering the positions detailed in paras.5(a) and 6(a).

6. (a). Officers Commanding Companies will reconnoitre routes to their new rendezvous and their new areas as soon as possible, and will hand over to the relieving Company all results of previous reconnaissances.
   (b). O.C."D" Company will in addition reconnoitre the ground south and south west of BIENVILLERS, with a view to defending the RED SYSTEM, for an attack from those directions.

7. ACKNOWLEDGE.

4/5/1918.

Lieut. Col.
Cmdg. 32nd. Battalion Machine Gun Corps.

Copies to:-
1. O.C.
2. Adjt.
3. O.C. "A" Coy.
4. O.C. "B" Coy.
5. O.C. "C" Coy.
6. O.C. "D" Coy.
7. Transport Officer.
8. Signals Officer.
9. Quartermaster.
10. 14th. Inf. Bde.
11. 96th. Inf. Bde.
12. 97th. Inf. Bde.
13. H.Q. 32nd. Division.
14. H.Q. 32nd. Division.
15. O.C. Guards. M.G. Battalion.
16. O.C. 37th. M.G. Battalion.
17. O.C. 2nd. M.G. Battalion.
18. O.C. 2nd. Canadian M.G. Bn.
19. C.M.G.O., VI Corps.
20. War Diary.
21. War Diary.
22. File.

SECRET.

Amendment No. 1 and Addendum No. 1 to 32nd Battalion Machine Gun Corps Instructions No. 10.

Cancel para. 1 (b).

Para. 5 (a) <u>1st Line</u> for words "CAUCHIE or BAZEQUE" substitute words "BERLES-AU-BOIS".

Para. 5 (a) Add:-

    The 97th Infantry Brigade will be prepared in case of emergency to send the remaining two Companies of the battalion at BERLES-AU-BOIS to occupy the MONCHY SWITCH from its junction with the QUESNOY - MONCHY Road to its junction with the PURPLE RESERVE and to gain touch with the 10th D.C.L.I.(Pioneers), 2nd Division, which will be holding the HAMEAU SWITCH and HAMEAU FARM. These Companies will be relieved by the 14th Infantry Brigade on the arrival of the Companies from BAVINCOURT (vide Para.6).

    <u>NOTE</u>: In the event of these Companies arriving before the 10th D.C.L.I. they will occupy HAMEAU FARM Locality until the arrival of the 10th D.C.L.I.

Para. 6 (a) Add:-

    and to gain touch with the 10th D.C.L.I. (Pioneers), 2nd Division, which will be holding the HAMEAU SWITCH and HAMEAU FARM.

    <u>NOTE</u>: In the event of these Companies arriving before the 10th D.C.L.I. they will occupy HAMEAU FARM Locality until the arrival of the 10th D.C.L.I.

1.   The following code will be used by Divisional Headquarters to order Brigades, 16th H.L.I. (Pioneers) and M.G. Battalion to move to rendezvous and outpost positions:-

    "Brigades PRAISE PUSH Rendezvous MOVE".

    On receipt of this order, the battalion will move as follows:-

2.

(i) "A" Coy. (less 1 Sect.) to rendezvous "A" and come under orders of 97th Inf. Bde.

1 Section "A" Coy. to move to outpost positions as ordered by 97th Inf. Bde.

(ii) "C" Coy. (less 1 Sect.) to rendezvous "B" and come under orders of 14th Inf. Bde.

1 Section "C" Coy. to move to outpost positions as ordered by 14th Inf. Bde.

(iii) "B" Coy. to rendezvous "C" and come under orders of 96th Inf. Bde.

(iv) "D" Coy. to remain at BIENVILLERS in Divisional Reserve.

NOTE. These moves will only come into force after move on 6th inst. until then the present orders remain good.

2. In the event of the battalion of 97th Inf. Bde. being required to find all the outpost positions normally found jointly by 14th and 97th Infantry Brigades, the following will be added to the message:-

"PRISM all outposts."

In this case "A" Coy. will detail 2 Sections to proceed direct and to occupy the whole outpost line.

The whole of "C" Coy. will then go to Rendezvous "B" but will be prepared to relieve the left Section of "A" Coy. in the outpost line later on if the situation permits.

3. ACKNOWLEDGE.

J. Reeve
Lt. Col.,
4/5/1918. Commanding 32nd Battalion M. G. C.

Issued to all recipients of M. G. Instructions No. 10.

SECRET.

Copy No. 23

32nd Battalion Machine Gun Corps Order No.23.

1. The 32nd Division (less Artillery) will relieve the 2nd Division (less Artillery) in the centre sector of the VI Corps front on the nights 11/12th and 12/13th May, as follows:-

    11/12th May. 14th Infantry Brigade will relieve 5th Infantry Brigade in <u>centre</u> sub-sector.

    12/13th May. 97th Infantry Brigade will relieve the 99th Infantry Brigade in the <u>Right</u> sub-sector.

    96th Infantry Brigade will relieve the 6th Infantry Brigade in the <u>Left</u> sub-sector.

2. The relief of the Machine guns will be carried out as under:-

    Night 12/13th May:-

    "A" Coy. 32nd Battn. will relieve "C" Coy. 2nd Battn. in centre.
    "D" " " " " "A" " " in reserve.

    Night 13/14th May:-

    "C" Coy. 32nd Battn. " "D" " " on right.
    "B" " " " " "B" " " on left.

3. Completion of relief on both nights will be reported in code to Battalion Headquarters as follows:-

    | Relief complete | ... | STUCK |
    | Little shelling | ... | FAST |
    | Much shelling | ... | AGAIN. |

4. Command of the M.G. defences will pass to O.C., 32nd Battalion M.G.C. on completion of the Infantry reliefs on night 12/13th May.

5. Coy. Commanders will mutually arrange all details of reliefs except as herein specified.

6. (a) All trench stores, orders, maps, range cards, lines of fire, bases, work in hand will be taken over and receipts given, a copy being forwarded to Battalion Headquarters.
    (b) Great care will be taken to ensure that all ranks know their lines of fire, positions of neighbouring guns etc.
    (c) Belt boxes will NOT be handed over.
    (d) 64 belt boxes per Coy. will be kept in reserve in limber; remainder, including all armour piercing S.A.A. will be taken into the line.

7. (a) Reliefs of back guns will be carried out by daylight, but relieving teams will not cross the PURPLE RESERVE line before 8.p.m.
    (b) Limbers will be taken as close to gun positions as possible in all cases.

8. "D" Coy. will put its heavy German guns at X.21.a.72.45 and X.20.c.65.66 respectively.

    The 10 light German Guns and 1 Section of Vickers Guns will be in reserve in vicinity of RANSART ready to move at 15 minutes notice on receipt of orders from Battalion Headquarters.

9./

2.

9. "A" and "D" Coys. will move to the line by march route; "B" and "C" Coys. by lorry starting SAULTY cross roads V.14.a.4.9. at 7.p.m. on 13th inst.

10. The following distances will be maintained by troops on the road:-

25 yards between Sections of infantry or of 6 vehicles.
100 yards between Coys.
100 yards between a Coy. and its transport.

11. (a) Echelon A of "A" "B" and "C" Coys! transport will be at BRETENCOURT (R.32.b.10.45).
(b) Echelon A of "D" Coy's. transport will be at RANSART (W.12.d.55.58).
(c) Echelon B of all transport will be at BAILLEULMONT (W.2.d.8.9.) with Battalion rear Headquarters.
(d) Move of all transport will be arranged by the Transport Officers.

12. (a) Great care will be taken to leave all billets and their vicinity in a scrupulously clean condition.
(b) All civilian claims for damages by troops must be settled before the Coy. leaves its billets.
(c) Certificates that (a) and (b) have been carried out will be sent to Battalion Headquarters.

13. All details left out of the line will proceed to the Divisional depot battalion at BAILLEULMONT. Further instructions as to this will be issued later.

14. Battalion Headquarters will close at SAULTY at 7.p.m. on 12th inst. and re-open at BRETENCOURT at same hour.

15. ACKNOWLEDGE.

J. Reeve

Lt. Col.,
Commanding 32nd Battalion M.G.C.

9/5/1918.

Copies to:-
1. C.O.
2. Adjutant.
3. O.C. "A" Coy.
4. O.C. "B" Coy.
5. O.C. "C" Coy.
6. O.C. "D" Coy.
7. Signalling Officer.
8. Transport Officer.
9. Medical Officer.
10. Quartermaster.
11. 14th Inf.Bde.
12. 96th Inf.Bde.
13. 97th Inf.Bde.
14/15. H.Q., 32nd Division.
16. 2nd Battn.M.G.C.
17. Guards M.G.Battn.
18. 2nd Canadian M.G.Battn.
19. C.M.G.O., VI Corps.
20. 32nd Div. Train.
21. Town Major, SAULTY.
22. " " BIENVILLERS.
23/24. War Diary.
25. File.

SECRET.   32nd. BATTALION MACHINE GUN CORPS.   Copy No. 13

OPERATION ORDER No. 24.

1. Alterations in accordance with attached table "A" will take place as soon as possible in the dispositions of machine guns in the Divisional Sector.

2. The map already forwarded under C.O. 110 shows the final dispositions of all guns and their main lines of fire.

3. One Section (4 guns) Vickers guns and 10 German light machine guns will remain in reserve near HAMMAM.

4. Companies will report to their respective Brigades when they move any guns to their new positions.
Officer Commanding "D" Company will report to both 97th and 14th. Infantry Brigades.

5. A C K N O W L E D G E.

J. Keare, Lieut. Col.
Cmdg. 32nd. Battalion Machine Gun Corps.

17/1/1918.

Copies to :-

1. C.O.
2. O.C. "A" Company.
3. O.C. "B" Company.
4. O.C. "C" Company.
5. O.C. "D" Company.
6. Transport Officer.
7. Signals Officer.
8. 14th. Infantry Brigade.
9. 96th. Infantry Brigade.
10. 97th. Infantry Brigade.
11. H.Q. 32nd. Division.
12. H.Q. 32nd. Division.
13. War Diary.
14. File.

"A" Form.
MESSAGES AND SIGNALS.

Army Form C.2121
(in pads of 100)
No. of Message

Code	Words	Charge	This message is on a/c of	Recd. at ...m.
Office of Origin and Service Instructions	45		A3	Date
	Sent At ...m. To		Service	From
	By	(Signature of "Franking Officer.")	By	

TO { POSE   QUHI
       QUHO
       QUVO

Sender's Number.	Day of Month.	In reply to Number.	A A A
G. 6.	18th.		

POSE
Reference Mxfx8m. Instructions No. 12 AAA
Times for night firing must be adjusted xmx so
as to meet requirements of Brigadiers as regards
patrols, etc. AAA E POSE will ascertain wishes
of Brigadiers AAA Addsd POSE reptd QUHI .QUHO
QUVO

From GEPA.
Place 4.15 p.m.
Time

The above may be forwarded as now corrected. (Z)

Lt.Col. GS.

Censor. Signature of Addresser or person authorised to telegraph in his name.

* This line should be erased if not required.

Table "A" issued with order No. 24.

Serial No.	M.G. Coy.	No. of Guns.	Present location.	Move to.	Instructions.
1.	B.Coy. H.Q.		X.4.a.70.25	X.5.b.5.4.	1. Positions marked x require very careful construction to avoid being seen by the enemy.
2.	B.	2.	M.31.d.05.30	X.6.a.0.0.	
3.	B.	2.	S.16.b.30.35	S.11.c.55.00.	
4.	B.	2.	S.12.c.45.50	S.18.a.0.8.	
5.	B.	2.	S.18.a.15.00	S.17.c.85.15.x	
6.	A.	2.	S.2.c.0.0.	S.7.b.65.50.	2. Several of the above moves have already taken place.
7.	A.	2.	S.16.c.2.2.	S.16.c.60.25.	
8.	A.	2.	S.22.b.80.05.	S.22.b.50.40.	
9.	C.	2.	X.21.a.30.92.	X.22.a.25.95.	3. Nos. 9,11,13,15,16 are particularly urgent.
10.	C.	2.	X.15.d.47.93.	X.15.b.05.50.	
11.	C.	2.	X.15.d.47.93.	X.23.a.25.05.	
12.	C.	2.	S.19.d.55.75.	S.19.b.40.25.	
13.	C.	2.	S.26.a.40.55.	S.20.d.95.30.	
14.	C.	2.	S.22.c.35.17.	S.21.d.80.70.x	
15.	D.	2.	W.24.a.85.26.	X.18.a.85.55.	
16.	D.	4.	X.19.a.17.91.	S.14.d.27.87.	
17.	D.	2.	X.12.c.03.21.	X.12.c.15.70.	

SECRET. 32nd. BATTALION MACHINE GUN CORPS.   Copy No. 18

INSTRUCTIONS No. 12.

S.O.S. LINES.

1. The present S.O.S. Lines for Machine Guns will be altered to cover a line from S.24.a.65.20 to S.24.c.00.42. and 4 guns on the N.W. exit of BOYEVILLE.

2. Attached table "A" shows dispositions of guns and target for each individual gun.

3. Company Commanders will submit detailed calculations to bring fire to bear in accordance with these instructions.

4. All guns firing on S.O.S. must have "T" or "V" bases, Zero aiming sticks and "T" aiming marks.
Companies will indent forthwith on Battalion Headquarters for any they require.
Zero posts will be always put out on a grid bearing of 90 and switches calculated from it.

5. All guns firing on S.O.S. will keep 8 belts per gun in addition to those detailed in C.O.100 of 15/5/18, (to Coys. only) to be used only on an S.O.S. call.

6. Fire will be at usual S.O.S. rates.

7. All S.O.S. guns must be kept mounted and laid <u>by day</u> and night ready to open fire at once on the Signal being made.
This is very important and will be rigidly complied with.
It is essential that a sentry should be on duty at each gun by day and that he should be constantly alert. A clinometer ready adjusted will be kept beside each gun.

8. If possible all guns that have to be kept mounted by day will be provided with shrapnel proof emplacements.

9. Company Commanders will arrange to test their S.O.S. Lines with a Machine Gun Officer in the front line trench to see that clearance is all right.

10. Company Commanders will forward a report to Battalion Headquarters when all guns are laid in their new lines and have been tested.

A.M.Humble Capt. & Adjt.
for Lieut. Col.
Cmdg. 32nd. Battalion Machine Gun Corps.

17/5/1918.

Copies to :-

1. C.O.
2. Adjt.
3. O.C. "A" Company.
4. O.C. "B" Company.
5. O.C. "C" Company.
6. O.C. "D" Company.
7. 14th. Inf. Brigade.
8. 96th. Inf. Brigade.
9. 97th. Inf. Brigade.
10. H.Q. 32nd. Division.
11. H.Q. 32nd. Division.
12. 32nd. Divnl. Artillery.
13. O.C. 2nd. Canadian M.G. Bn.
14. O.C. Guards M.G. Bn.
15. O.C. 2nd. M.G. Bn.
16. C.M.G.O. VI Corps.
17. War Diary.
18. War Diary.
19. File.

Table A issued with Instructions No 11.

Serial No	M G Coy	No of guns	Location	Target	Instructions
1.	A	2	S 22 b 52.41	S 22 a 65.20 S 24 a 60.13	If any of these guns change their positions their target will remain the same.
2.	B	4	S 16 b 33.36	S 24 a 54.05 S 24 c 48.97 S 24 c 42.89 S 24 c 36.81	
3.	A	6	S.16.c	S 24 c 30.75 S 24 c 24.69 S 24 c 18.62 S 24 c 12.55 S 24 c 06.48 S 24 c 00.42	
4.	C	4	S 20 d 95.20	S 28 c 35.45 to S 28 c 23.20	

S E C R E T.

Copy No. 16

32ND BATTALION MACHINE GUN CORPS INSTRUCTIONS NO. 12.

Harrassing Fire.

1. It is desired to considerably increase the amount of night harrassing fire done by machine guns in the Divisional Sector.

2. Company Commanders will make arrangements to bring fire to bear every night on some of the targets given in attached Appendix "A".

3. In order to render it harder for the enemy to locate the Machine Guns while firing, it is desired to synchronize their night firing as far as possible so that all guns fire simultaneous bursts (two belts at each burst).

4. Times for night firing for the next week are given in attached Appendix "B" (sufficient copies are attached for distribution down to gun positions).

5. The Signalling Officer will arrange to synchronize Coys. watches daily.

6. Reports on all night firing will be included as usual in the morning intelligence summary.

7. The targets engaged should be varied nightly.

8. ACKNOWLEDGE.

(signed) Capt. Adjt.
for Lt. Col.,
Commanding 32nd Battalion M.G.Corps

17/5/1918.

Copies to:-
1. C.O.
2. Adjutant.
3. O.C. "A" Coy.
4. O.C. "B" Coy.
5. O.C. "C" Coy.
6. O.C. "D" Coy.
7. Signalling Officer.
8. 14th Inf. Bde.
9. 96th Inf. Bde.
10. 97th Inf. Bde.
11/12. H.Q., 32nd Division.
13. 2nd Canadian M.G.Bn.
14. Guards M.G.Bn.
15. 2nd Bn. M.G.C.
16/17. War Diary.
18. File.

APPENDIX "A"
HARASSING FIRE TARGETS

TARGET	LOCATIONS
Orchard	A.4.a.15.50.
Orchard	A.4.a.20.10.
Garden	A.4.a.65.45.
Sunken Road	S.28.a.40.26.
Junction of tracks and railway	S.29.c.10.24.
Road in Hamelincourt	S.29.d.60.20. to S.29.c.00.
Trench	S.24.c.00.20.
Sunken Road	S.30.a.30.10. to S.30.a.00.
Trench	S.30.a.35.50.
Sunken Road	S.30.a.50.60 to S.30.a.80.
Road	S.24.c.90.30. to S.24.d.25.
Work	T.19.a.90.00.
Junction of trench and road	T.19.a.35.45.
Junction of trench and road	S.24.b.75.60.
Trench	S.24.b.15.82.
Movement on railway	S.18.d.70.40.
Boyelle	S.18.d.98.95.
Railway	T.13.c.30.20.
Movement	T.13.c.15.40.
Street in Boyelle	T.13.c.18.72.
Street in Boyelle	T.13.c.40.60.

APPENDIX "B"

Date	Times of Firing.					
May 18	9.30 pm	10.18 pm	12.20 am	1.30 am	2.10 am	2.50 am
" 19	10.15	11.20	12.50	2.40 am	3.5	3.30
" 20	10.30	11.5	12.30	1.10	2.15	2.45
" 21	11.00	11.55	12.40	1.30	2.8	2.30
" 22	10.45	11.10	12.10	1.23	2.5	3.10
" 23	10.10	11.10	12.35	1.18	1.59	2.55
" 24	10.19	10.40	12.15	1.45	2.29	3.00

Addendum No. 1 to M.G. Instructions No. 12.

1. Coys. must be careful to ascertain times and exact route of any patrols which may be going out and will adjust their targets so as not to cramp their action.

2. Any M.G. covering fire etc. that Infantry battalion commanders may require for their patrols will be arranged direct between M.G. Coy. commander and Infantry battalion concerned.

3. ACKNOWLEDGE.

A.M.Humble Capt. & Adjt.
for Lt. Col.,
Commanding 32nd Battalion M.G. Corps.

18/5/1918.

Issued to all recipients of M.G. Instructions No. 12.

SECRET.   Copy No. 17

32nd.BATTALION MACHINE GUN CORPS.

INSTRUCTIONS No. 12.

LIAISON.

1. To ensure close mutual cooperation between Machine Guns and Infantry the following scheme will be adopted forthwith.

2. Each Machine Gun Company Headquarters will communicate daily with its affiliated Brigade Headquarters and ascertain the wishes of the G.O.C.Brigade in Regard to any firing required etc.
It should not be necessary for the Company Commanders to go personally to Brigade Headquarters daily as this will prevent him effectively supervising his guns. It is suggested that the wishes of the G.O.C. Brigade should be ascertained on the telephone as to liaison for the following day and if anything special is required he will arrange to go personally to Brigade Headquarters.

3. O.C. "D" Company will communicate with both 14th. and 97th.Infantry Brigades.

4. Os.C. "B" and "C" Companies will establish close touch with the flank Machine Gun Company Commanders of neighbouring Divisions.

5. Their Headquarters are:- On the right X.29.c.35.35.
   On the left M.31.d.07.13.(Battery Hqrs.)

6. Machine Gun Section Commanders will establish close touch with Infantry Battalion or Company Headquarters situated in the same area.

7. The positions of Machine Gun Section Headquarters and the nearest Infantry Headquarters to them are given in Appendix "A", attached.

   Machine Gun Section Officers must make themselves thoroughly conversant with the dispositions and lines of fire etc., of all Lewis guns near them. They will often be able to offer suggestions for the better combination of Lewis and Machine Gun fire, so that the fullest effect may be gained from both.

8. Section Officers must not be content to know only their own little areas; they must get to know their whole Company Area at least and positions of all Section Headquarters on their flanks.
   This is particularly important on the flanks of the Division.
   Company Commanders will also take every opportunity of going round other Companies Areas.

9. It is hoped that Infantry Company Commanders may be encouraged to visit Machine Gun Section Headquarters and do their share in establishing close mutual liaison.

                                        A.W.Humble Capt + Adjt
                                        for Lieut. Col.
                                        Cmdg. 32nd.Battalion Machine Gun Corps.

12/8/1918.

Copies to :-
1. O.C.   10. H.Q.32nd.Division.
2. Adjutant.   11. H.Q. 2nd.Division.
3. O.C. "A" Company.   12. O.C. Guards M.G.Bn.
4. O.C. "B" Company.   13. O.C. 2nd.Canadian M.G.Bn.
5. O.C. "C" Company.   14. O.C. 2nd.Battalion M.G.C.
6. O.C. "D" Company.   15. C.M.G.O., VI Corps.
7. 14th.Infantry Bde.   16. War Diary.
8. 96th.Infantry Bde.   17. War Diary.
9. 97th.Infantry Bde.   18. File.

Appendix "A" issued with Instructions No. 15.

Serial No.	M.G. Coy.	Location of Section H.Q.	Location of Infantry H.Q.	Nature of Inf.H.Q.	Remarks.
1.	B.	S.18.a.0.8.	S.13.a.1.0.	Coy.	
2.	B.	S.16.b.2.6.	S.16.b.0.4.	Battn.	
3.	B.	S.2.a.5.1.	(S.10.a.5.5.	Battn.	
			(S.10.a.8.2.	Battn.	
4.	A.	S.22.b.6.0.	S.22.d.5.4.	Coy.	
5.	A.	S.16.c.	S.21.b.5.5.	Coy.	For both his own and B. Coys. guns.
6.	A.	S.9.d.5.2.	S.16.b.0.4.	Battn.	
7.	A.	S.7.b.6.5.	S.7.b.6.5.	Coy.	
8.	C.	S.22.c.30.15.	S.22.c.25.15.	Coy.	
9.	C.	S.10.d.9.5.	S.27.a.8.0.	Coy.	
10.	C.	S.13.d.6.8.	S.20.a.6.1.	Battn.	
11.	D.	S.14.b.5.9.	(S.15.c.1.0.	Battn.	
			(S.20.a.7.80.	Battn.	

SECRET.   Copy No... 13 ...

32nd. BATTALION MACHINE GUN CORPS.
M.G. Instructions for Raid of
14th. Infantry Bde.

1. **INTENTIONS.** The 14th. Infantry Brigade is carrying out a Raid with 2 Companies of the 1st. Bn. Dorset Regt. to kill and capture Germans and obtain identifications, documents etc.

2. **AREA TO BE RAIDED.**
   Eastern Boundary – Railway (inclusive) in S.22.b.
   and S.23.a. and c.
   Western Boundary – Road which runs N. and S. in S.
   22.b. and d.
   Southern Boundary – The bed of the COJEUL river
   in S.22.d.

3. **METHOD OF ATTACK.** Troops will be formed up just behind our present front line posts by Zero – 10.mins. and at Zero will advance under a creeping barrage mopping up the whole Area to be raided.

4. **ACTION OF ARTILLERY.** (A). The Artillery will provide a creeping barrage under which the raiders will advance.

   (B). A jumping barrage on the road and railway which will lift as the raiders advance.

   (C). Standing protective barrages on MOYENVILLE and beyond the final objective.

5. **ACTION OF MACHINE GUNS.** Machine Guns of "A", "B" and "C" Companies will bring fire to bear in accordance with Appendix "A" attached. Company Commanders will submit detailed firing calculations for checking by 12 noon 28th. inst.

6. All guns are to be ready in position by Zero – 10 minutes.

7. **COMMUNICATIONS.**
   (A). The Signalling Officer will arrange for a direct line from guns in S.15.c. to Battalion Headquarters S.15.a.9.6. He will arrange with O.C. "A" Company as to exact positions.

   (B). Guns of "B" Company will communicate by runner to Battalion Hqrs. at S.15.a.9.6.

8. **REPORTS.**
   (A). A report will be sent in at Zero – 10.min. that all guns are ready.

   (B). Reports during the raid will be sent in accordance with attached code (Appendix "B").

   (C). A report on the operation will be sent to Battalion Hqrs. on the following day by Company Commanders concerned.

9. **SYNCHRONIZATION OF WATCHES.** Watches will be synchronized under arrangements to be made by Battalion Hqrs on Z afternoon.

10. All guns firing will have flash screens and "T" or "Y" bases.

11. Arrangements will be made by Companies to give the men a hot drink at conclusion.

12. Guns will resume normal positions at Zero plus 60, if all is quiet.

13. **ZERO.** Zero day and hour will be notified later.

14. **ACKNOWLEDGE.**

1 c/5/1918-
                                                            Lieut. Col.
                                     Cmdr. 32nd. Battalion M.G. Corps.

Distribution of M.G. Instructions for Raid of 14th Inf. Bde.

1. O.C.
2. Adjutant.
3. O.C. "A" Coy.
4. O.C. "B" Coy.
5. O.C. "C" Coy.
6. O.C. "D" Coy.
7. Signalling Officer.
8. 14th Inf. Bde.
9. 96th Inf. Bde.
10. 97th Inf. Bde.
11/12. H.Q., 32nd Division.
13/14. War Diary.
15. File.

Appendix "A".

Serial No.	M.G. Coy.	No. of guns.	present Location.	Location During Raid.	Target.	Time.	Rate of fire.
1.	A.	6.	S.16.c.	S.16.c.7.5.	A.5.a.4.5. to A.5.a.70.85.	Zero+ 10 to Zero+ 40.	75 R.P.M.
2.	A.	6.	S.16.c.	S.16.c.7.5.	S.29.c.1.5. to S.29.c.55.80.	Zero+ 45 to Zero+ 75.	75 R.P.M.
3.	B.	4.	S.16.c.35.40. (2) S.17.a.15.15. (2)	S.16.c.35.40.	S.29.c.55.80. to S.29.a.7.0.	Zero+ 45 to Zero+ 75.	100 R.P.M.
4.	C.	4.	S.20.d.90.25.	S.20.d.90.25.	S.28.c.35.45. to S.28.c.25.20.	Frequent bursts from Zero onwards.	

Appendix "B".

Following Code is to be used in sending messages back by visual or phone:-

Assembly completed with no shelling	... succession of A's.
" " " little "	... " " B's.
" " " much "	... " " C's.
Little M.G.Fire.	... ... " " F's.
Much " "	... ... " " G's.
All going well.	... ... " " K's.

<u>Enemy Barrage.</u>

(1) On front posts.	... ... " " P's.
(2) On main posts.	... ... " " Q's.
(3) Between 1 & 2.	... ... " " R's.

      Followed by Light or Heavy
         Light L. Heavy Y.

Casualties Slight	... ... " " T's.
" Heavy	... ... " " U's.
Casualties	... ... " " E's.
Killed ...	... ... " "2A's.) Followed
Wounded ...	... ... " "2B's.) by numbers.
Missing ...	... ... " "2C's.)

SECRET.   Copy No. 13

32nd. BATTALION MACHINE GUN CORPS.
OPERATION ORDER No. 25.

1. The 64 O.R.(16 per Company) at the Divisional Depot Battalion BAILLEULMONT will be changed to-morrow, 21st. inst.

2. The ingoing men from the Depot Battalion will proceed to their respective Company Headquarters with the ration limbers on 21st inst.

3. (a). The outgoing men from the line will come down to Battalion Hqrs. leaving the line any time after 9-0.a.m., if all is quiet.

   (b). They will bath and get clean clothes and proceed to BAILLEULMONT leaving BRETENCOURT at 5-30.p.m. on 21st inst.

4. Both ingoing and outgoing parties will be marched as formed bodies, strict march discipline will be maintained.

5. N.C.O. instructors at present at BAILLEULMONT will remain there and start training the new class.

6. 2/Lieut.R.TICHENER is posted to the Battalion and will remain at BAILLEULMONT for the present in charge of all M.G.details there.

7. Should it be impossible, owing to the situation, to send men down from the line tomorrow Companies will notify Battalion Hqrs., as early as possible.

8.   A C K N O W L E D G E.

                                        A.M.Humble, Capt. & Adjt.
                                                   for Lieut. Col.
20/4/1918.   Cmdg. 32nd.Battalion Machine Gun Corps.

Copies to :-
   1. C.O.
   2. Adjutant.
   3. O.C. "A" Company.
   4. O.C. "B" Company.
   5. O.C. "C" Company.
   6. O.C. "D" Company.
   7. Quartermaster.
   8. Signalling Officer.
   9. O.C.Divnl.Depot Bn.
  10. 2/Lt.Tichener (at Div.Depot Bn).
  11. H.Q. 32nd.Division.
  12. H.Q. 32nd.Division.
  13. War Diary.
  14. War Diary.
  15. War Diary.

SECRET.

32nd BATTALION MACHINE GUN CORPS.
PROVISIONAL DEFENCE SCHEME.

Copy No 20

1. **FRONTAGE AND BOUNDARIES.**

   (a). The 32nd Division holds the Centre Sector of VI Corps Front.
   The Guards Division is on the right of the 32nd Division with Headquarters at HUMBERCAMPS.
   The 2nd Canadian Division is on the left with Headquarters at BASSEUX.

   (b). The front of the 32nd Division extends from S.27.a.0.1. to S.12.a.8.0.
   The extent of this front is approximately 5,300 yards.

   (c). The Divisional boundaries are marked on the attached map, A.

2. **TACTICAL FEATURES.**

   The most important Tactical Features on the Divisional Front are:-

   (a). The spur which runs North Eastwards from S.28 central.

   (b). The BOYELLES Spur in S.17 and S.18.
   This if captured would give the enemy observation.

   (c). The Spur running N.E. in S.27.a. and S.21.d.

   (d). ADINFER village Spur.

   (e). HENDICOURT LES RANSARTS.

   (f). Hill 115 (S.7.b. and S.1.d.).

   (g). HAMEAU FARM plateau.

3. **ORGANISATION OF DEFENCES.**

   FIRST SYSTEM.

   This system comprises all defences and positions in front of the PURPLE LINE.
   It consists of :-

   (a). An almost continuous Front Line.

   (b). A Support Line.

   (c). A line of defended localities on the Line SUGAR FACTORY - S.14.a. - S.9.a. organised to be held by one Infantry Company in each Brigade area.

   SECOND SYSTEM. (PURPLE).

   This system is situated at an average distance of 4,800 yards from the Front Line.
   It consists of the following Lines :-

   (a). An Outpost Line, Main Line, and Reserve Line, including the defended localities of ADINFER village, HENDICOURT and Hill 115 (S.7.b and S.1.d.).

   (b). The HAMEAU Switch which connects the PURPLE SUPPORT LINE with the PURPLE RESERVE.

   (c). The MERCATEL Switch joining the PURPLE LINE in S.2.c. to the Front Line held by the Left Division in M.35.d.

   (d). A new Switch called WINDMILL Switch connecting the Front Line N. of AYETTE about F5.b.5.5. to the PURPLE LINE at X.17.c.5.1.

3. SYSTEMS IN REAR OF PURPLE SYSTEM.

(a). MONCHY SWITCH joining the PURPLE SYSTEM to the RED LINE South of BIENVILLERS.

(b). BLAIRVILLE SWITCH joining the RED LINE to the PURPLE RESERVE LINE South of BLAIRVILLE.

(c). The RED LINE.

4. DISPOSITIONS.

The Divisional Front is divided into three Subsectors as shown on attached map.

(a). FRONT SYSTEM.

Each Brigade holds the Front system on a two Battalion Front, each Battalion being disposed in depth. In each Brigade Sector one Company from a Battalion in the front system is detailed as a permanent Garrison of a defended locality (Vide para.5(c).

(b). PURPLE SYSTEM.

One Battalion of each Brigade is definitely allotted for the defence of the PURPLE SYSTEM and will not be moved forward without orders from Divisional Headquarters.

(c). MACHINE GUNS.

1. One Machine Gun Company is allotted for the defence of each Brigade Sector.
The Machine Gun Company in each Brigade Sector is under the tactical orders of the Brigadier, but in stationary warfare the positions will be fixed by Officer Commanding Machine Gun Battalion and will not be changed without reference to him.
In the event of moving warfare developing (either forward or back) the Infantry Brigadier will be responsible for the tactical handling of the guns.

2. One Machine Gun Company is allotted for the defence of the PURPLE Line. For tactical purposes its guns will come under the orders of the G.O.C. Brigade in whose Subsector they are situated. (see Appendix "A" and map.)

3. 4 Vickers Guns, kept in limbers at W.12.d.55.55. and 10 Light German Machine Guns, at W.12.b.50.00. are in Divisional reserve. The 10 Light German Machine Guns will not be moved East of the PURPLE LINE.

(d). ARTILLERY.

The Field Artillery covering the Front is organised into three Groups, i.e. Right, Centre, and Left Group.
One Group covers each Infantry Brigade.
The greater part of the Artillery is placed in rear of the PURPLE Line. Forward Guns are placed at BOISLEUX-AU-MONT and BOIRY ST. MARTIN, with the object of harrassing fire and dealing with tanks.
The total number of guns in front of the PURPLE LINE and MERCATEL SWITCH is 14, 18 pdrs. and 12, 4.5 inch. Howitzers.

(e). 1 Section of Male Tanks is located at 3.20.a. central.
1 Section of Male Tanks is located at 3.15.b.8.7.

5. Machine Gun Dispositions are as shown in Appendix "A" and map.

6. PRINCIPLES OF DEFENCE.

(a). There will be no withdrawal from any one Line, to any other Line. All lines of defence will be held to the last, and every inch of the ground contested and as much loss inflicted on the enemy as possible.

(b). Defences must be organised in as great depth as possible, if the enemy should penetrate an adjacent portion of our defence Machine Guns must be ready to take up positions to support a defensive flank.

(c). The defence must be active and harrassing fire carried out at every opportunity.

7. PRELIMINARY MEASURES IN CASE OF ATTACK.

(a). Immediately an attack appears to be imminent owing to the opening of a heavy enemy bombardment etc., all gun teams will "stand to" but will remain under cover.
If it is by day, guns (except those firing on S.O.S. or Front Line positions) will be kept under cover safe from shell fire, ready to mount at once if necessary.

(b). The reserve guns will "stand to" and be ready to move at once on receipt of orders.

(c). All transport will harness up and be ready to hook in and move off. Each Company Transport Officer will send a mounted N.C.O. to his respective Company Headquarters for orders.

(d). All men out of the line (at BRETENCOURT etc) will return at once to their Company Headquarters, under command of the senior N.C.O. of the Company.

(e). All men at the Depot Battalion will remain under orders of Officer Commanding Divisional Depot Battalion.

(f). Should the Division wish these preliminary moves carried out it will send out the following code message, which will be repeated to Company's by Battalion Headquarters.
Preliminary moves AAA ACKNOWLEDGE.
On receipt of this all measures indicated in para 7. will be taken.

8. ACTION IN CASE OF S.O.S.

(a). As for para 7.

(b). All guns that have an S.O.S. line will at once open fire.
(see Appendix "B").
Section Officers must use their own descretion as to opening fire on their S.O.S. lines without having seen the signal or before the signal is made, if they consider circumstances demand it.
They must always however bear in mind the expenditure of belts involved and premature exhaustion of their gun teams.

9. HARRASSING FIRE.

(a). Harrassing fire on suitable targets (roads, tracks, and centres of movement) is carried out nightly by the forward guns.
(b). Attention is called to Machine Gun Instructions No.12. on Harrassing fire, which has been issued to all concerned.

(c). The targets are varied according to wishes of Infantry Battalion Commanders and Intelligence reports.

10. AMMUNITION SUPPLY.

(a). The amount of ammunition to be maintained at each gun is laid down in Appendix "C".

(b). Each gun on S.O.S. will have 8 additional belts kept for that special purpose.

(c). Each Company has about 4000 rounds of special anti-tank armour piercing S.A.A. distributed as shown on attached map "B" and Appendix "D".

11. ANTI-AIRCRAFT.

A certain number of guns are mounted by day in anti-aircraft positions to engage low flying enemy aircraft.
See attached map "B" and Appendix "E".

12. LIAISON.

(a). Machine Gun Company Commanders will keep in touch with their affiliated Infantry Brigades.

(b). Officers Commanding Machine Gun Sections will keep in close touch with the Infantry in whose area they are stationed and will report daily to the Battalion Commander concerned.

(c). The Officer Commanding Machine Gun Battalion will keep in close touch with Brigadiers and ascertain their requirements as to Machine Gun action.

(d). Attention is called to Machine Gun Instructions No.13. on

- 4 -

12. LIAISON. (Contd).

(d). on "Liaison" which has been issued to all concerned.

13. Battery Positions.

Eight gun battery positions.

Eight gun battery positions, with shelters, "T" bases and aiming marks are situated as follows:-

"A" Battery.....................X.21.a.35.95.
"B" Battery.....................X.15.d.40.90.
"C" Battery.....................X.10.a.60.35.
"D" Battery.....................X.8.b.50.40.

These Batteries are not occupied as gun positions but Company's will be responsible for their maintenance as under:-

"A" Battery.....................D" Company.
"B" Battery.....................C" Company.
"C" Battery.....................A" Company.
"D" Battery.....................B" Company.

14. RECONNAISSANCE.

(a). All reserve guns will reconnoitre the entire PURPLE SYSTEM and approaches to it. Special instructions with regard to their occupation of positions for the defence of the PURPLE SYSTEM are being issued.

(b). Company Commanders will reconnoitre positions to which their forward guns will "bound" back in the event of a fighting withdrawal being ordered.
N.B. This will not be communicated lower than Section Officers.

(c). Battalion Transport Officer will reconnoitre to and at p.20.c.7.4. to which place the transport will move from BAILLEULMONT should occasion arise.

15. COMMUNICATIONS.

See APPENDIX "F".

16. POSITION OF HEADQUARTERS.

(a). The positions of all Infantry Brigade and Battalion Headquarters and of the Machine Gun Company Headquarters are shown on map "A".

(b). Divisional Headquarters are at GASTINEAU (TUILERIES) W.11.b.90.20.

(c). Machine Gun Battalion Headquarters are at GASTINEAU W.5.d.00.5.0.

17. A C K N O W L E D G E.

J. Reeve
Lieut. Col.
22/3/1918. Cmdg. 32nd Battalion M.G. Corps.

Copies to:-

1. O.C.
2. Adjutant.
3. Signals Officer.
4. Transport Officer.
5. O.C. "A" Company.
6. O.C. "B" Company.
7. O.C. "C" Company.
8. O.C. "D" Company.
9. 14th Infantry Bde.
10. 95th Infantry Bde.
11. 97th Infantry Bde.
12. H.Q. 32nd Division.
13. H.Q. 32nd Division.
14. Divisional Artillery.
15. O.C. 2nd Canadian M.G.Bn.
16. O.C. 2nd Bn M.G. Corps.
17. C.M.G.O. VI Corps.
19. War Diary.
20. War Diary.
21. File.

LIST OF APPENDICES AND MAPS.

Map "A" — Boundaries. Trench lines. Positions of Headquarters. Positions of Machine Guns.

Map "B" — Distribution of armour piercing S.A.A. and A.A. Gun Positions.

Appendix "A".   Locations of Machine Guns.

Appendix "B".   S.O.S. Lines.

Appendix "C".   Establishment of ammunition.

Appendix "D".   Distribution of armour piercing S.A.A.

Appendix "E".   A.A. Gun positions.

Appendix "F".   Communications.

—:o:o:o:o:o:o:o:o:o:o:o:o:o:o:—

APPENDIX "A".

Machine Gun Dispositions.

"A" Coy. in centre sub-sector - Headquarters at X.10.a.35.50.
　　　　　　　　　　　　　　　Affiliated to 14th Infantry Brigade.

　　　S.7.b.62.45.
　　　S.7.b.62.52.
　　　S.7.b.91.95.
　　　S.7.b.99.99.
　　　S.9.d.55.84.
　　　S.9.d.60.19.
　　　S.16.c.03.10.
　　　S.16.c.10.18.
　　　S.16.c.20.25.　moving to S.16.c.48.36.
　　　S.16.c.24.30.　　　"　　　S.16.c.53.30.
　　　S.16.c.65.45.
　　　S.16.c.70.80.
　　　S.22.b.50.35.
　　　S.22.b.55.40.
　　　S.22.d.08.99.
　　　S.22.d.52.99.

"B" Coy. in left sub-sector - Headquarters at Y.5.b.50.40.
　　　　　　　　　　　　　　　Affiliated to 96th Infantry Brigade.
　　　S.10.c.09.95.　　　　S.9.d.75.02.
　　　S.16.a.12.00.　　　　S.9.d.73.04.
　　　S.16.a.05.75.　　　　S.3.c.52.52.
　　　S.16.a.00.80.　　　　S.3.c.44.58.
　　　S.17.a.00.05.　　　　S.3.c.00.85.
　　　S.17.a.05.09.　　　　S.3.c.05.85.
　　　S.16.b.55.59.　　　　Y.5.b.96.00.
　　　S.16.b.55.40.　　　　Y.6.a.02.05.

"C" Coy. in right sub-sector - Headquarters at Y.23.a.48.50.
　　　　　　　　　　　　　　　Affiliated to 97th Infantry Brigade.

　　　S.22.c.37.15.
　　　S.22.c.36.17.
　　　S.20.d.85.21.
　　　S.20.d.86.25.
　　　S.20.d.85.21.
　　　S.20.d.86.25.
　　　S.19.d.40.70.　moving to S.19.b.47.29.
　　　S.19.d.46.60.　　　"　　　S.19.b.40.25.
　　　Y.15.b.01.45.
　　　Y.15.a.98.55.
　　　Y.22.a.19.89.
　　　Y.22.a.24.90.
　　　Y.23.a.50.50.
　　　Y.23.a.55.50.
　　　Y.23.a.20.04.
　　　Y.23.a.22.00.

"D" Coy. in reserve - Headquarters at X.15.c.80.68.

1. Y.20.c.74.86.)
2. Y.20.c.72.85.)   German Heavy Machine Guns.
3. X.21.a.65.45.)
4. 2 guns at X.21.a.65.45.
5. X.21.d.08.03.
6. X.21.d.00.10.
7. X.17.b.10.12.
8. X.17.b.15.20.
9. X.12.c.15.40.
10. X.12.c.30.45.
11. X.18.a.30.45.
12. X.18.a.35.47.
13. S.14.d.25.81.
14. S.14.d.27.84.
15. S.14.d.23.88.
16. S.14.d.27.94.

Nos. 1 - 8 affiliated to 14th Infantry Brigade.
Nos. 9 - 16 affiliated to 97th Infantry Brigade.

4 Vickers guns at W.12.d.55.58.   ) In Divisional
10 German Light Machine Guns at W.18.b.50.00.)   reserve.

Transport lines :-

"A", "B", "C" advanced lines R.32.b.10.45.
"D"   "   W.12.d.55.58.

Battalion Rear Transport lines and Quartermaster Stores :-
                        BAILLEULMONT W.2.d.5.9.

Battalion Headquarters :- ~~BERTRANCOURT R.27.c.20.55.~~
                          GASTINEAU W.5d.00.90.

APPENDIX "B".

S.O.S. lines.

Serial No.	M.G. Coy.	No. of guns.	Location.	Target.
1.	A.	2.	S.22.b.52.41.	S.24.a.65.20. S.24.a.60.15.
2.	B.	2.	S.17.a.00.05.	S.24.a.54.05. S.24.c.48.97.
3.	B.	2.	S.16.b.95.38.	S.24.c.42.89. S.24.c.36.81.
4.	A.	6.	S.16.c.	S.24.c.30.75. S.24.c.24.69. S.24.c.18.62. S.24.c.12.55. S.24.c.06.48. S.24.c.00.42.
5.	C.	4.	S.20.d.95.20.	S.23.c.35.45. to S.23.c.23.20.

1. Fire at usual S.O.S. rates.

2. 1° Traverse each way.

3. Guns must be kept ready to open fire immediately a S.O.S. signal is made.

APPENDIX "C".

Establishment of Ammunition.

1. The following numbers of filled belts will be maintained in the line :-

   A. Guns West of the line from VALLEY WOOD (X.22.d.) to S.3.d.0.0. - 32 belts per gun.

   B. Guns between A. and a line from S.27.a.0.0. to S.11.d.6.3. - 24 belts per gun.

   C. Guns in front of B. - 16 belts per gun.

2. A minimum of 5 boxes of S.A.A. will also be kept at each gun position and 80,000 rounds at each battery position (para. 13.)

3. Companies will keep 64 filled belt boxes in reserve in a limber with their Echelon "A" transport.

4. Any belts surplus to above will be kept in reserve at Coy. Headquarters.

5. All belts must be re-filled as quickly as possible after firing.

APPENDIX "D".

Distribution of Amour piercing S.A.A.

"A" Coy.

    3 boxes at S.7.b.98.99.

    2   "   S.9.d.55.24.
    2   "   S.9.d.60.19.

    5   "   S.16.c.48.36.
    1   "   S.22.b.50.55.

    1   "   S.22.d.58.99.
    1   "   S.22.d.52.99.

"B" Coy.

    1   "   Y.5.b.98.00.
    1   "   Y.6.a.02.05.

    1   "   S.5.c.52.52.
    1   "   S.5.c.44.58.

    5   "   S.16.b.35.40.

    1   "   S.17.a.05.09.
    1   "   S.17.a.00.06.

    2   "   S.18.a.12.00.

    1   "   S.18.a.05.76.
    1   "   S.18.a.00.60.

    1   "   S.9.d.75.02.

"C" Coy.

    2 boxes at Y.15.b.00.46.
    5   "   S.20.d.85.21.
    1   "   S.22.c.37.15.
    2   "   S.19.d.40.70.
    2   "   Y.25.a.50.50.

"D" Coy.

    5   "   S.14.d.27.94.
    2   "   Y.18.a.88.45.
    2   "   Y.19.c.30.45.
    2   "   Y.17.b.10.15.
    2   "   Y.21.d.00.10.

APPENDIX "E".

A.A. Gun Positions.

"A" Coy.

    S.15.d.8.4.
    S.1.d.8.4.

"B" Coy.

    X.8.b.90.10.
    S.5.c.40.30.
    S.9.d.70.00.
    X.17.a.00.10.

"C" Coy.

    S.19.d.45.65.
    X.20.a.50.50.
    X.15.b.00.40.
    S.20.d.0.10.

"D" Coy.

    X.21.d.1.10.
    X.11.c.90.0.
    S.14.d.1.0.
    X.13.c.90.70.
    X.18.a.80.50.

APPENDIX "B".

COMMUNICATIONS.

Communications within the Battalion consist of :-

    (a) Telephone and Fullerphone.
    (b) Runner.
    (c) Visual.

(a) <u>Telephone and Fullerphone</u>. A combined forward Telephone Exchange and Runner Relay Post is established in BLAIRVILLE (N.4.a.9.3.). A line runs from Battalion Headquarters to this exchange which is in direct communication with "A", "B" and "C" Companies in the line.

    Each Company has a line direct to its affiliated Brigade.

    In addition lateral communication exists between Coys. This gives normally three different circuits for each Coy. There is a direct line between Battalion Headquarters and "D" Coy. (in reserve) and this Coy. is also connected to Right Brigade (97th).

    With the exception of one line from "B" Coy. to its Section Headquarters in S.2.b.65.00, no telephonic communication exists forward of Company Headquarters.

(b) <u>Runners</u>. There are five runners at Battalion Headquarters, three at BLAIRVILLE Relay Post, four at each Coy. H.Q. and two at each Section H.Q.

    The Battalion Headquarters runners work to BLAIRVILLE Relay Post, to the Coy. in reserve, and are available for special local runs as required. They are also familiar with the routes to the Coy. H.Q.

    The BLAIRVILLE runners work between the Relay Post and the Companies in the line.

    Company runners work between Coy. H.Q. and their Sections.

    Wherever possible all these runners are mounted on cycles. In addition, each Coy. has a mounted orderly at its Headquarters who is familiar with the routes from his Coy. to BLAIRVILLE Relay Post and to the Coy. H.Q. on either flank.

    The following are average times taken for messages by runner between Battalion Headquarters and Companies:-

Battalion Headquarters to "A" Coy.	...	30 mins.
"	"	" "B" "	...	40 "
"	"	" "C" "	...	1hr.25"
"	"	" "D" "	...	25 "

(c) <u>Visual</u>. Visual communication by day and night is established between :-

    (i) "B" Coy. H.Q. and Section in S.2.b.
    (ii) "A" " " " " " S.15.c.(through transmitting station in S.7.b.).

    In the event of abnormal activity, these stations will be manned. Test messages are sent through by day and night.

MAP "B"

AA

Map Shewing A-A Defence.

To be superimposed on Sheets 51 SE & 51 SW.

REFERENCE
A-A Position
A-A S.A.A. No. of Guns

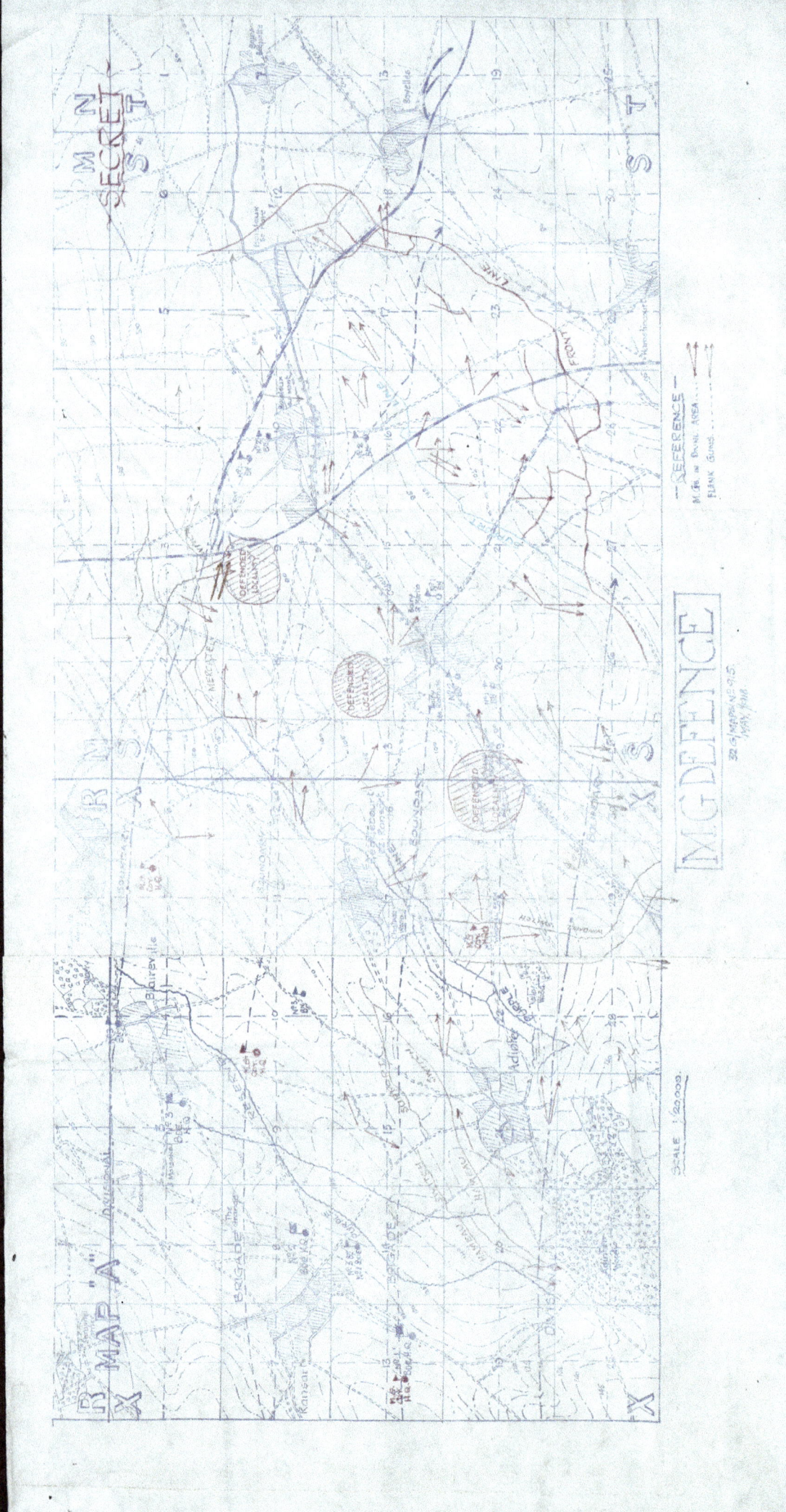

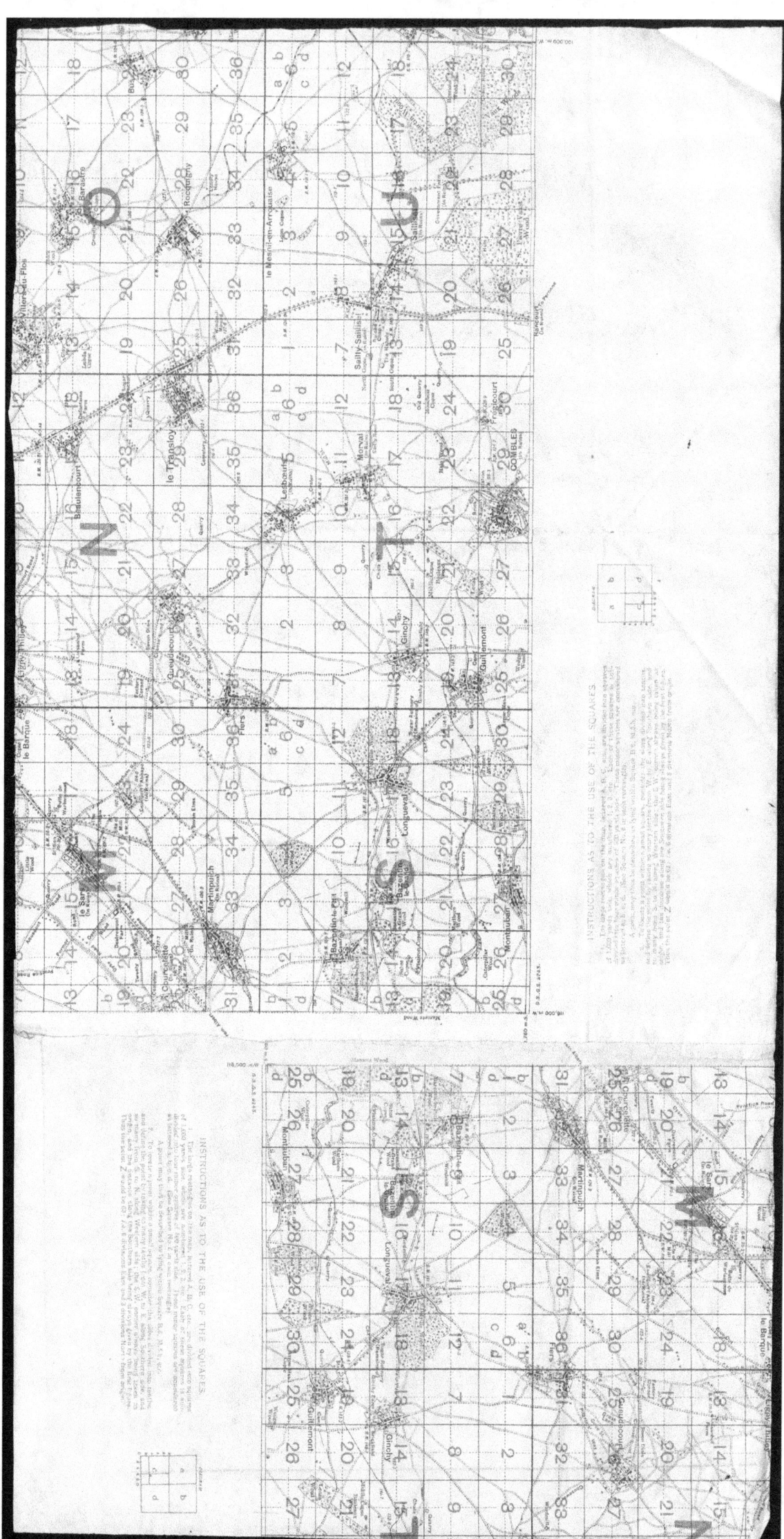

SECRET.
Copy No. 15

2ND BATTALION MACHINE GUN CORPS INSTRUCTIONS NO. 14.

Action of Reserve Guns.

1. These instructions are framed to provide as far as possible a settled plan of action, for the Reserve Machine Guns (4 Vickers and 10 German light Machine Guns) in the event of a big hostile attack developing on the VI Corps front.

2. It is recognised that circumstances may require them to be used otherwise and they must be prepared to do so if necessary.

3. The guns once in position will come tactically under the orders of the G.O.C. Brigade in whose sector they are situated.

4. The attached map shows three alternative sets of positions:-

   Scheme "A" in BLUE to meet an attack parallel to our front.

   Scheme "B" in GREEN to meet an attack on the left flank of the Division.

   Scheme "C" in RED to meet an attack on right flank of Division.

5. Gun positions at the places shown have been constructed.

6. In the event of the occupation of any of the positions becoming necessary, the following message will be sent to "D" Coy. from Battalion Headquarters and repeated to Infantry Brigades:-

   Scheme A (B. or C.) AAA Move AAA Acknowledge.

   N.B. In the event of a test being desired, the word "Test" will be inserted at the beginning of the message.

7. O.C. "D" Coy., 2nd Battalion M.G. Corps will see that all reserve gun teams know their way by day and night to all positions.

8. Range cards for each position will be prepared. Those for German guns should be made out in metres.

9. Thirty two belts per gun for the Vickers will be taken and all available German S.A.A. for the light guns.

10. Appendix "A" attached gives map locations of the guns.

11. A C K N O W L E D G E.

J. Reeve, Lt. Col.,
Commanding 2nd Battalion Machine Gun Corps.

27/3/1918.

Distribution of 32nd Battalion Machine Gun Corps Instructions No. 14.

1. C.O.
2. Adjutant.
3. O.C. "A" Coy.
4. O.C. "B" Coy.
5. O.C. "C" Coy.
6. O.C. "D" Coy.
7. 14th Inf. Bde.
8. 96th Inf. Bde.
9. 97th Inf. Bde.
10/11. H.Q., 32nd Division.
12. O.C., 4th Bn. M.G. Guards.
13. O.C. 2nd Canadian M.G. Bn.
14. O.C. 2nd M.G. Bn.
15/16. War Diary.
17. File.

Appendix "A" issued with X.G. Instructions No. 14.

Serial No.	Scheme.	No. of guns	Type of guns.	Location.	Brigade sector.
1.	A.	4	Vickers.	X.13.9.0.0.	14th Brigade.
2.		5	Light German.	X.8.a.80.85.	96th Brigade.
3.		5	"	X.14.b.0.0.	97th Brigade.
4.	B.	2	Vickers.	X.9.b.8.70.	96th Brigade.
5.		2	"	X.4.c.4.0.	96th Brigade.
6.		5	Light German.	X.5.b.85.80.	96th Brigade.
7.		5	"	X.5.c.80.25.	96th Brigade.
8.	C.	4	Vickers.	X.19.a.0.85.	97th Brigade.
9.		5	Light German.	X.19.a.95.10.	97th Brigade.
10.		5	"	W.24.b.1.5.	97th Brigade.

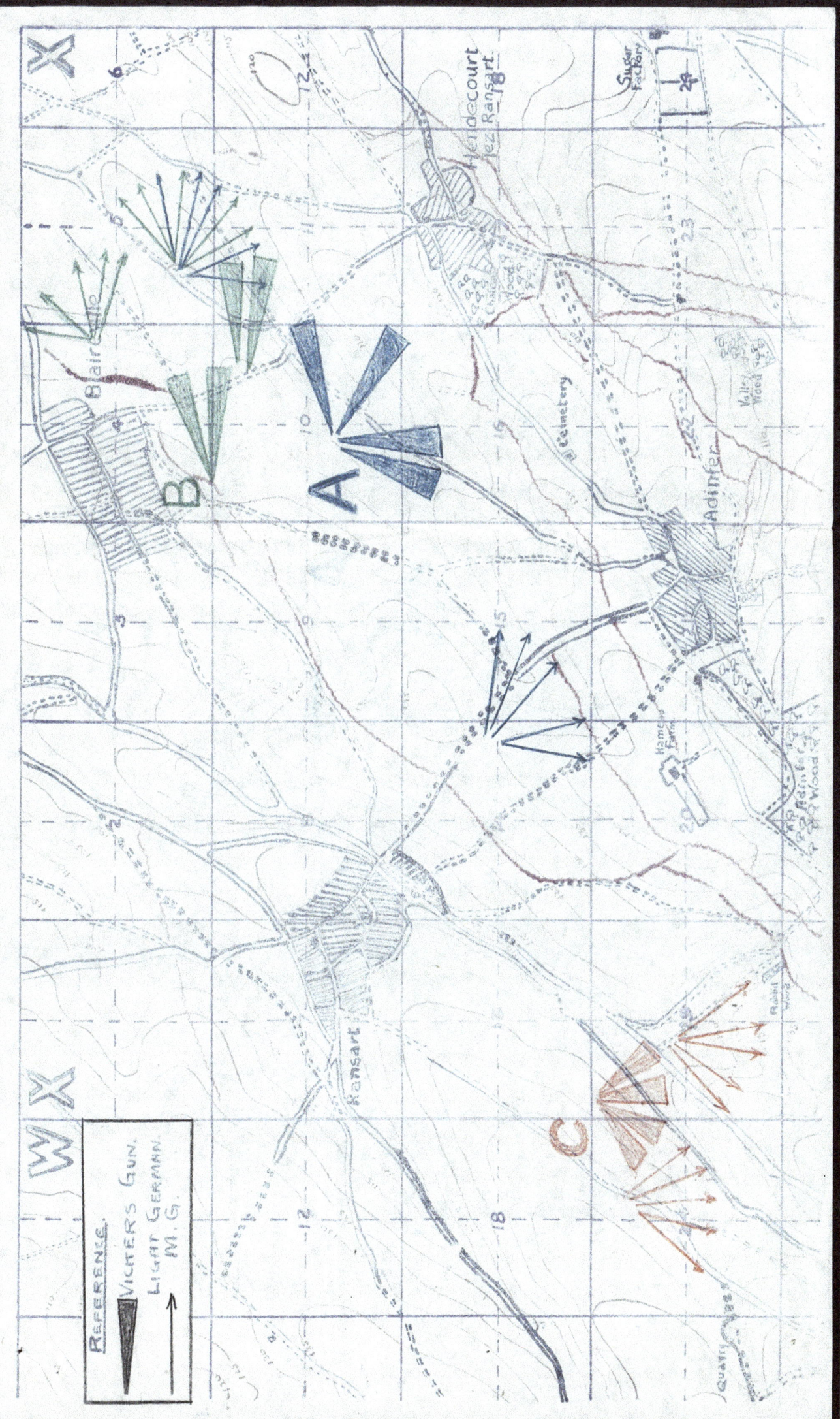

SECRET.   Copy No. 14

62ND BATTALION MACHINE GUN CORPS OPERATION ORDER NO. 26.

1.   The N.C.O.s. (15 per Company) at the Divisional Depot Battalion BAILLEULMONT, will be changed tomorrow, 28th inst.

2.   The ingoing men from the Depot Battalion will proceed to their respective Company Headquarters with the ration limbers on 28th inst.

3. (a). The outgoing men from the line will come down to BERTENCOURT, leaving the line any time after 5.a.m., if all is quiet.

   (b). They will bath and get clean clothes and proceed to BAILLEULMONT leaving BERTENCOURT at 2.30.p.m. on 28th inst.

4.   Both ingoing and outgoing parties will be marched as formed bodies, strict march discipline will be maintained.

5.   N.C.O. instructors at present at BAILLEULMONT will remain there and start training the new class.

6.   2/Lt. R.TITCHENER will remain at BAILLEULMONT for the present in charge of all M.G. details, there.

7.   Should it be impossible owing to the situation, to send men down from the line tomorrow morning, Companies will notify Battalion Headquarters as early as possible.

8.   ACKNOWLEDGE.

                                        A.M.Burall, Capt. Adjt.
                                        for Lieut. Col.,
                                Commanding 62nd Battalion M. G. Corps.

27/5/1918.

Copies to:-
   1. C.O.   9. O.C. Divl. Depot Bn.
   2. Adjutant.   10. 2/Lt. R.TITCHENER (at Div.Depot Bn.).
   3. O.C. "A" Coy.   11/12. H.Q., 62nd Division.
   4. O.C. "B" Coy.   13/14. War Diary.
   5. O.C. "C" Coy.   15. File.
   6. O.C. "D" Coy.
   7. Quartermaster.
   8. Signalling Officer.

CONFIDENTIAL.

Vol. 5

WAR DIARY.

of

32nd Bn. MACHINE GUN CORPS.

from 1st June 1918 to 30th June 1918.

No. 5.

Army Form C. 2118.

WAR DIARY
or
INTELLIGENCE SUMMARY.
(Erase heading not required.)

Place	Date	Hour	Summary of Events and Information	Remarks and references to Appendices
GOMIECOURT	1/6/18		CASUALTIES. 1. OR KILLED. 2. OR WOUNDED. 2. OR WOUNDED AT DUTY.	
			Situation Normal. Night Quiet. Enemy Artillery Active on Back Areas.	51.C.S.E.
			Throughout The Day Hendecourt Rampart Cojeul River,	
			Our M.Gs. Fired 27,750 Rounds On Special Targets. 5,500 Rounds	
			At E.R. 2/Lt A Dean Reported For Duty Posted To B. Coy 2/Lt J.W.V.W.K. Posted To C.C.Y.	
GOMIECOURT	2/6/18		CASUALTIES. 1. OR WOUNDED 4 OR GASSED	
			Situation Normal. Night Quiet. Enemy Artillery Below Normal During	51.B.S.W
			Day Boisleux Au Mont & East Of Boiry St Martin Shelled At Intervals.	
			Our M.Gs. Fired 26,000 Rounds. On Special Targets. 7,850 Rounds	
			At E.R. O.O. No 27 Issued	A.P.1.
GOMIECOURT	3/6/18		Situation Normal. Night Quiet Enemy Artillery Below Normal	51.B.S.W
			During Day Energetic Harassing Fire Throughout The Night Adineer	51.C.S.E.
			Hendecourt Boiry St Martin, Shelled At Intervals. Our M.Gs Fired	
			24,650 Rounds. On Special Targets. 2,500 Rounds At E.R.	
			O.O.28 Issued	A.P.2

WAR DIARY
or
INTELLIGENCE SUMMARY.

(Erase heading not required.)

Army Form C. 2118.

Place	Date	Hour	Summary of Events and Information	Remarks and references to Appendices
GRINCOURT	4/6/18		CASUALTIES 1.O.R. WOUNDED GAS. Situation Normal. Night Quiet. Enemy Artillery Very Active On Forward Areas Throughout The Day. Our MGs Fired 31,000 Rounds. Harassing Fire. 4,000 Rounds At E.A.	
GRINCOURT	5/6/18		CASUALTIES 2.O.R. WOUNDED. Situation Normal. Night Quiet. Enemy Artillery Normal Harassing During Day & Night. Enemy Put Down Heavy Barrage On Forward System Of Right Sub-Sector From 12.45AM To 1.15 AM. Our SOS Went Up In S.27a. No Infantry Action Followed Our MGs. 6,500 Rounds On SOS. 20,150 Rounds Harassing Fire 5000 Rounds At E.A.	51B.SW.
GRINCOURT	6/6/18		Situation Normal. Night Quiet. Enemy Artillery Normal Activity On Forward Areas. Roads & Tracks Harassed At Night. Hendecourt Bonfer. Wood + Boiry Shelled At Intervals Our MGs 27,500 Rounds On Special Targets. 3,500 Rounds At E.A.	51B.S.E. 51B.S.W.

Army Form C. 2118.

WAR DIARY
or
INTELLIGENCE SUMMARY.
(Erase heading not required.)

Place	Date	Hour	Summary of Events and Information	Remarks and references to Appendices
GATINEAU	7/6/18		Casualties. 1 O.R. Gassed. Situation Normal. Night Quiet. Enemy Artillery Active Throughout Day On Batteries. Heavy Barrages Put Down In Front Of POINFER. Boisleux Heavily Shelled At Intervals. Our M.G.s Fired 16000 Rounds S¹. S.W. On Special Targets. 4,500 Rounds At E.A. Bn. HQ. Shelled At Intervals During Night.	51 C.S.E.
				✓
GATINEAU	8/6/18.		Casualties. 5 O.R. Killed. 10 O.R. Wounded. Situation Normal. Night Quiet. Enemy Activity Below Normal During Day. Very Active From 9-30 P.M. 11-30 P.M. Our M.G. Fired 24500 Rounds On Special Targets 4,700 At E.A. 2/Lt. H.M. Corke, Reported Posted To B Coy.	✓
GATINEAU	9/6/18		Casualties. 1 O.R. Killed (Attached M.L.I.). Situation Normal. Night Quiet. Enemy Artillery Activity Below Normal. VENDECOURT Batteries In Rear Shelled During Afternoon. Our M.G.s Fired 26000 Rounds On Special Targets 3,750 At E.A.	51 C.S.E.

WAR DIARY
or
INTELLIGENCE SUMMARY.
(Erase heading not required.)

Army Form C. 2118.

Place	Date	Hour	Summary of Events and Information	Remarks and references to Appendices
GASTINEAU	10/6/18		Situation Normal. Night Quiet. Enemy Artillery Normal. Usual Harassing and Counter Battery Fire @ during the Night. (2 am) Gas Was Projected into Hamelincourt. Our M.G's. Fired 38,000 Rounds in Co-operation. 17,000 Rounds Harassing Fire. 1450 at E.A. O.O.8 issued.	51 B.S.W. A.P.3
GASTINEAU	11/6/18		Casualties. 10.R. Wounded. A.T. Deep. Bn. Situation Normal. Night Quiet. Enemy Artillery Normal. 96 Inf Bde. Carried Our Raid in Vicinity of Boyelles. Our M.G's Fired 9,000 Rounds 51 B.S.W. in Co-operation. 10,000 Rounds on Special Targets. 250 Rounds at E.A.	
GASTINEAU	12/6/18		Situation Normal. Night Quiet. Enemy Artillery Below Normal. Our M.G's Fired 13,200 Rounds on Special Targets. 1,250 Rounds at E.A. O.O.30 issued.	A.P.4
GASTINEAU	13/6/18		Situation Normal. Night. Enemy Artillery Quiet on Right Sub Sector. Otherwise Normal. Hendecourt + Batteries in Vicinity. Boiry St Martin & Adinfer were shelled. Our M.G's Fired 42,500 Rounds in Co-operation. Why Gas Protector Discharge into Hamelincourt 10,750 Rounds Harassing Fire. 1450 Rounds at E.A.	51 B.S.W. 51 C.S.E.

Army Form C. 2118.

WAR DIARY
or
INTELLIGENCE SUMMARY.
(Erase heading not required.)

Place	Date	Hour	Summary of Events and Information	Remarks and references to Appendices
Gaskinean	14/6/18		CASUALTIES. Lt. C.E. Duggan, M.C. Wounded. Situation Normal. Night Quiet. Enemy Artillery carried out normal Harassing & Counter Battery work. Our M.G. 16600 Rounds. Harassing Fire.	
Gaskinean	15/6/18		CASUALTIES. 1.O.R Wounded. Situation Normal. Night Quiet. Enemy Artillery Normal on left & Centre. Quiet on Right. Boisleux Station Hendecourt & Boiry St Martin Shelled at intervals. Our M.G's Fired 18,500 Rounds Harassing Fire. 2,500 Rounds F.A.	51.B.S.W. 51.C.S.E.
Gaskinean	16/6/18		Situation Normal. Night Quiet. Enemy Artillery Normal on left & Centre. Quiet on Right. Boisleux au Mont. Boisleux St Marc & Boiry St Martin Shelled at intervals. Enemy carried out counter Battery Work. Our M.G's Fired 22,500 Rounds Harassing Fire. 27,500 Rounds At. E.A.	51.B.S.W. 51.C.S.E.

Army Form C. 2118.

WAR DIARY
or
INTELLIGENCE SUMMARY.
(Erase heading not required.)

Instructions regarding War Diaries and Intelligence Summaries are contained in F. S. Regs., Part II. and the Staff Manual respectively. Title pages will be prepared in manuscript.

Place	Date	Hour	Summary of Events and Information	Remarks and references to Appendices
Gastineau	17/4/18		Situation Normal. Night Quiet. Enemy Artillery Normal. Boisleux Station Pointer Wood Valley Wood & Coseul Valley Shelled At Intervals. Our M.G.s 14750 Rounds. On False S.O.S. Lines In Response To False S.O.S. Signal Sent Up With Object Of Deceiving The Enemy 13,000 Rounds Harassing Fire. 1800 Rounds At E.A. O.O.31 Issued	51 c S.W. 51 c S.E. A.P.s ⟨sig⟩
			Casualties. 1 O.R. Wounded At Duty	
Gastineau	18/4/18		Situation Normal. Night Quiet. Enemy Artillery Normal. Boiry St. Martin Coseul Valley. Boisleux Station Shelled At Intervals. Our M.G. Fired 25,000 Rounds On Special Targets 2550 Rounds At E.A.	51 B S.W. 51 f S.E. ⟨sig⟩
			Casualties 2 O.R. Wounded	
Gastineau	19/4/18		Situation Normal. Night Quiet. Enemy Artillery Active On Forward Areas Our M.G.s Fired 31,000 Rounds. In Support Of Raids By The 14th And 96th Inf. Bdes. 11,750 Rounds On Special Targets. 500 Rounds At E.A.	⟨sig⟩

Army Form C. 2118.

WAR DIARY
or
INTELLIGENCE SUMMARY.
(Erase heading not required.)

Place	Date	Hour	Summary of Events and Information	Remarks and references to Appendices
Gezaincourt	20/4/18		Casualties 10 O.R. Wounded. Situation Normal. Night Quiet. Enemy Artillery Activity Below Normal. Our M.G. Fired 11,500 Rounds on Special Targets. 1,500 Rounds at E.A.	
Gezaincourt	21/4/18		Casualties. 1 O.R. Wounded. 1 O.R. Wounded at Duty. Situation Normal. Night Quiet. Enemy Artillery Activity Normal on Left & Centre, Below Normal on Right. Our M.G. Fired 27,000 Rounds on Special Targets. 1,200 Rounds at E.A.	
Gezaincourt	22/4/18		Situation Normal. Night Quiet. Enemy Artillery Below Normal. Boisleux au Mont, Gonfer, Boiry St. Martin & Mendecourt Were Shelled. Our M.G. Fired 20,500 Rounds on Special Targets. 650 Rounds at E.A.	51.b.SV 51.B.SE

Army Form C. 2118.

WAR DIARY
or
INTELLIGENCE SUMMARY.
(Erase heading not required.)

Instructions regarding War Diaries and Intelligence Summaries are contained in F. S. Regs., Part II. and the Staff Manual respectively. Title pages will be prepared in manuscript.

Place	Date	Hour	Summary of Events and Information	Remarks and references to Appendices
GEZAINCOURT	27/6/18		CASUALTIES 2/Lt H. DEAN WOUNDED	
			SITUATION NORMAL NIGHT QUIET. ENEMY ARTILLERY ACTIVITY Gs BELOW	51 B SW
			NORMAL ON LEFT. CENTRE & RIGHT NORMAL BOINFFER BOIRY WINDMILL	
			FARM SUGAR FACTORY SHELLED. OUR MGs FIRED 3,000 ROUNDS IN	51 C SE
			SUPPORT OF FIGHTING PATROL OF CENTRE BDE. 17000 ROUNDS ON	
			SPECIAL TARGETS. 850 ROUNDS AT E.A.	
GEZAINCOURT	28/6/18		SITUATION NORMAL NIGHT QUIET. ENEMY ARTILLERY ACTIVITY ABOVE NORMAL	
			ON RIGHT OTHERWISE NORMAL. SPECIAL ATTENTION BEING PAID TO	
			TRACKS IN THE SECTOR. OUR MGs FIRED 22,000 ROUNDS ON SPECIAL TARGETS	AP6
			7,650 ROUNDS AT E.A. 00. 32 + 33 ISSUED.	AP7
GEZAINCOURT	29/6/18		SITUATION NORMAL NIGHT QUIET. ENEMY ARTILLERY ACTIVITY NORMAL	51 S SW
			BOISLEUX AU MONT WINDMILL FARM SUGAR FACTORY VALLEY WOOD BOIRY	
			& VENDECOURT SHELLED DURING DAY. OUR MGs. 17000 ROUNDS SPECIAL	51 C SE
			TARGETS. 3,000 ROUNDS AT E.A.	

WAR DIARY
or
INTELLIGENCE SUMMARY.

Army Form C. 2118.

Place	Date	Hour	Summary of Events and Information	Remarks and references to Appendices
GOSTINEAU	26/6/18		CASUALTIES 1.O.R. WOUNDED	
			Situation Normal. Night Quiet. Enemy Artillery Normal Principal	
			Areas Shelled Pioneer Hendecourt Sugar Factory Railway Cutting	51.S.W
			in S.R. & S.16C. Our MG8 Fired 12000 Rounds. 1,200 Rounds At.	51.S.E.
			E.9.	
GOSTINEAU	27/6/18		CASUALTIES 2 O.R. WOUNDED.	
			Situation Normal. Night Quiet. Enemy Artillery Normal. Principal	
			Areas Shelled. Boisleux Au Mont Station. Pioneer - Boyelles	51.S.W
			Road. Boiry. Considerable Harrassing Fire Carried Out on	51.S.E.
			Roads Tracks. Our MGs. Fired 20,000 Rounds on Special Targets	
			4,500 Rounds At E.9.	
GOSTINEAU	28/6/18		CASUALTIES 2 O.R. 1. ACCIDENTALLY	
			Situation Normal. Night Quiet Enemy Artillery Active On Tracks	
			And Battery8. Railway Cutting in S.R. & Hendecourt Sugar Factory	51.S.W
			And Boiry Shelled At Intervals. Our MGs Fired 8000Rounds	51.S.E.
			On Special Targets. 4,350 Rounds At E.9.	

Army Form C. 2118.

WAR DIARY
or
INTELLIGENCE SUMMARY.
(Erase heading not required.)

Instructions regarding War Diaries and Intelligence Summaries are contained in F. S. Regs., Part II, and the Staff Manual respectively. Title pages will be prepared in manuscript.

Place	Date	Hour	Summary of Events and Information	Remarks and references to Appendices
Gouzeaucourt.	29/6/18		Situation Normal. Night Quiet. Enemy Artillery Activity Below Normal During Day. Our M.G's Fired 16,500 On Special Targets. 2450 Rounds By E.A.	
Gouzeaucourt	30/6/18		Situation Normal. Night Quiet. Enemy Artillery Below Normal On Centre Sub-Sector. Pioneer, Boiteux, Bory, Sugar Factory Herdecourt & Reigart. Shelled Our M.G. 20,000 Rounds On Special Targets. 5,150 Rounds By E.A.	51 S.E. 51 S.W.

S E C R E T.   Copy No. 13

33RD BATTALION MACHINE GUN CORPS ORDER NO. 37.

1. **GAS DISCHARGE.**

   "J" Special Company R.E. will carry out a Gas Projector Discharge into HAMELINCOURT on the night June 4/5th, if the wind is favourable, or on the first subsequent favourable night.

2. **TARGETS ENGAGED.**

   The following targets will be engaged :-

   A.5.a. central   ....   500 drums.
   A.5.b. central   ....   500 drums.

   All projectors will be discharged from emplacements at S.25.a.3.5.

3. **ZEROS.**

   In order to allow for variations in the wind there will be two alternative Zeros :-

   First Zero   ...   12 midnight.
   Second Zero ...   2.a.m.

   All the projectors will be fired at the one Zero.

4. **R.E. OFFICER IN CHARGE.**

   O.C. "J" Special Coy. R.E. will be in charge of the operation.

5. **WIND LIMITATIONS.**

   The wind limitations for the operation are S.W. to N.N.E. (through W.).

   The O.C. "J" Special Coy. R.E. will be responsible for deciding if the wind is safe.

6. **CODE.**

   All concerned will be informed by wire at 6.30.p.m. on June 4rd (and on subsequent dates if the discharge does not take place on June 4th), if the discharge is to take place that night or not, and the Zero hour.

   This information and any subsequent alterations necessary owing to changes in the wind will be circulated in code as under :-

   Operation will take place.
   First Zero   ...   JOHN.
   Operation will not take place
   First Zero   ...   CANCEL JOHN.
   Operation will take place
   Second Zero   ...   GEORGE.
   Operation will not take place
   Second Zero   ...   CANCEL GEORGE.
   Operation will not take place
   to-night   ...   WILLIAM

7. **MACHINE GUNS.**

Machine guns will co-operate in accordance with Appendix "A" attached, searching the objectives and all approaches within 400 yards of it.

8. **ARTILLERY.**

The Artillery are arranging to sweep the same area with shrapnel. Their times of fire will be identical with the machine guns.

9. **ZERO HOUR.**

Machine guns will take the flash of the projectors as their zero hour and time their firing, accordingly.

10. **SPECIAL INSTRUCTIONS.**

Special instructions for Machine Guns are issued in Appendix "B" attached.

11. **PRECAUTIONS.**

All ranks engaged in the operation and all other machine gunners in forward positions will have their respirators ready for instant adjustment in case of the slightest smell or suspicion of gas.

12. **SYNCHRONIZATION OF WATCHES.**

Battalion Headquarters will send an Officer to "D" and "A" Coy. Headquarters at 6.30.p.m. and 7.p.m. respectively. Watches will not be synchronised on the telephone.

13. **ACKNOWLEDGE.**

J. Reeve
Lt. Col.,
Commanding 62nd Battalion M. G. Corps.

2/6/1918.

Copies to:-
1. C.O.
2. Adjutant.
3. O.C. "A" Coy.
4. O.C. "B" Coy.
5. O.C. "C" Coy.
6. O.C. "D" Coy.
7. Signal Officer.
8. H.Q. 62nd Division.
9. "   "
10. 14th Inf. Bde.
11. 15th Inf. Bde.
12. 17th Inf. Bde.
13/14. War Diary.
15. File.

APPENDIX "A".

Serial No.	M.G. Coy.	No. of guns.	Present Location.	Location during operation.	Target.
1.	A.	6	S.15.c.	S.22.a.00.55. (right gun)	4 guns A.5.a.80.55. to A.5.a.55.75. 2 guns) A.5.a.40.25.
2.	B.	2	S.15.b.5.4.	"	2 guns) to A.5.a.80.45.
3.	D.	4	S.14.d.5.2.	S.19.a.65.10. (right gun)	A.5.b.80.55. to A.5.b.60.75.
4.	D.	4	Reserve	"	A.5.b.45.20 to A.5.b.60.40.

1. **Times of fire.**

   Zero plus 2 to zero plus 7.
   and zero plus 25 to zero plus 35.

2. **Rates of fire.**

   250 rounds per minute.

3. **Traverse.**

   2° each side of zero line.

APPENDIX "B".

1. The guns will be formed in two night gun batteries.

2. The 4 guns of "B" Coy. participating will come under the orders of the O.C. "A" Coy. for the operation.

3. Approximate locations of night guns are given in Appendix "A". Battery commanders will be responsible for choosing the exact sites.

4. O's. C. "A" and "B" Coys. will forward detailed firing calculations for checking as soon as possible.

5. Should the operation not take place on first night (June 3/4th) these orders will hold good for subsequent nights. *H/S.M.*

6. As the clearances over friendly troops are large and great accuracy not essential "T" bases need not be used, but tripods will be dug in or sandbagged to keep them steady.

7. Each gun will have a clinometer.

8. A small amount of searching (2 minutes) may also be employed with the traversing, but great care will be taken that guns are not depressed unduly. Searching should extend away from the guns during the last 2 minutes of each shoot.

9. Spare water will be taken so that barrel casings may be refilled if necessary between shoots. It is essential that casings should be absolutely full owing to high rate of fire and long range.

10. Only such numbers as are absolutely necessary to fire and direct the guns will be close by; spare numbers will be kept under cover to flank or rear.

11. Signalling Officer will arrange for visual communication from guns back.

12. Reports.
    (a) A report that all guns are ready will be sent in at zero minus 5 minutes.
    (b) A report during operation will be sent in code in accordance with Appendix "C" attached. (To Coys. only)
    (c) A report on the operation, stoppages encountered, casualties etc. will be rendered on following morning by Coys. concerned.

13. All guns will resume their positions as soon as possible after conclusion of shoot and relay where necessary on their S.O.S. lines.

14. Coys. will arrange to give men firing, a hot drink at conclusion of operation.

15. Sticks should be driven in on either side of gun casing to regulate traverse.

SECRET   Copy No. 13

32ND BATTALION MACHINE GUN CORPS ORDER No. 28.

1. The Class (16 per Company) at the Divisional Depot Batt. BAILLEULMONT, will be changed tomorrow, 4th inst.

2. The ingoing men from the Depot Battalion will proceed to their respective Company Headquarters with the ration limbers on 5th inst.

3. (a). The outgoing men from the line will come down to BRETENCOURT leaving the line any time after 9 a.m. if all is quiet.

   (b). They will bath and get clean clothes and proceed to BAILLEULMONT leaving BRETENCOURT at 5.30 p.m. on 4th inst.

4. Both ingoing and outgoing parties will be marched as formed bodies, strict march discipline will be maintained.

5. N.C.O. instructors at present at BAILLEULMONT will remain there and start training the new class.

6. 2/Lt. R. KITCHENER will remain at BAILLEULMONT for the period in charge of all M.G. details, there.

7. Should it be impossible owing to the situation, to send men down from the line tomorrow morning, companies will notify Battalion Headquarters as early as possible.

8. ACKNOWLEDGE

                                            A.W. Trimble Capt. Adjt.
                                            for Lieut. Col.
                                            Commanding 32nd Battalion M.G. Corps.

3/6/18.
Copies to:-
  1. C.O.
  2. Adjutant
  3. O.C. "A" Coy.
  4. O.C. "B" Coy.
  5. O.C. "C" Coy.
  6. O.C. "D" Coy.
  7. Quartermaster
  8. Signalling Officer
  9. O.C. Div. Depot Bn.
  10. 2/Lt. R. KITCHENER (at Div. Depot Bn.)
  11/12. H.Q. 32nd Division
  13/14. War Diary
  15. File.

SECRET.   Copy No. 13

62ND BATTALION MACHINE GUN CORPS ORDER NO. 29.

1.   The 24 O.R. (6 per Company) at the Divisional Depot Battalion BAILLEULMONT, will be changed tomorrow 11th inst.

2.   The ingoing men from the Depot Battalion will proceed to their respective Company Headquarters with the ration limbers on 11th inst.

3.   (a) The outgoing men from the line will come down to BIENVILLERS leaving the line any time after 9.a.m., if all is quiet.
(b) They will bath and get clean clothes and proceed to BAILLEULMONT leaving BIENVILLERS at 5.30.p.m. on 11th inst.
(c) All No.1's proceeding to BAILLEULMONT will take their revolvers with them.

4.   Both outgoing and ingoing parties will be marched as formed bodies, strict march discipline will be maintained.

5.   N.C.O. instructors at present at BAILLEULMONT will remain there and start training the new class.

6.   2/Lt. TITCHENER will remain at BAILLEULMONT for the present in charge of all M.G. details there.

7.   Should it be impossible owing to the situation, to send men down from the line tomorrow, Companies will notify Battalion Headquarters as early as possible.

8.   Nominal Rolls will be sent to O.C., Depot Battalion.

9.   ACKNOWLEDGE.

                                                    Capt. Adjt.
                                                    fr Lieut. Col.,
                                            Comndg. 62nd Battalion M. G. Corps.
10/6/18.

Copies to :-
1. C.O.
2. Adjutant.
3. O.C. "A" Coy.
4. O.C. "B" "
5. O.C. "C" "
6. O.C. "D" "
7. Quartermaster.
8. Signalling Officer.
9. O.C., Divl. Depot Bn.
10. 2/Lt. R.TITCHENER (at Divl. Depot Bn.)
11/12. H.Q., 62nd Division.
13/14. War Diary.
15. File.

SECRET.   Copy No. 10

32ND BATTALION MACHINE GUN CORPS ORDER NO. 50.

1. GAS DISCHARGE.

"J" Special Company R.E. will carry out a gas projector discharge into HAMELINCOURT on the night 12/13th June, if the wind is favourable, or on the first subsequent favourable night.

2. TARGETS ENGAGED.

The following targets will be engaged :-

A.5.a. central.
A.5.b. central.

All projectors will be discharged from emplacements at S.35.a.5.3.

3. ZEROS.

In order to allow for variations in the wind there will be two alternative Zeros :-

First Zero   ...   1. a.m.
Second Zero   ...   2.15.a.m.

All the projectors will be fired at the one Zero.

4. R.E. OFFICER IN CHARGE.

O.C. "J" Special Coy. R.E. will be in charge of the operation.

5. WIND LIMITATIONS.

The wind limitations for the operation are S.W. to N.N.E. (through W.).   Special
The O.C. "J"/Coy. R.E. will be responsible for deciding if the wind is safe.

6. CODE.

All concerned will be informed by wire at 6.30.p.m. on June 12th (and on subsequent dates if the discharge does not take place on June 12/13th), if the discharge is to take place that night or not, and the Zero hour.

This information and any subsequent alterations necessary owing to changes in the wind will be circulated in code as under:-

Operation will take place,
First Zero   ...   JOHNSON.

Operation will not take place,
First Zero   ...   CANCEL JOHNSON.

Operation will take place,
Second Zero   ...   TOM.

Operation will not take place,
Second Zero   ...   CANCEL TOM.

Operation will not take place
to-night   ...   JAMES.

7./

7. **MACHINE GUNS.**

    Machine Guns will co-operate in accordance with Appendix "A" attached, searching the objective and all approaches within 400 yards of it.

8. **ARTILLERY.**

    The Artillery are arranging to sweep the same area with shrapnel. Their times of fire will be identical with the Machine Guns.

9. **ZERO HOUR.**

    Machine guns will take the flash of the projectors as their Zero hour and time their firing accordingly.

10. **SPECIAL INSTRUCTIONS.**

    Special instructions for Machine Guns are issued in Appendix "B" attached.

11. **PRECAUTIONS.**

    All ranks engaged in the operation and all other machine gunners in forward positions will have their respirators ready for instant adjustment in case of the slightest smell or suspicion of gas.

12. **SYNCHRONIZATION OF WATCHES.**

    Battalion Headquarters will send an Officer to "D" and "A" Coy. Headquarters at 6.30.p.m. and 7.p.m. respectively. Watches will not be synchronized on the telephone.

13. A C K N O W L E D G E.

J. Reeve
Lt. Col.,
Commanding 32nd Battalion M. G. Corps.

12/6/18.

Copies to :-
1. C.O.
2. Adjutant.
3. O.C. "A" Coy.
4. O.C. "B" Coy.
5. O.C. "C" Coy.
6. O.C. "D" Coy.
7. Signal Officer.
8/9. H.Q., 32nd Division.
10. 14th Inf.Bde.
11. 96th Inf.Bde.
12. 97th Inf.Bde.
13/14. War Diary.
15. File.

APPENDIX "A".

Serial No.	M.G. Coy.	No. of guns.	Present Location.	Location during operation.	Target.
1.	A.	6	S.16.c.	S.22.a.00.38. (right gun)	4 guns A.5.a.20.55. to A.5.a.55.75.
2.	B.	2	S.16.b.3.4.	"	2 guns) A.5.a.45.25. 2 guns) to A.5.a.60.45.
3.	D.	4	S.14.d.5.9.	S.16.c.65.10. (right gun)	A.5.b.20.55. to A.5.a.60.75.
4.	D.	4	Reserve	"	A.5.b.45.20. to A.5.b.60.40.

1. **Times of fire.**

    Zero plus 2 to Zero plus 7
    and Zero plus 45 to Zero plus 55.

2. **Rates of fire.**

    250 rounds per minute.

3. **Traverse.**

    5° each side of Zero line.

APPENDIX "B".

1. The guns will be formed in two eight gun batteries.

2. The 2 guns of "B" Coy. participating will come under the orders of O.C. "A" Coy. for the operation.

3. Approximate locations of right guns are given in Appendix "A". Battery commanders will be responsible for choosing the exact sites.

4. O's.C. "A" and "D" Coys. will forward detailed firing calculations for checking as soon as possible.

5. Should the operation not take place on first night (June 12/13th) these orders will hold good for subsequent nights.

6. As the clearances over friendly troops are large and great accuracy not essential, "Y" bases need not be used, but tripods will be dug in and sandbagged to keep them steady.

7. Each gun will have a clinometer.

8. A small amount of searching (30 minutes) may also be employed with the traversing, but great care will be taken that guns are not depressed unduly. Searching should extend away from the guns during the last 2 minutes of each shoot.

9. Spare water will be taken so that barrel casings may be refilled if necessary between shoots. It is essential that casings should be absolutely full owing to high rate of fire and long range.

10. Only such numbers as are absolutely necessary to fire and direct the guns will be close by; spare numbers will be kept under cover to flank or rear.

11. Signalling Officer will arrange for visual communication from guns back.

12. REPORTS.
    (a) A report that all guns are ready will be sent in at Zero minus 5 minutes.
    (b) A report during operation will be sent in code in accordance with Appendix "C" attached to M.G.Order No.27 (To Coys. only).
    (c) A report on the operation, stoppages encountered, casualties etc., will be rendered on following morning by Coys. concerned.

13. All guns will resume their positions as soon as possible after conclusion of shoot, and relay where necessary, on their S.O.S. lines.

14. Coys. will arrange to give men firing a hot drink at conclusion of operation.

15. Sticks should be driven in on either side of gun casing to regulate traverse.

SECRET.

                                                                                            Copy No. 14

32ND BATTALION MACHINE GUN CORPS ORDER NO. 51.

1. The 64 O.R. (16 per Company) at the Divisional Depot Battalion BAILLEULMONT, will be changed tomorrow 18th inst.

2. The ingoing men from the Depot Battalion will proceed to their respective Company Headquarters with the ration limbers on 18th inst.

3. (a) The outgoing men from the line will come down to BIEFENCOURT leaving the line any time after 9.a.m. if all is quiet.
   (b) They will bath and get clean clothes and proceed to BAILLEULMONT leaving BIEFENCOURT at 5.30.p.m. on 18th inst.
   (c) All No. 1's proceeding to BAILLEULMONT will take their revolvers with them.

4. Both outgoing and ingoing parties will be marched as formed bodies, strict march discipline will be maintained.

5. N.C.O. instructors at present at BAILLEULMONT will remain there and start training the new class.

6. 2/Lt. R.TISCHNER will remain at BAILLEULMONT for the present in charge of all M.G. details there.

7. Should it be impossible owing to the situation, to send men down from the line tomorrow, Companies will notify Battalion Headquarters as early as possible.

8. Nominal Rolls will be sent to O.C., Depot Battalion.

9. ACKNOWLEDGE.

                                                                  Lieut. Col.,
                                 Comdg., 32nd Battalion M.G. Corps.

17.6.18.

Copies to :-
   1. C.O.
   2. Adjutant.
   3. O.C. "A" Coy.
   4. O.C. "B" Coy.
   5. O.C. "C" Coy.
   6. O.C. "D" Coy.
   7. Quartermaster.
   8. Signalling Officer.
   9. O.C., Divl. Depot Bn.
 10. 2/Lt. R.TISCHNER (at Divl. Depot Bn.)
11/12. H.Q., 32nd Division.
13/14. War Diary.
 15. File.

S E C R E T.

Copy No. 14

32ND BATTALION MACHINE GUN CORPS ORDER NO. 58.

1. The 64 O.R. (16 per Company) at the Divisional Depot Battalion BAIZIEUX, will be changed tomorrow, 25th inst.

2. The ingoing men from the Depot Battalion will proceed to their respective Company Headquarters with the ration limbers on 25th inst.

3. (a) The outgoing men from the line will come down to BEHENCOURT, leaving the line any time after 9.a.m. if all is quiet.
   (b) They will bath and get clean clothes and proceed to BAIZIEUX-MONT leaving BEHENCOURT at 1.30.p.m. on 25th inst.
   (c) All No. 1's proceeding to BAIZIEUX will take their revolvers with them.

4. Both outgoing and ingoing parties will be marched as formed bodies, strict march discipline will be maintained.

5. N.C.O. instructors at present at BAIZIEUX will remain there and start training the new class.

6. 2/Lt. R. T CHESER will remain at BAIZIEUX for the present in charge of all M.G. details there.

7. Should it be impossible owing to the situation, to send men down from the line tomorrow, Companies will notify Battalion Headquarters as early as possible.

8. Nominal Rolls will be sent to O.C., Depot Battalion.

9. ACKNOWLEDGE.

Lieut. Col.,
Comdg., 32nd Battalion M. G. Corps.

24. 6. 18.

Copies to :-
1. C.O.
2. Adjutant.
3. O.C., "A" Coy.
4. O.C., "B" Coy.
5. O.C., "C" Coy.
6. O.C., "D" Coy.
7. Quartermaster.
8. Signalling Officer.
9. O.C., Divl. Depot Bn.
10. 2/Lt. R. T CHESER (a Divl. Depot Bn.).
11/12. H.Q., 32nd Division.
13/14. War Diary.
15. File.

S E C R E T.   Copy No. 15.

32ND BATTALION MACHINE GUN CORPS ORDER NO. 33.

1. The method of holding the divisional front is being reorganized on night June 25/26th, and each Infantry Brigade will then hold its sector with one battalion in the front system, one battalion in the PURPLE system and one battalion in reserve.

2. Some of the forward machine guns will also be withdrawn and will move to new positions as detailed below:-

Gun No.	M.G. Coy.	Move to.
F.45) F.46)	B.	X.6.c.04.95.
F.33) F.34) F.38) F.36)	A.	X.10.c.80.75.
F.27) F.28)	C.	X.15.b.00.40.

3. Relief of the forward guns will not commence before 9.30.p.m. Completion will be reported to Battalion Headquarters in code by word THINNER.

4. Positions vacated will not be destroyed, and number boards (F.45 etc.) will be left there. New numbers will be assigned to the guns that withdraw. All S.A.A. will be taken back.

5. All ranks must realize that the thinning out of infantry and machine guns in the forward area entails increased vigilance and activity on the part of those remaining. It is absolutely essential that the enemy should not get to know of the redistribution.

6. The same amount of night firing will be carried on as usual. Os.C. Companies will arrange either for the remaining guns to fire more, or to send up guns from behind to fire at night.

7. Permanent infantry escorts with Lewis Guns are being detailed for the special purpose of affording local protection for the machine guns left in the forward area. This applies to the 5 pairs of guns as follows:-

Nos. F.47)	F.43)	F.31)	F.29)	F.25)
F.48)	F.44)	F.32)	F.30)	F.26).

   The very closest liaison and mutual co-operation between machine guns and their escorts must be established. Os.C. Companies will ensure that every man of the forward machine gun teams knows exactly who is protecting him, and the dispositions of the escort.

8. Generally speaking, the machine guns will fire to the flanks in enfilade and the escort will be responsible for their frontal protection, and for dealing with hostile snipers and bombers.
   It is only by the closest liaison and mutual confidence that the best results can be obtained.

2.

9. All forward machine guns must be imbued with the determination to "fight it out" in their position to the last. There must be no idea of withdrawing under any circumstances.

No attack will be able to reach them as long as the guns continue firing and machine gunners and escorts both do their jobs.

10. Amendments to the M.G. Defence Scheme and positions for reserve guns of "D" Company will be issued separately.

11. ACKNOWLEDGE.

J. Reeve.
Lieut. Col.,
Commanding 32nd Battalion M. G. Corps.

24. 6. 18.

Copies to :-

1. O. C.
2. Adjutant.
3. O. C., "A" Coy.
4. O. C., "B" Coy.
5. O. C., "C" Coy.
6. O. C., "D" Coy.
7. 14th Inf. Bde.
8. 96th Inf. Bde. 17 97th Inf. Bde.
9/10. H. Q., 32nd Division.
11. O. C., 2nd Bn. M'. G. C.
12. O. C., 2nd Canadian M. G. Bn.
13. O. C., 4th Guards M. G. Bn.
14/15. War Diary.
16. File.

Confidential 986

War Diary
of
32 Bn. M.G.C.
From July 1st/18 — July 31st/18.

No. 6.

Army Form C. 2118.

WAR DIARY
or
INTELLIGENCE SUMMARY.
(Erase heading not required.)

Place	Date	Hour	Summary of Events and Information	Remarks and references to Appendices
Berle Au Bois Wood O.1.	1/7/18		Situation Normal. Night Quiet. Enemy Artillery more active than usual on Centre Sub-Sector. Otherwise Normal. Our M.G'. Fired 20,000 Rounds on Special Target. 3,450 Rounds at E.9. Bombs were dropped on Ransart at 1.30 AM.	51.c SE
Berle Au Bois Wood.O.1.	2/7/18		Situation Normal. Night Quiet. Enemy Artillery Normal. Boisleux Cemetery. Hendecourt Sugar Factory. Quarry S.7.b & Rohfer. Principal Areas Shelled. Our M.G's Fired 119,000 Rounds in Support of Raids By Left & Right Bdes. 6750 Rounds Harrassing Fire. 3,300 Rounds at E.9.	51.c SE 51.b SW
Berle Au Bois Wood O.1.	3/7/18		Situation Normal. Night Quiet. Enemy Artillery Normal. On Left & Centre Quiet on Right Transport Aero Drome Hendecourt & Batteries in vicinity Received Attention Our N°8. 17,756 Rounds on Special Target. 950 Rounds at E.9. OO.34 Issued Relief Orders	51.c SE 51.S.W 9.R.1.c

WAR DIARY
or
INTELLIGENCE SUMMARY.

Army Form C. 2118.

Place	Date	Hour	Summary of Events and Information	Remarks and references to Appendices
Berles Au Bois	4/7/18		Situation Normal. Night Quiet. Enemy Artillery Normal. Blett. Sugar Factory and Pointer Shelled. Usual Harassing Fire on Tracks at Night. Our M.G. Fired 6,000 Rounds on Special Targets. 800 Rounds At E.9.	51˚S.W. 51˚S.E.
N10101				
Berles Au Bois	5/7/18		Situation Normal. Night Quiet. Enemy Artillery Below Normal on Left and Centre. Increased Activity on Right. Pointer, Hendecourt, Sugar Factory & Bart. Were Shelled. Our M.G. Fired 17,750 Rounds on Special Targets 4,550 Rounds At E.9.	51˚S.W. 51˚S.E.
N10101			Casualties. 1 O.R. Wounded	
Berles Au Bois	6/7/18		Situation Normal. Night Quiet. Enemy Artillery Normal. Defence Scheme A.P.N.62 Issued. Bn HQ Moved to Saulty. P & D Coys were Relieved by No 1 & No 2 Coys 4 Bn Guards M.G. Regt. & Proceeded by Light Railway to Saulty. Billets In Saulty.	51˚S.W.
No 20.1 & N7.7.5.5				
Saulty				

WAR DIARY or INTELLIGENCE SUMMARY.

Army Form C. 2118.

Place	Date	Hour	Summary of Events and Information	Remarks and references to Appendices
SAULTY	7/7/18		B & C Coys were relieved by 3 & 4 Coys of the 47th Bn Queens M.G. Regt. A & D Coys Resting.	
SAULTY	8/7/18		Coys spent the day in cleaning up M.G. Instructors No K Bruce P.P.3	
SAULTY	9/7/18		Coys carried out training as per programme.	
SAULTY	10/7/18		Coys carried out training as per programme	
SAULTY	11/7/18		Coys. carried out training as per programme	
SAULTY	12/7/18		Coys. carried out training as per programme.	
SAULTY	13/7/18		Coys. carried out training as per programme	
SAULTY	14/7/18		Church Parade.	

Army Form C. 2118.

WAR DIARY
or
INTELLIGENCE SUMMARY.

(Erase heading not required.)

Instructions regarding War Diaries and Intelligence Summaries are contained in F. S. Regs., Part II. and the Staff Manual respectively. Title pages will be prepared in manuscript.

Place	Date	Hour	Summary of Events and Information	Remarks and references to Appendices
Sally	19/7/18		Coy. Carried on Training as per Programme.	
Sally	16/7/18		Coy. Carried on Training as per Programme.	
Sally	17/7/18		Coys. Carried out Training as per Programme. Warning order Received for Moving.	
Sally	18/7/18		Bn. Moved to Proven, By Strategical Trains as per O.O. 35 A.P.A. Bn. In G.H.Q. Reserve.	Sheet 27
Proven	19/7/18		Bn. In G.H.Q. Reserve.	
Proven	20/7/18		Bn. Spent Day In Cleaning Up Camps.	
Proven	21/7/18		Church Parade.	

Army Form C. 2118.

WAR DIARY
or
INTELLIGENCE SUMMARY.
(Erase heading not required.)

Place	Date	Hour	Summary of Events and Information	Remarks and references to Appendices
PROVEN	22/7/18		Bn. WENT OUT FOR ROUTE MARCH. COY. CMDRS. RECONNOITRED 6 DIVISIONAL AREA.	
PROVEN	23/7/18		COYS. CARRIED OUT TRAINING AS PER PROGRAMME.	
PROVEN	24/7/18		COYS. CARRIED OUT TRAINING AS PER PROGRAMME.	
PROVEN	25/7/18		COYS. CARRIED OUT TRAINING AS PER PROGRAMME.	
PROVEN	26/7/18		COYS. CARRIED OUT TRAINING AS PER PROGRAMME.	
PROVEN	27/7/18		COYS. CARRIED OUT TRAINING AS PER PROGRAMME.	
PROVEN	28/7/18		COYS. CARRIED OUT TRAINING AS PER PROGRAMME.	

Instructions regarding War Diaries and Intelligence Summaries are contained in F. S. Regs., Part II. and the Staff Manual respectively. Title pages will be prepared in manuscript.

Army Form C. 2118.

WAR DIARY
or
INTELLIGENCE SUMMARY.

(Erase heading not required.)

Place	Date	Hour	Summary of Events and Information	Remarks and references to Appendices
Proven	29/7/18		Coys. Carried Out Training As Per Programme. Boxing Tournament Held In The Afternoon.	
Proven	30/7/18		Coys. Carried Out Training As Per Programme.	
Proven	31/7/18		Coys. Carried Out Training As Per Programme.	

SECRET. Copy No. 22

32ND BATTALION MACHINE GUN CORPS ORDER NO.54.

1. The Guards Division is relieving the 32nd Division in the centre sector of the VI Corps front.

2. Infantry reliefs will be carried out as follows :-

   (a) <u>On July 5th and night July 5/6th.</u>   The 1st Guards Brigade will relieve the 14th Infantry Brigade in the centre sub-sector.

   (b) <u>On July 6th and night July 6/7th.</u>   The 2nd Guards Brigade will relieve the 97th Infantry Brigade in the Right sub-sector.

   The 3rd Guards Brigade will relieve the 96th Infantry Brigade in the Left sub-sector.

3. Machine Gun Companies will be relieved as follows:-

   <u>Night July 6/7th.</u>

   "A" Coy. will be relieved by No.1 Coy. 4th Batn. Guards M.G. Regt.
   "D" "   "   "   "   " No.2 Coy.   "   "   "   "   "

   <u>Night July 7/8th.</u>

   "B" Coy. will be relieved by No.3 Coy. 4th Batn. Guards M.G. Regt.
   "C" "   "   "   "   " No.4 Coy.   "   "   "   "   "

4. On relief the 32nd M.G. Battalion will move to SAULTY and the 32nd Division will be in Third Army Reserve.

5. Completion of reliefs on both nights will be reported in code to Battalion Headquarters as follows :-

   Relief complete   ...   DAILY.
   Little shelling   ...   MAYL.
   Much shelling   ...   TOPSY.

6. (a) All details of relief except those herein specified will be arranged direct between Company Commanders concerned.
   (b) Os.C. Guards M.G. Coys. will visit their opposite numbers on Thursday 4th inst.
   Guides to meet them will be sent as follows:-

   "A" "C" and "D" Coys. - Cross Roads RANSART K.6.c.60.85 at 10.a.m.
   "B" Coy.   - Cross Roads BLAIREVILLE K.4.a.8.8. at 10.30.a.m.

7. Command of the M.G. defences of the Divisional sector will pass to O.C., 4th Batn. Guards M.G. Regt. at 10.a.m. on July 7th

at which hour the Command of the Divisional sector will pass to G.O.C., Guards Division.

8. (a) M.G. Coys. of the Guards Division moving into the 56th Divisional area will come under the tactical orders of the G.O.C., 56th Division on reaching the line MONCHY – RANSART – BELLACOURT Road.

(b) "A" and "D" Coys. will similarly come under the tactical orders of G.O.C. Guards Division when west of above road until 10.a.m. on July 7th.

9. (a) "A" and "D" Coys. will move to SAULTY by rail from RANSART on night 6/7th July. Further instructions will be issued.

(b) "C" Coy. will similarly entrain at RANSART and "B" Coy. at BLAIREVILLE on night July 7/8th.

10. The Headquarter Transport at BAILLEULMONT will be relieved on morning of July 7th. Details will be arranged between Transport officers concerned. Coy. Transport lines will be relieved under Coy. arrangements.

11. (a) The strictest march discipline must be observed on the march to SAULTY both by personnel and transport.

(b) The following distances will be maintained :-

100 yards between Coys.
100 yards between a Coy. and its transport.

A gap of 20 yards will be left between each section of 6 vehicles.

(c) No restrictions as to routes.

12. No reference as to the relief will be made in front of Brigade Headquarters by any means of communication except by D.R. and runners, except as to the reporting in case of completion of relief.

13. (a) All belts and boxes containing anti-tank armour piercing S.A.A. will be handed over on relief but all other gun stores, tripods, belts and boxes will be brought out and NOT handed over.

(b) All defence schemes, lines of fire, alternative emplacements, marked maps, information about the line, dug-outs, gas sentries and appliances etc., will be handed over.

(c) The following will be brought out:-

1. Petrol tins which belong to limbers and one per gun in addition.
2. Range card boards. Copies of all the range cards will be handed over.
3. Section reserves of food and spare clothing.
4. Maps which have not been used.
5. Gas rattles which form part of Coy. equipment.

3.

    (d) Especial care will be taken in handing over the forward groups of Machine Guns so that their action and co-operation with their escorts is perfectly clear.

    (e) Receipts for all stores handed over will be taken in triplicate and two copies sent to Battalion Headquarters.

14.   It is absolutely essential that all dug-outs, gun positions transport lines etc. should be handed over in a perfectly-clean condition. All latrines must be absolutely clean and old refuse pits filled in. Coys. will ensure that Section Officers obtain a certificate of cleanliness from the Officer relieving them. The same applies to all Coy. Headquarters and transport lines.

    Copies of these receipts will be sent to Battalion Headquarters.

15.   Personnel now at the Divisional Depot Battalion will join their Coy. transport lines on 6th inst. after completion of morning's training.

    They will march with their transport to SAULTY.

16.   The Signal Officer will send an advance party to take over communications on 6th inst.

17. (a)   While in Third Army reserve, Units of 32nd Division will be prepared to move at one hour's notice from 6 to 10.a.m. daily and 3 hours notice for remainder of the day.

    (b)   Further instructions will be issued as to counter-attack schemes etc. of the M.G. Battalion while in Reserve.

18.   Battalion Headquarters will close at W.10.a.1.2. at 10.a.m. on July 7th and re-open at SAULTY on arrival.

19.   ACKNOWLEDGE.

                                Lieut. Col.,
                Commanding 32nd Battalion M.G. Corps.

5.7.18.

Copies to :-
1. C.O.
2. Adjutant.
3. O.C., "A" Coy.
4. O.C., "B" Coy.
5. O.C., "C" Coy.
6. O.C., "D" Coy.
7. Quartermaster.
8. Transport Officer.
9. O.C., 4th Bn. Gards M.G.Regt.
10. 14th Inf.Bde.
11. 96th Inf.Bde.
12. 97th Inf.Bde.
13/14. H.Q., 32nd Division.
15. O.C., 32nd Divl. Depot Bn.
16. 2/Lt. R. KITCHENER.
17. O.C., 2nd Bn. M.G.C.
18. O.C., 3rd Cand. M.G. Bn.
19. Town Major, BAILLEULMONT.
20.   "   SAULTY.
21/22. War Diary.
23. File.

APPENDIX "A".

Machine Gun Dispositions.

"A" Coy. in centre Sub-sector - Headquarters at Y.10.a.35.30.
                    Affiliated to 14th Infantry Brigade.

Gun No.	Position.		
R.31	S.8?.b.?8.00.		
R.32	S.8?.b.60.00.		
S.13	S.9.a.5?.80.		
S.14	S.9.d.70.0?.		
R.47	S.7.b.68.?0.	Moving to	Y.8.a.46.18.
R.48	S.7.b.6?.4?.	"	Y.8.a.40.21.
R.49	S.7.b.99.8?.	"	Y.8.a.3?.24.
R.50	S.7.b.91.9?.	"	Y.8.a.37.27.
R.36	S.16.c.10.00.		
R.38	S.16.c.70.20.		
R.39	S.20.b.90.70.		
R.40	S.20.b.92.70.		
	Y.10.c.6?.6?. (From R.3)		
	Y.10.c.7?.70. (From R.37)		
	Y.10.c.90.90. (From R.33)		
	Y.10.c.99.97. (From R.34)		

"B" Coy. in left Sub-sector - Headquarters at Y.?b.?.?0.
                    Affiliated to 96th Infantry Brigade.

R.45	S.18.a.0?.75.	S.15	S.9.c.7?.02.
R.47	S.18.a.?0.80.	S.16	S.9.c.75.04.
R.44	S.17.c.7?.60.	S.17	S.3.c.?.48.
R.43	S.17.c.79.62.	S.18	S.?.c.44.3?.
R.42	S.16.a.0?.84.	S.21	S.?.c.14.81.
R.41	S.16.a.07.82.	S.22	S.?.c.17.82.
	Y.?.c.92.79. (From R.46)	R.??	Y.?b.98.00.
	Y.?.c.95.82. (From R.4?)	R.51	Y.6.a.08.0?

"C" Coy. in right Sub-sector - Headquarters at Y.1.c.4?.80.
                    Affiliated to 97th Infantry Brigade.

R.28	S.20.c.79.80. Moving to S.26.a.9?.82.	
	Y.1.a.8?.5?. (From R.27)	
	Y.1.b.10.4?. (From R.26)	
R.2?	S.20.c.9.3?. Moving to S.26.a.95.89.	
R.3?	Y.22.a.84.90.	
R.36	Y.22.a.19.89.	
R.35	Y.1?.b.01.4?.	
R.34	Y.1.a.98.5?.	
S.7	S.19.b.?5.?.	
S.8	S.19.b.60.40.	
R.30	S.21.c.70.04.	
R.29	S.21.c.67.20.	
R.40	Y.22.a.?0.19.	
R.39	Y.22.a.?5.40.	
R.37	Y.21.c.08.1?.	
R.38	Y.21.c.0?.20.	

"D" Coy.

"D" Coy. in reserve - Headquarters at X.15.c.80.68.

Affiliated to 14th Infantry Brigade :-

    R.29   X.20.c.90.48.)
    R.30   X.20.c.75.85.) German Heavy Machine Guns.
    R.30a   X.20.c.90.32.)
    R.31 & R.32 X.21.a.6 .4.
    R.28   X.21.a.08.08.
    R.27   X.21.a.00.10.
    R.42   X.17.b.10.15.
    R.41   X.17.b.15.20.

Affiliated to 97th Infantry Brigade :-

    R.46   X.12.c.15.40.
    R.45   X.12.c.30.45.
    R.45   X.18.a.20.45.
    R.44   X.18.a.83.47.
    S.12   S.14.a.2 .81.
    S.11   S.14.a.27.84.
    S.10   S.14.a.28.88.
    S. 9   S.14.a.27.94.

    4 Vickers guns at W.12.d.5.8.   ) In Divisional
    10 German Light Machine Guns at W.18.b. 0.00.) reserve.

Transport lines :-
        Coys' Transport Lines W.10.d.2. .
    "A" "B" "C"   "   "
    "D"   "   "   W.12.d.5.6.

Advanced Battalion Headquarters :- W.10.d.0.1.

Rear Battalion Headquarters and Quartermaster Stores BAILLEULMONT W.2.d.4.2.

6. PRINCIPLES OF DEFENCE.

(f). Our general method of defence must be as active and as aggressive as possible.
   Raids will be carried out on each Brigade Front.
   The enemy will be continually harassed by Machine Gun-fire trench mortars and artillery.
   Artillery concentrations on enemy trench mortars and centres of activity will be constantly arranged.

(g). Should the enemy gain a footing in any portion of our defences by a small and merely local attack he will be ejected by an immediate counter-attack.
   Such a counter-attack will have the best chance of success if delivered from the flanks, and if delivered as a surprise (i.e. under cover of smoke, darkness or the dust of the battle-field.)
   Counter-attack troops should be us on the flanks of the enemy and thus take the enemy in flank. *& therefore be moved to positions still held.*

7. PRELIMINARY MEASURES IN CASE OF ATTACK.

(a). Immediately an attack appears to be imminent owing to the opening of a heavy bombardment etc., all gun-teams will "Stand to" but will remain under cover. *

   * If it is by day, guns (except those firing on S.O.S. or Front Line positions) will be kept under cover safe from shell fire, ready to mount at once if necessary.

(e). All men at the Depot Battalion will remain under orders of Officer Commanding Divisional Depot Battalion.

(f). Should the Division wish these preliminary moves carried out it will send out the following code message which will be repeated to Companies by Battalion Headquarters. Preliminary moves AAA ACKNOWLEDGE. On receipt of this all measures indicated in para.7 will be taken.

8. ACTION IN CASE OF S.O.S.

(a). As for para.7.

(b). All guns on front line (YELLOW) S.O.S. will at once open fire (See Appendix "B").
   Section Officers must use their own discretion as to opening fire on their S.O.S. lines without having seen the signal or before the signal is made, if they consider circumstances demand it. They must always however bear in mind the expenditure of belts involved and premature exhaustion of their gun teams.

9. ACTION IN CASE OF ATTACK.

1. FORWARD GUNS AND ESCORTS.

The role of all Machine Gun Posts and their escorts is to defend their posts to the last whether their flanks are turned or not, and to inflict as much loss as possible on the enemy.

2. OTHER GUNS.

The nature of the country gives admirable scope for Machine Gun action and no enemy can succeed if the Machine Guns fulfil their *attack*

10. HARASSING FIRE.

(a). Harassing fire on suitable targets (roads, tracks and centres of movement) is carried out nightly by the forward guns.

6. PRINCIPLES OF DEFENCE.

(f). Our general method of defence must be as active and as aggressive as possible.
Raids will be carried out on each Brigade Front.
The enemy will be continually harassed by Machine Gun-fire trench mortars and artillery.
Artillery concentrations on enemy trench mortars and centres of activity will be constantly arranged.

(g). Should the enemy gain a footing in any portion of our defences by a small and merely local attack he will be ejected by an immediate counter-attack.
Such a counter-attack will have the best chance of success if delivered from the flanks, and if delivered as a surprise (i.e. under cover of smoke, darkness or the dust of the battle-field.)
Counter-attack troops should by us on the flanks of the enemy and thus take the enemy in flank. *& they have be moved to positions still held.*

7. PRELIMINARY MEASURES IN CASE OF ATTACK.

(a). Immediately an attack appears to be imminent owing to the opening of a heavy bombardment etc., all gun-teams will "Stand to" but will remain under cover. *

(b). The Reserve guns will "Stand To" and be ready to move at once on receipt of orders.

* (c). All transport will harness up and be ready to move at once hook in and move off. Each Company Transport Officer will send a mounted N.C.O. to his respective Company H.Q. for orders.

(d). All men out of the line (at BRETENCOURT etc.) will return at once to their Company Headquarters, under Command of the Senior N.C.O. of the Company.

(e). All men at the Depot Battalion will remain under orders of Officer Commanding Divisional Depot Battalion.

(f). Should the Division wish these preliminary moves carried out it will send out the following Code message which will be repeated to Companies by Battalion Headquarters. Preliminary moves AAA ACKNOWLEDGE. On receipt of this all measures indicated in para.7 will be taken.

8. ACTION IN CASE OF S.O.S.

(a). As for para.7.

(b). All guns on front line(YELLOW) S.O.S. will at once open fire (See Appendix "D").
Section Officers must use their own discretion as to opening fire on their S.O.S. lines without having seen the signal or before the signal is made, if they consider circumstances demand it. They must always however bear in mind the expenditure of belts involved and premature exhaustion of their gun teams.

9. ACTION IN CASE OF ATTACK.

1. FORWARD GUNS AND ESCORTS.

The role of all Machine Gun-Posts and their escorts is to defend their posts to the last whether their flanks are turned or not, and to inflict as much loss as possible on the enemy.

2. OTHER GUNS.

The nature of the country gives admirable scope for Machine Gun action and no enemy can succeed if the Machine Guns fulfil their *attack* role

10. HARASSING FIRE.

(a). Harassing fire on suitable targets(roads,tracks and centres of movement)is carried out nightly by the forward guns.

/- (b).

10. HARASSING FIRE. (Contd.)

(b). Attention is called to Machine Gun Instructions No.14 on harassing fire, which has been issued to all concerned.

(c). The targets are varied according to wishes of Infantry Battalion Commanders and Intelligence reports.

11. AMMUNITION SUPPLY.

(a). The amount of ammunition to be maintained at each gun is laid down in Appendix "C".

(b). Each gun on S.O.S. as detailed in Tables "A" and "B" of Appendix "B" will have 3 additional belts kept for that special purpose. Guns detailed in Tables "C" and "D" 12 belts.

(c). Each Company has about 4000 rounds of special anti-tank armour piercing S.A.A. distributed as shown in APPENDIX "D".

12. ANTI-AIRCRAFT.

A certain number of guns are mounted by day in anti-aircraft positions to engage low flying enemy aircraft.

See Appendix "E"

13. LIAISON.

(a). Machine Gun Company Commanders will keep in close touch with their affiliated Infantry Brigade.

(b). Officers Commanding Machine Gun Battalion Sections will keep in close touch with the Infantry in whose area they are stationed and will report daily to the Battalion Commander concerned.

(c). The Officer Commanding Machine Gun Battalion will keep in close touch with Brigadiers and ascertain their requirements as to Machine Gun action.

(d). Attention is called to Machine Gun Instructions No.15 on "LIAISON" which has been issued to all concerned.

14. BATTERY POSITIONS.

Eight Gun Battery Positions.

Eight Gun Battery positions, with shelters, "T" bases and aiming marks are situated as follows:-

"A" Battery.	X.21.a.35.80.
"B" Battery.	X.16.d.40.90.
"C" Battery.	X.16.d.80.20.
"D" Battery.	X.6.b.50.40.

These Batteries are not occupied as gun positions, but Companies will be responsible for their maintenance as under:-

"A" Battery.	"D" Company.
"B" "	"C" Company.
"C" "	"A" Company.
"D" "	"B" Company.

15. RECONNAISSANCE.

(a). All reserve guns will reconnoitre the entire PURPLE SYSTEM and approaches to it. Special Instructions with regard to their occupation of positions for the defence of the PURPLE SYSTEM are being issued.

(b). Company Commanders will reconnoitre positions to which their forward guns will "bound back" in the event of a fighting withdrawal. N.B. This will not be communicated lower than Section Officers.

(c). Battalion Transport Officer will reconnoitre all roads to and at F.29.c.7.4. to which place the transport will move from BAILLEULMONT should occasion arise.

16. COMMUNICATION.

See Appendix "F".

/- 17. Position of H.Q.

- 6 -

17. POSITION OF HEADQUARTERS.

   (a). Divisional Headquarters are at W.5.d.4.4.

   (b). Machine Gun Battalion Headquarters are at W.10.c.0.1.

18. ACKNOWLEDGE.

                                                   J. Reeve. Lieut. Col.

                              Cmdg., 2nd. Battalion Machine Gun Corps.

4/7/18.

Copies to :-

1. O.C.
2. Adjutant.
3. Signal Officer.
4. Transport Officer.
5. O.C. "A" Company.
6. O.C. "B" Company.
7. O.C. "C" Company.
8. O.C. "D" Company.
9. ~~5th. Infantry Bde.~~ 1st Guards Bde.
10. 96th. Infantry Bde.
11. 97th. Infantry Bde.
12. H.Q. 2nd. Division.
13. H.Q. 32nd. Division.
14. Divisional Artillery.
15. O.C. 2nd. Canadian M.G.Bn.
16. O.C. Guards M.G.Bn.
17. O.C. 2nd. Bn.M.G.Corps.
18. C.M.G.O., VI Corps.
19. War Diary.
20. War Diary.
21. File.

TABLE "A".

Front Line S.O.S. - YELLOW.

Serial No.	No. of guns.	M.G. Coy.	Location.	Target.
1.	2.	"B"	S.13.d.0.8.	(S.24.a.5.00. (S.24.c.48.05.
2.	2.	"A"	(S.16.c.6.10. (S.16.c.10.09.	(S.24.c.40.87. (S.24.c.53.80.
3.	2.	"A"	S.20.b.8.7.	S.23.c.30.30.
4.	2.	"C"	S.20.d.80.2.	S.23.c.30.40.
5.	2.	"C"	S.19.b.60.5.	S.23.c.0.5.6.

TABLE "B".

BLUE Line S.O.S. - BLUE.

Serial No.	No. of guns.	M.G. Coy.	Location.	Target.
6.	2.	"B"	S.9.d.60.10.	S.17.b.6.30.
7.	2.	"A"	S.9.d.65.20.	S.22.c.30.70.
8.	2.	"D"	S.14.d.30.90.	S.22.b.9.70.
9.	2.	"D"	S.14.d.50.80.	S.22.c.40.00.
10.	2.	"C"	S.19.b.60.5.	S.27.a.6.5.

TABLE "C".

RED Line S.O.S. - RED.

Serial No.	No. of guns.	M.G. Coy.	Location.	Target.
11.	4.	"A"	X.3.a.5.30.	S.13.a.00.70.
12.	2.	"D"	X.13.d.80.0.	S.14.b.7.25.
13.	4.	"B"	S.5.c.	S.14.b.60.50.
14.	2.	"D"	S.12.c.30.4.	S.1.d.2.00.

N.B. - Left end of target given in each case.

AXE "D".

BARRAGE Line S.O.S. - GREEN.

Serial No.	No. of guns.	M.G. Coy.	Location.	Target.
15.	4.	"B"	X.6.a.0.0.	S.8.c.20.5. to S.8.c.0.0.
16.	4.	"A"	X.10.c.	X.18.c.2.50.
17.	4.	"C"	X.1.b.95.55.	X.18.c.0.0.
18.	2.	"D"	X.21.d.0.0.	X.23.b.80.7.

N.B. - Left end of target given in each case.

APPENDIX "B".

S.O.S. Lines.

1. The S.O.S. lines of Machine Guns will be divided into 4 parts:-

    A. Front Line S.O.S.

    B. BLUE Line S.O.S.

    C. RED Line S.O.S.

    D. PURPLE Line S.O.S.

2. The guns firing on each of these lines are shown on attached tables.

3. (a) Guns detailed in table "A" will open fire immediately in response to the S.O.S. Signal.

    (b) Further instructions as to opening fire of guns in tables "B", "C" and "D" will be issued.

4. All guns must realize that indirect fire can never be as effective as direct fire.
    Fire therefore will <u>never</u> be opened or continued on S.O.S. lines if a direct target presents itself.

5. The positions of all guns firing, targets and trace of BLUE and RED lines are shown on attached tracing (to Coys. Brigades, 52nd Div. and C.R.A. only).

6. (a) In the case of barrages "A" and "B" not more than 8 belts per gun will be expended.

    (b) In the case of barrages "C" and "D" not more than 10 belts will be expended.

7. Fire at usual S.O.S. rates. Traverse 1° each side of Zero line.

APPENDIX "D".

Distribution of Amour Piercing S.A.A.

"A" COY.

    3 boxes at S.7.b.99.99.
    2 " " S.9.d.5.24.
    2 " " S.9.d.70.0.
    2 " " S.23.b.60.00.
    2 " " X.10.c.8.6.

"B" COY.

    1 " " X.4.b.98.00.
    1 " " X.6.a.02.05.
    1 " " S.3.c.32.48.
    1 " " S.3.c.44.8.
    1 " " S.16.d.04.80.
    1 " " S.16.d.04.82.
    1 " " X.4.d.92.79.
    1 " " X.4.d.95.82.
    1 " " S.16.a.00.80.
    1 " " S.9.d.80.00.
    1 " " S.9.d.79.02.

"C" COY.

    2 belts at X.1.b.01.43.
    2 " " S.20.d.9.3.
    2 " " S.19.b.5.35.
    2 " " X.23.a.5.40.
    2 " " X.23.c.02.15.
    2 " " X.1.a.84.5.

"D" COY.

    2 boxes at S.14.d.27.94.
    2 " " X.18.a.80.4.
    ~~2 " " X.18.a.80.4.~~
    2 " " X.12.c.30.4.
    2 " " X.17.c.10.15.
    2 " " X.21.d.00.10.
    2 " " X.20.c.73.8. (German).

APPENDIX "E"
A.A. Gun Positions.

M.G. Coy.	Zone.	Location.
A.	No. 1.	S.22.b.90.00. *
A.	2.	S.16.c.10.18.
C.	2.	S.20.d.5.05.
A.	3.	S.9.d. 0.00.
B.	3.	S.9.d.70.15.
C.	3.	S.10.b.2.2.
D.	3.	S.14.d.10. 0.
C.	3.	Y.23.a.40.4.
D.	3.	Y.13.a.80. 0.
B.	3.	S.3.c.40.80.
D.	4.	Y.13.a.10.90.
A.	4.	S.9.b.40.25. *
B.	4.	Y.5.b.95.10.
D.	4.	Y.21.d.10.00.
C.	4.	Y.15.a.9.2.
D.	4.	Y.15.c.90.75.
A.	4.	Y.10.a.95.10.
A.	4.	Y.10.c.65.8.

* Only used in case of very low flying aeroplanes.

APPENDIX "F".

COMMUNICATIONS.

Communications within the battalion consist of :-

    (a) Telephone and Fullerphone.
    (b) Runners.
    (c) Visual.

(a) <u>Telephone and Fullerphone</u>. A line runs from Battalion Headquarters to the Divisional Exchange which is in direct telephonic communication with the Brigades. Each Company has a line direct to its affiliated Brigade, "D" Company (in reserve) being connected to the Right Brigade (97th).
    In addition lateral communication exists between "A""B""C" Companies.
    Communications forward of Company Headquarters consist of :-
    (i) Telephone connecting "B" Company to its Section Headquarters at S.2.b.60.00.
    (ii) Fullerphone connecting Infantry Battalion at S.15.c.1.1. and 14th Brigade forward station at S.14.a.0.0. with "B" Company Section Headquarters at S.14.d.20.30.
    (iii) Telephone connecting "C" Company to its Section Headquarters at X.25.a.4.4.

(b) <u>Runners</u>. There are five runners at Battalion Headquarters, four at each Company Headquarters and two at each Section Headquarters.
    The Battalion Headquarters runners work direct to the Companies, and are available for special local runs as required.
    Company runners work between Company Headquarters and their Sections.
    Wherever possible all these runners are mounted on cycles. In addition each Company has a mounted orderly at its Headquarters who is familiar with the routes to the Company Headquarters on either flank.
    The following average times taken for messages by runner between Battalion Headquarters and Companies:-

    Battalion Headquarters to "A" Coy. ... 30 mins.
    "   "   to "B" Coy. ... 40 "
    "   "   to "C" Coy. ... 30 "
    "   "   to "D" Coy. ... 20 "

(c) <u>Visual</u>. Visual communication by day and night is established between :-
    (i) "B" Coy. Headquarters and Section in S.2.b.
    (ii) "B" Coy. Headquarters and "A" Coy. Headquarters.
    (iii) "A" Coy. Headquarters and Section in S.14.c. (through transmitting station in S.7.b.).
    (iv) "A" Coy. Headquarters and "C" Coy. Headquarters.

    In the event of abnormal activity these stations will be manned. Test messages are sent through by day and night.

SECRET.   Copy No. 14

32ND BATTALION MACHINE GUN CORPS INSTRUCTIONS NO.16.

Defence orders for Battalion in Reserve.

1. **DISPOSITIONS.**

    The VI Corps front is now held as follows:-
    - Right sector ... 2nd Division.
    - Centre   " ... Guards Division.
    - Left   " ... 3rd Canadian Division.
    - Reserve   ... 32nd Division.

2. **ORGANIZATION OF DEFENCES.**

    The following description of defences are in amplification of those detailed in 32nd Battn. M.G.C. Defence Scheme para.3.

    A. **THE THIRD SYSTEM (RED).**

    1. This includes the following defended localities:-

        BIENVILLERS AU BOIS.
        BERLES AU BOIS.
        GASTINEAU.
        BRAINBETZ.
        BAC DU NORD.

    2. The following switches connect the second and third systems:-

        FONCHEVILLERS SWITCH facing N.E.
        MONCHY SWITCH facing E.
        BLAIREVILLE SWITCH facing S.

    B. **REARWARD ZONE.**

    1. Consisting of :-

        SAULTY - GOUY SWITCH.
        FOURTH SYSTEM - (G.H.Q.).

    2. The following switches connect the third and fourth systems:-

        HUMBERCAMP SWITCH facing S.
        BAILLEULMONT SWITCH facing N.E.

    C. The positions of all lines, defended localities and switches are shown on Map "A" attached. (½ coys only)

3. **SITUATIONS.**

    There are two situations with which the 32nd Division may be called upon to deal with while in Reserve :-

    A. An attack taking place on the VI Corps front.

    B. An attack on the XV Corps (south) front which does not involve the VI Corps front.

4. **ROLE OF 32ND DIVISION IN CASE OF PARA.3 A.**

    The Division will be prepared for any of the following tasks:-

    (a) To hold as ordered any part of the PURPLE RESERVE line N. of MONCHY Switch, Old German line, Old British line, or MONCHY

    SWITCH

CHURCH from the Corps Boundary to the BLANGEVILLE - HENINCOURT Road.

(b) To hold the third System (RED) from BASSEUX (exclusive) to the VI Corps Northern Boundary.

(c) To regain by counter-attack any of the following :-

(i) BUCQUOY RISE and GUEMOY PARK.
(ii) The old British trenches in N.16.d, & b, and N.11.a. and c.
(iii) The "OLD GUNPIT" locality.
(iv) The "ORION TRENCH" locality.
(v) The "AJAX TRENCH" locality.
(vi) The "ACHICOURT" locality.
(vii) The "BEAUCOURT" locality.
(viii) The "Hill 110" locality.
(ix) The Second System as a whole, North of the FICHEUX - BOISLEUX au MONT Road.
(x) The "MERCATEL HILL Switch".

4. PRELIMINARY MOVES.

In view of the above Brigades and Units will be prepared to move immediately on receipt of orders as under :-

(a) 98th Inf. Bde.   ...   Valley South-west of BERLES on
    (Right Bde.)   ROAD in W.20.d. and W.26.b.
                             (Rendezvous A.).

(b) 16th Inf. Bde.   ...   Valley North-east of BERLES on
    (Centre Bde.)   ROAD in W.10.c. and d. (Rendezvous B)

(c) 97th Inf. Bde.   ...   Valley South-west of BUNCHUX in
    (Left Bde.)   Q.26.c. and b. (Rendezvous C.).

(d) Machine Gun   ...   "B" Coy. to rendezvous A. to come
    Battalion.   under orders of 98th Inf. Bde.
                             on arrival there.

                             "A" and "D" Coys. to rendezvous B.

                             "A" Coy. to come under orders of
                             16th Inf. Bde. on arrival there.
                             "D" Coy. to remain in Divisional
                             reserve.

                             "C" Coy. to rendezvous "C" to
                             come under orders of 97th Inf.
                             Bde. on arrival there.

                             Battalion Headquarters to OLD
                             GUN PITS W.16.d. with advanced
                             Divisional Headquarters.

(e) Transport. ...   (a)   Will accompany Coys. to rendezvous
                             and will then be disposed of as re-
                             quired by G.O.C. Brigades concerned.

                             "D" Coy's transport will remain at
                             rendezvous B.

                             Rear Battalion Headquarters and

                      (b)   personnel to be left out of action
                             (R.E.M.S. Sec.,etc and O.D. 1619 dated
                             14.3.18.) will be left behind at present
                             billets. Orders as to their disposal
                             will be issued.

(f) The above movements will be ordered by Divisional Headquarters by the code "Assembly move".

5. ROLES OF INFANTRY BRIGADES. 96 Infantry Brigade (Right Brigade)

(a) The 98th Infantry Brigade and 1 M.G. Coy. attached will be prepared to move from Rendezvous A. to occupy either:

(1)/

either :-

(i) The old British line and the "old German" locality from the HAMESCAMPS - LA BRAYELLE Road (inclusive) to the MONCHY - GUEMAPPE Road (exclusive).

(ii) The "Old German" and "MONCHY SWITCH" Localities.

In either case not less than one Battalion will be held in reserve to guard the right flank of the Brigade.

7. **142ND INFANTRY BRIGADE.** (Centre Brigade)

(a) The 142nd Infantry Brigade and 1 M.G. Coy. attached will be prepared to move from Rendezvous "B".

(i) To Valley in W.23.a. and W.17.d.

(ii) To occupy the MONCHY SWITCH Locality and the PURPLE Reserve line from the MONCHY - GUEMAPPE Road (inclusive) to the NAREAU FARM Locality (exclusive).

(iii) To occupy the PURPLE Reserve line from the RANSART - ADINFER Road (inclusive) to the BLAIREVILLE - BIENVILLERS Road.

(b) In either case strong patrols will be pushed forward to reconnoitre the "ADINFER" Locality with a view to either

(i) Reinforcing the garrison of the locality, if weak.
(ii) Recapturing the Locality immediately, if lost.

8. **97TH INFANTRY BRIGADE.** (Left Brigade)

The 97th Infantry Brigade and 1 M.G. Coy. attached will be prepared to move from Rendezvous C. to occupy either

(a) The PURPLE Reserve from the RANSART - ADINFER Road (inclusive) to the BLAIREVILLE - BIENVILLERS Road.

(b) A position of reserve to the other two Brigades.

(c) The Third System from BASSEUX (exclusive) to the Northern Corps boundary.

9. **FLANK DIVISIONS.**

(a) A Battalion of the Reserve Brigade of the Left Division of the IV Corps has been allotted a battle station in the old British System as far North as the HAMESCAMPS - ROSARIE Road.

The Right (Bab) Brigade will be prepared to take this position over, if the Battalion of the IV Corps moves forward.

(b) The Pioneer Battalion of the Guards (Centre) Division will be holding NAREAU Locality.

Brigades holding the MONCHY Locality or PURPLE Reserve North of the NAREAU Locality will keep in close touch with the garrison of the latter locality.

10. **ROLE OF 32ND DIVISION IN CASE OF PARA.3 B.**

(a) The Division will be prepared to move to assembly positions in the area FONCQUEVILLERS (exclusive) MONCHY SWITCH (South) - Third System (RED) East and South of BIENVILLERS.

(b) The role of the Division in this contingency would be to carry out a counter-attack (probably under the orders of the IV Corps) in a South-easterly direction.

(c) Further orders will be issued as to Rendezvous for Brigades in this contingency.

11. **RECONNAISSANCES.**

O's.C. Coys. will reconnoitre :-

(a) All lines of defence which their affiliated brigade may be called upon to occupy (vide paras. 6, 7, and 8).

(b) The areas over which the Division may have to counter-attack (vide para.4 (c)).

(c) O.C. "D" Coy. will reconnoitre areas of right and centre Brigades and as in (b) above.

Special attention will be paid by Coy. Commanders to the contingency of counter attacks by Brigades as under :-

(i) 96th and 14th Bdes. ... To recover GUEUDECOURT FARM and SAUSAGE ROW.

(ii) All Brigades ... To recover MORCHY SWITCH, CHATEAU FARM and AUTUMN.

(iii) 97th and 14th Bdes. To recover PURPLE System in the Canadian Divisional area TELEGRAPH SWITCH HENIN-COURT and all its localities.

(d) All Coys. will reconnoitre routes and cross country tracks to their Rendezvous and thence to their various lines of defence.

(e) Attached map "A" shows routes to Rendezvous, but this will not absolve Coys. from responsibility of reconnoitring them thoroughly.

12. **DEGREE OF READINESS.**

(a) While in reserve, units of the 32nd Division will be prepared to move at one hours notice from 6.a.m. to 10.a.m. daily and at 3 hours notice for the remainder of the day.

(b) Practices in turning out and moving to rendezvous positions will be carried out from time to time by order of the Division.

(c) The following Code will be used to order practice Turning Out and Moving to Rendezvous :-

(i) "TEST ASSEMBLY MOVE" will mean that the preliminary moves indicated in para.5 will take place at once.

(ii) "TEST TURN OUT" will mean that Brigades and units are to turn out at once as for moving to their Rendezvous positions but will not move beyond their starting points.

(iii) If only certain Brigades or units are intended to move or turn-out the name of the unit or formation will precede the word 'Test', i.e. "97th TEST TURN OUT" or "102D TEST ASSEMBLY MOVE".

In this case M.G. Coys to be attached to Infantry Brigades on arrival at the Rendezvous will turn out or move in accordance with the orders issued to the Infantry Brigades to which they are to be attached.

(d) (i) Coys. will not march (without special sanction from Battalion Headquarters) away from their normal training area in a direction which will increase the distance to their rendezvous.

(ii) If Coys. move from their normal areas towards their rendezvous they must be in battle order and their exact location known.

13. LIAISON.

(a) O.C. Coys. will report to G.O.C. Infantry Brigades immediately on arrival at rendezvous.

(b) They will keep Battalion Headquarters informed of their movements.

(c) O.C. "D" Coy. will send a runner to Battalion Headquarters at the OLD GUN PITS W.14.d.2.5. two hours after the order to move is issued.

14. COMMUNICATIONS.

(a) Coys. will work with Brigades to whom they are affiliated.

(b) Signal Officer will lay a line from Battalion Headquarters to "D" Coy. at rendezvous B.

15. POSITIONS OF HEADQUARTERS.

(a) Headquarters of all brigades in the line are shown in Appendix "A" attached.

(b) Headquarters of brigades of 32nd Division will be at their respective rendezvous.

16. ACKNOWLEDGE.

J. Raeve
Lieut. Col.,
Commdg. 32nd Battalion M. G. Corps.

8.7.1918.

Copies to :-

1. C.O.
2. Adjutant.
3. O.C. "A" Coy.
4. O.C. "B" Coy.
5. O.C. "C" Coy.
6. O.C. "D" Coy.
7. Transport Officer.
8. Signal Officer.
9. 14th Inf. Bde.
10. 96th Inf. Bde.
11. 97th Inf. Bde.
12/13. H.Q. 32nd Division.
14/15. War Diary.
16. File.

APPENDIX "A"

Positions of Headquarters of Infantry Brigades
VI Corps Front.

RIGHT DIVISION.

    Right Brigade, ... E.4.c,d,f,
    Centre Brigade, ... N.4.6.j-9.
    Left Brigade, ... N.33.c/d.4

CENTRE DIVISION.

    Right Brigade, ... X.10.d. central.
    Centre Brigade, ... X.8.6.4.4.6c,
    Left Brigade, ... X.9.d.5,70.

LEFT DIVISION.

    Right Brigade, ... R.34.d,4,4,0,
    Left Brigade, ... R.16.6.5.6.
    Reserve Brigade, ... HERMICOURT CHATEAU.

Herewith revised Provisional Defence Scheme.
Appendix "C" of former Defence Scheme to be attached.

> 82ND BATTALION,
> MACHINE GUN
> CORPS.
>
> No..............
> Date............

Lt. Col.,
Commanding 82nd Battalion M.G. Corps.

6.7.1918.

Issued to all recipients of 82nd Battn. M.G. Corps
Provisional Defence Scheme.

SECRET.   Copy No. ~~19~~ 20.

32ND. BATTALION MACHINE GUN CORPS
~~PROVISIONAL~~ DEFENCE SCHEME.

1. FRONTAGE AND BOUNDARIES.

(a). The 32nd. Division holds the Centre Sector of the VI Corps Front.
The 2nd. Division is on the right of the 32nd. Division with Headquarters at HUMBERCAMPS.
The 3rd. Canadian Division is on the left with Headquarters at BASSEUX.

(b). The front of the 32nd. Division extends from S.27.a.01 to S.12.a.80.
The extent of this Front is approximately 6,500 yards.

2. TACTICAL FEATURES.

The most important Tactical Features in the Divisional Front are :-

(a). The Spur which runs North Eastwards from S.28 central.

(b). The BOYELLES Spur in S.17 and S.18. This if captured would give the enemy observation.

(c). The Spur running N.E. in S.27.a. and S.21.d.

(d). ADINFER village Spur.

(e). HENDICOURT LES RANSARTS.

(f). HILL 116 (S.7.b. and S.1.d.).

(g). HAMEAU FARM PLATEAU.

3. ORGANISATION OF DEFENCES.

FIRST SYSTEM.

This system comprises all defences and positions in front of the PURPLE LINE. It consists of :-

(a). An Outpost Zone organised into an Outpost Line, a Support (BLUE) Line and a Main (RED) Line of resistance.

(b). A line of defended localities on the line SUGAR FACTORY-S.14.a.-S.9.a. organised to be held by one Infantry Company in each Brigade Area.

SECOND SYSTEM. (PURPLE).

This system is situated at an average distance of 4,800 yards from the Front Line.
It consists of the following lines :-

(a). An Outpost Line, Main Line and Reserve Line, including the defended localities of ADINFER village, HENDICOURT and HILL 116 (S.7.b. and S.1.d.)

(b). The HAMEAU SWITCH which connects the PURPLE/LINE with the PURPLE RESERVE. SUPPORT

(c). The MERCATEL SWITCH joining the PURPLE LINE in S.2.c. to the Front Line held by the Left Division in M.33.d.

(d). A new Switch called the WINDMILL SWITCH connecting the Front Line N. of AYETTE about F.e.b.4.0. to the PURPLE LINE at X.17.c.0.1.

THIRD SYSTEM.

(a). This system includes a Front, Support, and Reserve Lines.
It includes the BLAINVILLE SWITCH running North of RANSART, which joins the RED LINE at W.12.c.00.00 to the Purple Reserve Line at X.9.b.50.40.

(b). Included in the THIRD System is the MONCHY SWITCH running from the THIRD system EAST of VILLERS-AU-BOIS to the Second System West of ADINFER WOOD.

(c). A new switch is under construction from BERLES AU BOIS to GOUY EN ARTOIS.

/- 4. DISPOSITIONS.

4. DISPOSITIONS.

(a) FRONT SYSTEM. (No.1.Battalions).

One Battalion in each Brigade is detailed as Outpost Battalion and is responsible for the defence of the Outpost Zone within the Brigade Sector.

A half Company is detailed from the Outpost Battalion of No.1 Brigade as permanent garrison of the Sugar Factory locality and will not be used in front of this locality without the sanction of the Divisional H.Q.

(b) PURPLE SYSTEM. (No.2.Battalions).

The No.2 Battalion in each Brigade is definitely allotted for the defence of the PURPLE LINE (and WINDMILL SWITCH in the case of the right Brigade).

(c) DIVISIONAL RESERVE. (No.3.Battalions).

The No.3.Battalion of each Brigade is in Divisional Reserve in the vicinity of the PURPLE Reserve Line within its Brigade Area.

If communication with Divisional H.Q. is cut out, the Brigadier has a direct call on his No.3.Battalion in case of emergency.

It is to be clearly understood that he is not to use it without reference to Divisional H.Q. unless communication is cut and the situation urgent.

(d) MACHINE GUNS.

1. One Machine Gun Company is allotted for the defence of each Brigade Sector.

   The Machine Gun Company in each Brigade Sector is under the Tactical orders of the Brigadier, but in stationary warfare the positions of of guns will be fixed by Divisional H.Q. and will not be changed without sanction of the Divisional Commander.

   In the event of moving warfare developing (either forward or back) the Infantry Brigadier will be responsible for the tactical handling of the guns. These positions are sited as much as possible so as to be hidden from direct observation and so as to enfilade the reverse slopes of the ridges.

   Concealment of Machine Gun positions is all important.

2. One Machine Gun Company is allotted for the defence of the PURPLE LINE. For tactical purposes its guns will come under the orders of the G.O.C. Brigade in whose Sub-Sector they are situated. (See Appendix "A").

3. 4 Vickers guns Res-C in limbers at W.15.d.44.48 and 10 Light German Machine Guns at W.15.b.50.00 are in Divisional Reserve.

   The 10 Light German Machine Guns will not be moved East of the PURPLE LINE.

   The Brigadier is responsible for the protection of Machine Guns placed tactically under his orders.

   Immediately the situation becomes one of open warfare the Brigadier becomes responsible for the moving and handling of the Machine Guns under his orders.

   For this purpose definite Machine Gun Sections in each Brigade area will be affiliated to definite Battalions, which will assist them with carrying parties for belt boxes, etc., in the event of an advance or withdrawal.

   In the event of a defensive battle
   (a) The Machine Gun Groups and their escorts at

   S.20.d.10.10. S.21.d.7.6. S.22.b.66.10.
   S.17.c.80.60. and S.18.a.00.80.

   are not to be moved without reference to Divisional H.Q.

   (b) It should be very exceptional for it to be advisable for a Brigadier to move any of the guns under his Command from their defensive positions, which have been carefully chosen to cover a definite area of ground.

   Brigadiers will therefore only move any guns from their defensive positions under very exceptional circumstances and will inform Divisional Headquarters if they have done so, as soon as possible.

-/ (e) Artillery.

- 3 -

4. (a) ARTILLERY.

1. FIELD ARTILLERY.

Field Artillery will be disposed in depth, a proportion being silent batteries. Certain guns are sited forward of the Main Line of resistance for close defence and Anti-Tank defence. No guns other than close defence guns and anti-tank guns will normally be disposed in front of the main line of Resistance. The Field Artillery covering the front is organised into three Groups, i.e. Right Group, Centre Group, Left Group. One Group covers each Infantry Brigade Sub-Sector.

2. HEAVY ARTILLERY.

Colonel BRUCES Group is allotted to the Divisional Front for carrying out destructive shoots and harassing fire beyond the Field Artillery Zone.

4. Machine Gun dispositions are shown in Appendix "A".

5. SCHEMES OF DEFENCE.

There are two alternative situations which have to be dealt with in drawing up our Schemes of Defence.

(a). The normal case in which the enemy delivers an attack or opens an intense bombardment previous to an attack without previous warning.

(b). The case in which reliable information is received in good time that an enemy attack is imminent.

(c). The normal situation (a) is dealt with in succeeding paragraphs. The defence of the Divisional Front will be governed by the following principles:-

(a). There will be no withdrawal without definite orders from Div. H.Q.
~~across~~ ~~from~~ ~~any one line to an other.~~
All defensive positions will be held to the last whether their flanks are turned or not.

(b). Troops holding any positions of defence if driven in are to contest every inch of ground, covering their movements by fire, and inflicting as much loss as possible on the enemy.
Any ground lost will be regained as soon as possible.

(c). All defences will be organised in depth and mutually supporting localities, prepared for all round defence, will be prepared as far as possible.

(d). The Front and Support (BLUE) lines in the Outpost Zone will be held with the minimum number of troops to fulfil the following roles :-

(1). To retain observation.

(2). To prevent enemy reconnaissance and retain control of the ground immediately in front of the Front line.

(3). To keep out hostile raids and reconnaissances.

(4). To mislead the enemy as to the strength in which we are occupying the Front line.

(5). Particular attention will be paid to preserving the more important tactical points.

(e). In order to fulfil the policy indicated in (d) above, front line troops must be very active. Patrolling must be unusually vigorous. The position of posts in the front line must be constantly changed. Very lights must be fired in plenty. In short every device must be employed to induce the enemy to believe that we are holding the Front line in strength.

/- (f).

SECRET.   M.G.No.C.O.345.

Copy No. 11.

32ND BATTALION MACHINE GUN CORPS OPERATION ORDER NO.53.

Extracts from 32nd Div. No.S.Q.232.

1. Attached table gives entraining programme for Brigade Groups and Divisional Artillery.

2. Detraining Stations will be :-
   PROVEN,   WAYENBERG,   & HERDEBEEK.

   The Station at which each Brigade Group will detrain will be notified later.

3. Composition of Brigade Groups.

14th Brigade Group.	96th Brigade Group.	97th Brigade Group.
14th Inf. Brigade.	96th Inf. Brigade.	97th Inf. Brigade.
206th Field Coy. R.E.	218th Field Coy. R.E.	219th Field Coy. R.E.
90th Field Ambce.	91st Field Ambce.	92nd Field Ambce.
No.2 Coy. Div. Train.	No.3 Coy. Div.Train.	No.4 Coy.Div.Train.
1 M.G. Company.	1 M.G. Company.	2 M.G. Companies.
Divisional H.Q.	16th High L.Inf.	H.Q. M.G.Battn.
No.1 Sec. Div.Sig.Co.	Mob.Vet.Section.	H.Q. Divl.Arty.
H.Q. Divl.Train.		
H.Q. Divl.Engineers.		

4. Brigade Groups will move to embussing points, embuss and entrain under orders of Brigade Group Commanders.

5. Detraining parties must be told off beforehand for each train, so that no delay may occur at the far end.

6. 14th Brigade Group will move to Entraining point by March Route.
   Lorries for the conveyance of personnel and baggage of Brigade Groups to the Entraining point will be allotted as follows:-
   PERSONNEL. Lorry accommodation for 1450 men will report as below:-
   96th Brigade Group:
   on LA COUCHIE - GAUDIEMPRE Road at HUMBERCAMP - SAULTY Cross Rds. facing N.E. at 12 noon ~~tomorrow~~.
   97th Brigade Group:
   on BARLY - SOMBRIN Road facing West, at 12 noon 18th inst.

   Lorries will in both cases be used at discretion of Group Commanders.

   Lorries for Baggage: Lorries are allotted as under :-

96th Brigade Group:	4 at BAZEQUE FARM - HUMBERCAMP Cross Rds., at 11.30.a.m.
14th Brigade Group:	6 at SAULTY Chateau at 11.30.a.m.
97th Brigade Group:	4 at BARLY Chateau at 11.30.a.m.
M.G.Battalion:	1 at SAULTY, V.7.b.6.c. at 12 noon.
D.T.M.O. (for Light T.M.Btys.)	6 at L'ARBRET Church at 2.p.m.

   Lorries will work until movement of Formation to which they are allotted is completed, and will then receive orders from Brigade Staff representative or O.C. Unit to rejoin park.

   Drivers will be given written orders for each journey.

7. Brigade Group Commanders and C.R.A. will arrange for Billeting Officers and representatives of Units to travel by the first train.

8. Entraining and Detraining Officers will be detailed by Brigade Group Commanders and C.R.A.

9. Officers of the Divisional Staff will meet trains at Detraining Stations and give instructions regarding billeting areas.

10. ACKNOWLEDGE.

18.7.1918.

Major,
Commanding 32nd Battalion M.G.Corps.

S E C R E T.

ENTRAINING PROGRAMME.

Entraining Stations.

A: BOUQUEMAISON
B: DOULLENS
C: MONDICOURT.

Train No. From Stations			UNIT.	Date 1918.	MARCHE	Time of Dept.
A.	B.	C.				
1	-	-	97th Bde. H.Q. Bde Signal Sec. Bde.M.G.Co. Lt.T.M.Bty. 1 Co. 1 Am Cooker & Team of "A" Bn. of 97th Bde.	18/7	T.59	17.04
-	2	-	96th Bde. H.Q. Bde Signal Sec. Bde. M.G.Co. Lt.T.M.Bty. 1 Co. 1 Cooker & Team of "A" Bn. of 96th Bde.	"	T.60	18.22
-	-	3	14th Bde. H.Q. Bde Signal Sec. Bde M.G.Co. Lt. T.M.Bty. A Co. 1 Cooker & Team of "A" Bn. of 14th Bde.	"	DA212/761	18.38
x 15	-	-	Div.M.G.Co. H.Q. M.G.Bn. 1 Co. Cooker & Team of "A" Bn. of 97th Bde., H.Q. Div. Arty.	19/7	W.71	5.54

x 4th Company M.G.Bn. & H.Q. M.G. Bn.

Confidential

WD 7

War Diary
of
32nd Bn. Machine Gun Corps
From 1st August 1918 to 31st August 1918

No 7

Army Form C. 2118.

WAR DIARY
or
INTELLIGENCE SUMMARY.

(Erase heading not required.)

Instructions regarding War Diaries and Intelligence Summaries are contained in F. S. Regs., Part II. and the Staff Manual respectively. Title pages will be prepared in manuscript.

Place	Date	Hour	Summary of Events and Information	Remarks and references to Appendices
Proven F14.a.0.3	1/9/18		Battalion Sports Held On Proven Aerodrome.	Sheet 27 N.E.
Proven	2/9/18		Coys. Carried Out Training As Per Programme.	
Proven	3/9/18		Coys Carried Out Training As Per Programme.	
Proven	4/9/18		Church Parade. Anniversary of 4th Year of the War. Warning Order Received To Move By Strategical Trains. Commencing On 6th	
Proven	5/9/18		Coys Carried Out Training As Per Programme	
Proven	6/9/18		Bn. Commenced Move By Strategical Trains O.O.26. Issued	9.P.1.

(A788J) Wt. W897/M1672 350,000 4/17 Sch. 52a Forms/C/2118/14
D. D. & L., London, E.C.

Army Form C. 2118.

WAR DIARY
or
INTELLIGENCE SUMMARY.
(Erase heading not required.)

Place	Date	Hour	Summary of Events and Information	Remarks and references to Appendices
PROVEN	7/8/18		M.G. Bn. Entrained at HEROEBEEK. X.21.C. Sheet 19.	
HENGIST	8/8/18		M.G. Bn. Detrained at HENGIST. Marched to CROUY. Arriving at 2 a.m. Bn. Enbussed at 1 p.m. & Debussed at GENTELLE WOOD Bn. Bivouacked for the night	Sheet 62.D T.17 Cent.
GENTELLE WOOD	9/8/18		Bn. Moved to Wood. D.14.C. Sheet.66.E Cops Attached to Bdes.	
D.14.C.	10/8/18		Division Attacked. With 36TH Bde on right. & 27TH Bde on left. And Reached Line. LA CAMODE - Western Edge of BOIS EN EQUERRE - L.28.a.5.0. - L.21.Central. - L.17.Central Casualties Heavy due to M.G. Fire.	Sheet 66.E
K.15.a.	11/8/18		Attacked Resumed at 9.30am 14TH Bde Leap Frogged through 36TH Bde.	

Army Form C. 2118.

WAR DIARY
or
INTELLIGENCE SUMMARY.
(Erase heading not required.)

Instructions regarding War Diaries and Intelligence Summaries are contained in F. S. Regs., Part II. and the Staff Manual respectively. Title pages will be prepared in manuscript.

Place	Date	Hour	Summary of Events and Information	Remarks and references to Appendices
K15a	14/9/18		CASUALTIES. 2/Lt. G.G. BOLER WOUNDED 12.0.R KILLED 35.0.R WOUNDED. ON HELD UP AT O.O. BOSCHE FRONT LINE ON. RELIEVED BY 3RD CANADIAN DIV.	
K15a & Q22c	15/9/18		Bn. MOVED TO WOOD DUMP.	
Q11d	16/9/18		Bn. MOVED TO C.2.C CENTRAL BIVOUACS.	
C.2.C.	17/9/18		Bn. RESTING.	
C.2.C.	18/9/18		Bn. RESTING.	
C.2.C.	19/9/18		Bn. RESTING. THE FOLLOWING OFFICERS REPORTED FOR DUTY. LT. E. BOND & 2/LT. A. CHANDLER POSTED TO B.Coy. 2/Lt. H.C. EVANS. POSTED TO D. Coy.	
C.2.a.	20/9/18		Bn. RESTING. O.O. 36.A ISSUED. B.&.C. Coys MOVED INTO SUPPORT WITH THEIR RESPECTIVE BDES.	App.2

WAR DIARY
or
INTELLIGENCE SUMMARY.

Army Form C. 2118.

Place	Date	Hour	Summary of Events and Information	Remarks and references to Appendices
C.2.C.9.	8/6/18		Bn. HQ. At O.Cors. Moved By Busses. At O.Cors. In Dn. Reserve. Bn. HQ.	62.P.S.W.
Villers Breton'eux			Established At. O.28.b.5.8	
Villers Bretonneux	19/8/18		Situation Normal. Night Quiet. Enemy Artillery Active On Front & 00.37/8060. Support Lines Prior To Assault By Enemy At 10-30 PM When The Enemy Entered Our Front Line In S.7b+d. The Enemy Were Ejected By Counter Attack At 11.15 PM. Our M.G.8. Fired 400 Rounds At Direct Targets Until Forced To Fall Back. Resumed Positions After Counter Attack	A.P.3. 62.S.E. 62.S.E.
Villers Bretonneux	20/8/18		Situation Normal. Night Quiet Artillery Active On Back Areas Framerville, Harbonnieres, & Vauvillers. Shelled M.G8 Fired 4,000 62.P.S.E Rounds Harassing Fire.	
Villers Bretonneux & Q.32.a.22.	21/8/18		Situation Normal. Night Quiet. Artillery Normal. Usual Harassing Fire Carried Out. Our M.G8. Fired 6,000 Rounds Harassing Fire. 62.P.S.E OS 82.M.G.1 No. 17. Issued. Bn Hq. Moved Forward To Q.37.d.22.8834	

WAR DIARY
or
INTELLIGENCE SUMMARY.

Army Form C. 2118.

Place	Date	Hour	Summary of Events and Information	Remarks and references to Appendices
Q.32.a.22	21/9/18		Casualties. L/Col. J.T.W. Reeve Wounded. Shell.	Ref Sheet Gipsé
			1.O.R Wounded	
			Situation Normal. Night. Quiet. O. Coy. Made. Battery Position For The Attack. Major R.G. Pettle Assumed Command Of Br. I/O.c. L/Col. J.T.W Reeve Wounded.	
Q.32.a.21	27/9/18		Casualties. 2/Lt H.C. Evans Killed In Action	Ref Sheet Gipse
			Lt. R.J. Morley Wounded At Duty	
			1 O.R Killed	
			8 O.R Wounded	
			1 O.R Wounded At Duty.	
			The Division Attacked On Two Bde Front In Conjunction With 4th Australian Div. On Left. Zero 4-45 a.m. All Objectives Gained. Casualties Light. 00.28. Issued	A.P.O. 5

WAR DIARY
or
INTELLIGENCE SUMMARY.
(Erase heading not required.)

Place	Date	Hour	Summary of Events and Information	Remarks and references to Appendices
Qardiff.22	24/9/18		SITUATION NORMAL. NIGHT QUIET. ARTILLERY BELOW NORMAL. MIDNIGHT RIGHT SUB. SECTOR SHELLED WITH H.E. GAS. OUR M.G's. FIRED 8000 ROUNDS. ON TRACK Etc. O.O. 39. ISSUED.	Ref. Sheet 62.D.S.E. A.P.6.
Q31.a.22.	25/9/18		CASUALTIES 2/Lt. R.J.MORLEY WOUNDED GAS 2/Lt. C.L. HARDY DITTO 53. O.R. DITTO SITUATION NORMAL. NIGHT QUIET. ARTILLERY BELOW NORMAL DURING DAY Rd. To 2 Ray Bde ACTIVE ON MOEUVRE WOOD, HERLEVILLE QUARRY IN X.23.b. COPSE IN X.4.B. RIDGE IN X.2.a. ENEMY M.G's. ACTIVE ON SAVRIEN QUAY. OUR M.G's FIRED 3,000 ROUNDS ON SPECIAL TARGETS.	62.D.S.E. 62.C.S.W.

WAR DIARY
or
INTELLIGENCE SUMMARY.

Army Form C. 2118.

Place	Date	Hour	Summary of Events and Information	Remarks and references to Appendices
Q32.q.22	20/3/18		Situation Normal. Artillery Activity Below Normal. A Few Gas Shells Were Fired On X.15.d.7d During The Night. Harbonnieres-Lyons Road Harassed. Enemy M.G. Active On Right Of Sector. Our M.G.s. Fired 11000 Rounds On Tracks Etc.	62 S.W 62 S.E
			Casualties 1 O.R. Wounded	
Q32.q.22	21/3/18		Enemy Retired Infantry Advanced Keeping Touch With Enemy. Approx Line At 6 P.M. Foucacourt – Vermandovillers – Chaulnes Wood.	62 Q S.W
			2/Lt Q.T. Beresford Reported For Duty And Posted To D. Coy.	
Q32.q.22 and Quarry X.23.b	28/3/18		Enemy Carried On His Retreat. Approx Line. 6 P.M. Estrees – West Of Berny En Santerre – Marchelpot. Bn H.Q. Moved To Quarry X.23.b.	62 D 8 E 62 S.W

Army Form C. 2118.

WAR DIARY
or
INTELLIGENCE SUMMARY.
(Erase heading not required.)

Place	Date	Hour	Summary of Events and Information	Remarks and references to Appendices
Quarry X.21.b	29/8/18		Enemy carried on his retreat. Our Infantry met with little resistance. Cross roads mined in many cases. Approx line at 6 p.m. line of Canal De La Somme. During night several parties crossed canal but failed to get over the swamp. O.O. 90 issued. D. Coy. withdrawn. B. Coy. relieved by C. Coy. Lt. Col. F.C. Aldous assumed active command.	62.D.S.E. 62.C.S.W. APP.7
Quarry X.21.b	30/8/18		Casualties 2 O.R. killed. 4 O.R. wounded. 1 O.R. wounded duty. Situation normal. Night quiet. Enemy Artillery active. Villers Carbonnel & Estrees shelled. Patrols crossed Somme but held up in marsh. O.O. 91 issued.	62.C.79 APP.8

D.D. & L., London, E.C. (A)883) Wt. W809/M1672 350,000 4/17 Sch.52a Forms/C/2118/14

Army Form C. 2118.

WAR DIARY
or
INTELLIGENCE SUMMARY.
(Erase heading not required.)

Instructions regarding War Diaries and Intelligence Summaries are contained in F. S. Regs., Part II. and the Staff Manual respectively. Title pages will be prepared in manuscript.

Place	Date	Hour	Summary of Events and Information	Remarks and references to Appendices
QUARRY X.23.b.	31/7/18		Situation Normal. Night Quiet. Enemy Artillery Active throughout Day & Night. Villers Carbonnel & Estrees Shelled Further. Attempts to cross Somme Failed.	62 SW

S E C R E T. Copy No. 16

32ND BATTALION MACHINE GUN CORPS ORDER NO.36.

1. The 32nd Division is moving on 7th and 8th inst. from the Second Army to the Fourth Army area.

2. The 32nd Battalion M.G. Corps (in the 96th Brigade Group) will entrain at HEIDEBEEK X.21.c. as follows :-

   H.Q.)
   "A" Coy.) at 5.p.m. on 7th (6th train).
   "B" Coy.)

   "C" Coy.)
   "D" Coy.) at 8.p.m. on 7th (7th train).

3. The detraining station will be HANGEST.

4. Approximate length of journey will be 10 hours.

5. (a) Billeting parties (Quartermaster, 1 N.C.O. for Battalion H.Q., 1 N.C.O. per Coy.) will proceed by the first train starting from HEIDEBEEK at 2.a.m. on 7th.

   (b) Instructions as regards Billeting will be issued to them on detraining.

6. Companies will render to Battalion Headquarters by 12 noon on 7th inst. a complete marching out state showing numbers of men, horses, G.S., Limbered G.S. and 2 wheeled wagons and bicycles. A duplicate copy will be sent with each Coy's transport for the information of the R.T.O.

7. (a) Supply and baggage wagons will move with the Battalion.

   (b) Water carts will be entrained full.

   (c) Breast ropes for horse trucks will be provided by the Transport Officer.

8. Companies will detail a picquet (1 Officer and 2 N.C.O's) on their half of the train to prevent men leaving the carriages during halts.

9. All doors of trucks and carriages on the right hand side of the train must be kept closed.

10. (a) The entrainment of all Companies must be completed half an hour before time of departure of the train.

    (b) Transport will reach entraining station 3 hours before departure of train, personnel 1½ hours before.

11. (a) The following intervals on the march will be maintained :-

    100 yards between Coys.
    25 yards between every 6 vehicles.

    (b) Route. Cross roads F.1.c.4.1. - F.3.a. - road junction X.27.a.3.6. - X.21.c.6.0. Coy. Commanders will ensure that they know the road.

12. Dress. Marching Order with water bottles full. Caps.

13. Rations. (a) Rations for 7th will be carried on the man.
    (b) Rations for 8th will be loaded on G.S. Wagons and accompany unit.
    (c) Rations for 9th will be delivered in new area by M.T. except those for "C" and "D" Coys. which will accompany them on train.

14. Great care will be taken to see that all huts, tents, cook-houses Latrines, Transport Lines etc. are left perfectly clean. Certificates will be obtained from the Town Major and forwarded to Battalion Headquarters.

15. Battalion Headquarters will close at PIGEON CAMP at 3.p.m. on 7th inst.

16. A C K N O W L E D G E.

J. Reeve
Lieut. Col.,
Commdg. 32nd Battalion M. G. Corps.

6.8.1918.

Copies to :-

1. C.O.
2. Adjutant.
3. O.C., "A" Coy.
4. O.C., "B" Coy.
5. O.C., "C" Coy.
6. O.C., "D" Coy.
7. Quartermaster.
8. Transport Officer.
9. Signal Officer.
10. 96th Inf. Bde.
11/12. H.Q., 32nd Division.
13. Town Major, PROVEN.
14. R.T.O. HEIDEBEEK.
15/16. War Diary.
17. File.

SECRET.

ADDENDUM NO. 1 to 32nd Battalion M. G. Corps Order No. 36.

1. The following Divisional Artillery will be covering the 32nd Division front and will come under the orders of G.O.C. 32nd Division at 10.a.m. on Aug. 19th :-

    2nd Australian Divnl. Artillery.
    14th Army Brigade R.F.A.

2. The 32nd Divisional Artillery will relieve the 2nd Australian Divisional Artillery on the nights August 18/19th and 19/20th.

    One Section per Battery will be relieved on the first night.

    All details of relief will be arranged direct between C.R.As. concerned.

                                                                              Capt & Adjt
                                                                              Lieut. Col.,
19.8.18.   Commanding 32nd Battalion Machine Gun Corps.

    Issued to all recipients of 32nd Battn. M.G.Corps Order No.36.

SECRET.   Copy No. ......15....

32ND BATTALION MACHINE GUN CORPS ORDER NO.56.(A)

1. The 32nd Division (less Artillery) is relieving the 2nd Australian Division on nights 17/18th and 18/19th August.

2. (a) The 5th Australian Division will be on the <u>Left</u> with 14th Australian Infantry Brigade on its right with Headquarters at O.30.d.6.5.
   (b) The 4th Australian Division will be on the <u>Right</u> with 4th Australian Infantry Brigade on its left with Headquarters in W.18.

3. (a) The 32nd Division will hold the line with the 96th Infantry Brigade on right on a one battalion front and two battalions in support and 97th Infantry Brigade on left with 2 battalions in front and one in support.
   (b) The 14th Infantry Brigade will be in Divisional Reserve.

4. Distribution of Machine Gun Companies will be as follows :-

   "B" Coy. will remain under orders of 96th Infantry Brigade.
   "C" Coy. will remain under orders of 97th Infantry Brigade.
   "A" and "D" Coys. will be in Divisional Reserve.

5. (a) Orders for the moves and taking over of the front system by "B" and "C" Coys. have been issued direct by the Brigades concerned.
   (b) Headquarters, "A" and "D" Coys. will enbus at O.5.d.3.4. at 8.p.m. 18th August and debus at W.11.c.8.7. about 12 midnight 18/19th August.
   (c) After debussing on night 18/19th, "D" Coy. will take over positions occupied by "B" Coy. on night 17/18th.
   "A" Coy. will take over positions occupied by "C" Coy. on night 17/18th.
   (d) Advanced Battalion Headquarters will proceed to P.34.d. "D" and "A" Coys. will be met by guides from "B" and "C" Coys. on debussing.

6. (a) Transport of Battalion Headquarters (except that proceeding to VILLERS-BRETONNEUX) "A" and "D" Coys. will proceed by road under orders of 14th Infantry Brigade Transport Officer. Head of column will pass starting point O.5.d.9.9. at 9.a.m. 18th.
   (b) Final destination of transport will be as follow :-
      Headquarters (less that for VILLERS-BRETONNEUX) - P.35.a.5.2.
      "A" Coy.   ...   .   - P.35.a.5.2.
      "D" Coy. just west of BARBONNIERES in W.10.

      Note. "D" Coy. will branch off at MARCEL CAVE on route.

7. Troops will come under the tactical orders of 2nd Australian Division on debussing and will revert to command of G.O.C. 32nd Division at 10.a.m. on 19th August.

8. Completion of all reliefs on night 18/19th will be reported to Battalion Headquarters in code by word - KANGAROO.

9. The following distances will be maintained on the march by transport and troops :-

          Between Companies   ...   100 yards.
          Between transport of Companies   500 yards when
   E. of a N. and S. line drawn through VILLERS-BRETONNEUX.

10. Position of Headquarters will be as follows :-

    32nd Divisional Headquarters   ...   quarry O.28.c.4.5.
    Battalion Headquarters   small quarry O.28.d.5.6.
    Advanced Battalion Headquarters ...   P.34.d.
    96th)
    97th) Infantry Brigade Headquarters   ...   W.18.c.7.7.
    14th Infantry Brigade Headquarters   ...   W.32.

2.

11. All personnel to be left out of action will be concentrated at Advanced Battalion Headquarters P.34.d. under orders to be issued later. Major PETTLE will be in command of all details.

12. ACKNOWLEDGE.

                                          J. Reeve
                                          Lieut. Col.,
               Commdg. 32nd Battalion Machine Gun Corps.

17.8.18.

Issued to :-

    1. C.O.
    2. Adjutant.
    3. Signal Officer.
    4. O.C., "A" Coy.
    5. O.C., "B" Coy.
    6. O.C., "C" Coy.
    7. O.C., "D" Coy.
    8. Quartermaster.
    9. 14th Inf. Bde.
  10. 96th Inf. Bde.
  11. 97th Inf. Bde.
12/13. H.Q., 32nd Division.
  14. O.C., 2nd Aust. M.G. Battn.
15/16. War Diary.
  17. File.

S E C R E T.   Copy No ....

32ND BATTALION MACHINE GUN CORPS ORDER NO. 37.

1. Details Camp will be established at rear Headquarters at XXXXXX P.34.d., tomorrow, 20th inst.

2. Each Coy. will send as many men as possible. (a minimum of 1 Officer and 16 O.R.) to report not later than 6. p.m. 20th inst.

3. Lieut. TITCHENER of "D" Coy. will assume duties of Assistant Adjutant forthwith and will superintend training of all details.

4. Surplus gun complete with tripod, spare parts etc., from "A", "B", and "C" Coys. will be sent down tomorrow for instructional purposes. Instructional guns will not be taken away by Coys. to replace casualties without reference to Battalion Headquarters.

5. Training programmes will be made out on the assumption that the course of instruction will last a week. R.S.M. SHERWOOD will superintend Company Drill and C.S.M.I. OSBORNE Physical Training.

6. All details will be under the command of Major PETTLE.

7. One gun will be mounted for A.A. work during the night.

8. ACKNOWLEDGE.

                                        (sd) A.M.Humble,
                                              Capt. & Adjutant,
                                              for Lieut-Col.
                            Commanding 32nd. Battalion Machine Gun Corps.

19.8.18.

Copies to :-

   1. C.O.
   2. Adjutant.
   3. Second-in-Command.
   4. Quartermaster.
   5. O.C., "A" Coy.
   6. O.C., "B" Coy.
   7. O.C., "C" Coy.
   8. O.C., "D" Coy.
   9. Lieut. Titchener.
   10. H.Q., 32nd. Division.
   11. File.

S E C R E T.

Copy No. 12

32ND BATTALION MACHINE GUN CORPS OPERATION ORDER NO.38.

Ref. Sheet :-

HATTENCOURT 1/20,000.

1. 96th Infantry Brigade will extend its right and relieve 4th Australian Division as far South as S.20.central, on night 23/24th August.

2. 12 guns of "D" Company will relieve 12 guns of 4th Australian Machine Gun Battalion at the following gun positions on night 24/25th:-

S.13.d.20.75.	X.17.d.60.15.	X.16.d.10.15.
S.13.d.30.45.	X.23.b.70.97.	X.16.d.10.00.
S.19.b.30.60.	X.23.b.90.70.	X.22.b.10.85.
S.20.a.05.60.	X.24.a.75.90.	X.22.b.05.70.

3. All details of relief will be arranged direct between Company Commanders concerned.

4. All defence lines, S.O.S. lines etc., will be carefully taken over and particulars of same with exact map location of guns will be sent in to Battalion Headqarters on 25th.

5. Relief complete will be reported to Battalion Headquarters by code word "WHISKEY".

6. ACKNOWLEDGE.

Major,
Comndg. 32nd Battalion M. G. Corps.

23.8.18.

Copies to :-

1. C.O.
2. Adjutant.
3. O.C., "D" Coy.
4. O.C., "A" Coy.
5. O.C., "B" Coy.
6. O.C., "C" Coy.
7. 14th Inf.Bde.
8. 96th Inf.Bde.
9. 97th Inf.Bde.
10. H.Q., 32nd Division.
11. C.R.A., 32nd Division.
12.)
13.) War Diary.
14. File.

W.D.

SECRET.
Copy No. 11

32ND BATTALION MACHINE GUN CORPS OPERATION ORDER NO.39.

1. 14th Infantry Brigade (less 15th H.L.I. already in line) will relieve 97th Infantry Brigade (less 10th A. & S.H. already relieved) on night 24/25th August.

2. "A" Coy. will relieve "C" Coy. in the left sub-sector of the 32nd Divisional Front on the night 25/26th.

3. All details of the relief will be arranged direct between Coy. Commanders concerned.

4. All defence lines, S.O.S. lines etc. will be carefully taken over.

5. Relief complete will be reported to Battalion Headquarters by code -

Relief complete	...	MARTINI.
Much shelling	...	RIFLE.
Little shelling	...	COCKTAIL.

6. ACKNOWLEDGE.

R.C. State.
Major,
Commdg. 32nd Battalion M.G.Corps.

24.8.18.

Copies to :-

1. C.O.
2. Adjutant.
3. O.C., "A" Coy.
4. O.C., "B" Coy.
5. O.C., "C" Coy.
6. O.C., "D" Coy.
7. 14th Inf.Bde.
8. 96th Inf.Bde.
9. 97th Inf.Bde.
10. H.Q., 32nd Division.
11/12. War Diary.
13. File.

SECRET.   Copy No. 11

32ND BATTALION MACHINE GUN CORPS OPERATION ORDER NO.40.

1. 97th Infantry Brigade will relieve 96th Infantry Brigade in the right Brigade Sector of the Divisional Front on 29th August.

2. "C" Company, M.G. Battalion will relieve "B" Company on 29th.

3. "D" Company will be withdrawn and will, together with "B" Coy. come under the tactical orders of G.O.C., 96th Infantry Brigade in Divisional Reserve.

4. One Section of "D" Coy. at present with "C" Coy. will return to "D" Coy. as soon as possible.

5. All details of relief will be arranged direct between Coy. Commanders concerned.

6. Relief complete will be reported to Battalion Headquarters and Brigades concerned by code word - "CHAMPAGNE".

7. ACKNOWLEDGE.

28.8.18.

                                                    _____
                                                    for Major,
                                            Comdg. 32nd Battalion M.G.Corps.

Copies to :-

    1. C.O.
    2. Adjutant.
    3. O.C., "A" Coy.
    4. O.C., "B" Coy.
    5. O.C., "C" Coy.
    6. O.C., "D" Coy.
    7. 14th Inf.Bde.
    8. 96th Inf.Bde.
    9. 97th Inf.Bde.
   10. H.Q., 32nd Division.
11/12. War Diary.
   13. File.

S E C R E T.　　　　　　　　　　　　　　　　　　　　　　　　　Copy No. 12

32ND BATTALION MACHINE GUN CORPS OPERATION ORDER NO.41.

1. The 32nd Division is ordered to take over that portion of the 5th Australian Divisional Front between present left Brigade boundary of 32nd Divisional Front and line running through O.8.c.0.0., O.7.c.0.0. - N.12.c.0.0. - N.11.c.0.0. - LAMIERE FARM being exclusive to 32nd Division.

2. 14th Infantry Brigade will take over outpost line West of the Canal on the above front with one Battalion, tonight. Front now held by 14th Brigade will be taken over by 97th Brigade. Divisional Front will then be held by two Brigades each on a one battalion front with remaining battalions disposed in depth. 96th Brigade will remain in Divisional Reserve.

3. "D" Coy. M.G. Battalion will take over Machine Guns of 5th Australian Division in Sector to be taken over by 14th Brigade.

   "C" Coy. will extend its left and take over guns of "A" Coy. on present 14th Brigade front.

   "A" and "B" Coys. will be in Divisional Reserve under the orders of the G.O.C. 96th Brigade.

4. All details of relief will be arranged direct between Coy. Commanders concerned.

5. Relief complete will be sent in to Battalion Headquarters and Brigades concerned by code word - "VERMOUTH".

6. ACKNOWLEDGE.

　　　　　　　　　　　　　　　　　　　　　　　　　　　　　　　Lieut. Col.,
　　　　　　　　　　　　　　　　　　　Commdg. 32nd Battalion M. G. Corps.

30.8.18.

Copies to :-

  1. C.O.
  2. Adjutant.
  3. O.C., "A" Coy.
  4. O.C., "B" Coy.
  5. O.C., "C" Coy.
  6. O.C., "D" Coy.
  7. 14th Inf. Bde.
  8. 96th Inf. Bde.
  9. 97th Inf. Bde.
 10. H.Q., 32nd Division.
11/12. War Diary.
 13. File.
 14. 5th Aust. M.G. Battn.

SECRET.

Copy No. 14

32ND BATTALION MACHINE GUN CORPS INSTRUCTIONS NO.17.

1. The Australian Corps will attack the enemy on the front HERLEVILLE - CHUIGNES at an early date and hour to be notified later.

2. The 1st Australian Division will be on the left on a front of two Brigades, the 32nd Division on the right on a one brigade front.

3. The attached map (to Coys. only) shows the area to be taken by the 32nd Division. The attack will be carried out by the 97th Infantry Brigade.
The 96th Infantry Brigade will remain holding its present defensive front and the 14th Infantry Brigade will remain in Divisional Reserve.

4. The attack will be carried out under a creeping artillery barrage, moving in a N.E. direction. The attacking troops will advance due East.

5. Twelve tanks of the 8th Tank Battalion will assist in the attack of 97th Infantry Brigade and will assemble in concealed forward positions on X/Y night, moving forward from there in time to catch up the attacking infantry at Zero plus 3 minutes. When the 97th Infantry Brigade has reached its final objective the tanks will become available to move N. and assist the 1st Australian Division.

6. (a) Machine Guns of "A" "B" and "D" Coys. will co-operate in accordance with Appendix "A" attached and map (to Coys. only).
   (b) Special Instructions for Machine Guns are detailed in Appendix "B" attached.

7. Guns of "C" Coy. will co-operate as follows :-

   (a) One Section will be allotted to each attacking battalion and will assemble in positions of readiness in rear of them, reporting to the Battalion Commander concerned.
   (b) An Officer will go forward with the last party of the assaulting troops and reconnoitre suitable positions for guns at about -
      R.35.d.25.50.
      X.5.b.60.40.
   (c) Having found positions he will send back a runner to guide all teams up there and one sub-section will come into action at each place.
   (d) The Officer will meanwhile proceed forward to the new front line, select suitable positions for his other sub-section, and return to guide them up personally.
   (e) Above method will ensure teams arriving at the best positions with a minimum of exposure and uncertainty.
   (f) Arrangements are being made by 97th Infantry Brigade for 4 carriers per gun from 5th Border Regt. to be attached for the operation. O.C. "C" Coy. will arrange details of this.

8. (a) A Contact aeroplane will fly along line of final objective at Zero plus 2 hours and call for flares by sounding "A's" on klaxon horn, and firing a White Very Light, which process will be repeated 10 minutes later if it fails to mark the line accurately at the first attempt.
   (b) From Zero hour onwards counter attack aeroplanes will be constantly on the alert to watch for any concentration of hostile infantry or artillery or abnormal movement.
   If the enemy are seen to be preparing for a counter attack, the aeroplane will fire a white parachute flare in the direction of the impending counter attack.
   (c) Certain aeroplanes will be detailed to carry ammunition. If it is required, Vickers guns will display a white "V" with arms 6 feet by 1 foot and apex towards the enemy.
   Ammunition carrying aeroplanes will have the under side of the lower planes painted black for a distance of 2½ feet from the
   tips/

tips.

This only applies to guns of "C" Coy. moving forward to consolidate new area.

9. Communications.

The Signal Officer will arrange for lines from the batteries to 97th Infantry Brigade advanced Headquarters just W. of WALL of MILL X.8.b.5.8.

He will also arrange for a lateral line between "C" and "B" Coys' Headquarters.

10. Synchronization of Watches.

All Coys. will send an officer to "D" Coy. Headquarters W.11.a.8.8. at 2.p.m. and 8.p.m. on Y day. Watches will not be synchronized on the telephone.

11. ACKNOWLEDGE.

Reeve

Lieut. Col.,
Commdg. 32nd Battalion M. G. Corps.

21.8.18.

Issued to :-

1. C.O.
2. Adjutant.
3. O.C., "A" Coy.
4. O.C., "B" Coy.
5. O.C., "C" Coy.
6. O.C., "D" Coy.
7. Signal Officer.
8. 97th Inf.Bde.
9. 96th Inf.Bde.
10. 14th Inf.Bde.
11/12. H.Q., 32nd Division.
13/14. War Diary.
15. File.

S E C R E T.

Amendment No.1 and Addendum No.1 to 32nd Battalion M.G.Corps Instructions No.17.
----

1. **Maps.**

   1/20,000 message map are being issued down to N.C.O's of attacking troops. No other maps will be carried by Officers or men of "C" Coy. taking part in the attack.

2. **Consolidation.**

   It is of the utmost importance that all guns going forward should consolidate as strongly as possible in their final positions, so that good cover for personnel and gun stores may be obtained combined with good concealed fire position for gun. O.C., "C" Coy. will arrange for necessary tools to be taken forward.

3. **Action on front of 96th Infantry Brigade.**

   (a) In order to deceive the enemy the creeping barrage on 97th Infantry Brigade front will be prolonged over the 96th Infantry Brigade front and on right flank Divisional front.
   (b) This barrage will come down 200 yards in advance of our front line and creep outwards.
   (c) The 96th Infantry Brigade will push out strong patrols under cover of the barrage and establish posts in trench line S.14.a.00.00. - S.13.b.95.95. - S.7.b.80.00. - S.7.b.40.61. - VERMANDOVILLERS ALLEY.
   (d) When 96th and 97th Brigades have reached their objectives a new line from about X.12.a.9.9. to X.6.c.8.6. will be established to gain depth in front of the crucifix.

4. **Artillery.**

   (a) The barrage will have 10% of smoke in it.
   (b) The protective barrage will cease on 32nd Divisional front at Zero plus 60 unless continuation is asked for by Brigadiers.
   (c) The S.O.S. signal will be inoperate between Zero minus 15 and Zero.

5. **Action of Machine Guns.**

   In order to conceal the noise of the tank engines, O.C. "B" Coy. will arrange for bursts of harassing fire on usual targets from Zero minus 15 to Zero. This fire will not be of any unusual intensity.

6. Reference Appendix "A" of Instructions No.17., Serial No.8.

   Owing to action of 96th Infantry Brigade, O.C., "B" Coy. will lift off all targets west of STARRY WOOD at Zero and fire on western edge of wood.

7. Reference Appendix "A". Serial Nos. 5,6, & 7 in Time Column read :-

   No.5 ... Zero to Zero plus 5.
   No.6 ... Zero plus 5 to Zero plus 10.
   No.7. ... Zero plus 10 to Zero plus 60.

8. Owing to adjustment of line detailed in para.3 (d), care must be taken by section of "A" Coy. not to impede this work. This can best be done by moving to their right if necessary to newly captured portion of VARMANDOVILLERS ALLEY about S.7.b.2.7.

9. Reference Instructions No.17. Operation detailed will take place on 23rd August.
   Zero hour will be 4.45.a.m.

10. ACKNOWLEDGE.

22.8.18.   *J Reeve*   Lieut. Col.,
                      Commdg. 32nd Battalion M. G. Corps.

Issued to all recipients of Instructions No.17.

APPENDIX "A".

Serial No.	No. of guns.	M.G. Coy.	Position.	Target.	Time.	Rate of Fire.	Remarks.
1.	8	"A"	X.4.d.6.5. (right battery)	S.1.b.0.1.- X.6.a.65.55.	Zero to Z. plus 8.	100 R.P.M.	1. Serial No.1 lifts to Serial No.2 target at Zero plus 8.
2.	24	"D" 16 "A" 8	X.4.b. & d.	S.1.b.55.20 to R.36.c.45.40.	Zero to Z. plus 15.	100 R.P.M.	2. Forward section of "A" Coy. (Nos.5,6,7) will sweep all ground up to 800 or 1000 yards from gun with grazing fire.
3.	24	"	"	S.2.a.0.3. to R.36.c.8.5.	Zero plus 15 to Z.plus 21.	100 R.P.M.	3. Attached map shows various barrage lines.
4.	24	"	"	S.2.a.20.35.- M.32.a.50.00.	Zero plus 21 to Z. plus 60.	100 R.P.M.	
5.	4	"A"	VERMANDOVILLERS ALLEY	Bearing 335°	Zero to Z. plus 5.	100 R.P.M.	
6.	4.	"A"	"	Bearing 0°	Zero plus 5 to Z. plus 12.	"	
7.	4.	"A"	"	Bearing 35°	Zero plus 12 to Z. plus 60.	"	
8.	8	"B"	Battle Positions	Trench area in S.8.a. to W. edge of STARRY WOOD.	Zero to /Zero plus 60.	50 R.P.M.	

APPENDIX "B".

1. Major HOOPER will be in command of the group of batteries.

2. Each battery will have its own commander.

3. All guns will be in position ready to fire at Zero minus 20 minutes.

4. "V" shaped bases will be used which will be put in position on X/Y night.

5. Dumps of belt boxes, extra S.A.A. and water will be formed at the battery positions on X/Y night. Belt filling stations will also be established there.

6. Each gun will have a clinometer.

7. Arrangements will be made to give all men hot tea and rum before Zero and a further issue to "A" and "D" Coys. after withdrawal.

8. "D" Coy. will be prepared to take over all positions from "C" Coy. on Zero plus one, or Zero plus two nights.

9. Reports.

    (a) A report will be sent in at Zero minus 20 minutes that all guns are in position.
    (b) Subsequent reports every half hour or whenever anything unusual occurs.
    (c) A report of withdrawal of "A" and "D" Coys. will also be sent.
    (d) Attached code (to Coys. and 97th Inf.Bde. only) will be used.
    (e) A detailed report of operations from O.C., "B" "C" and "D" Coys. and forward section Commander of "A" Coy. will be forwarded to Battalion Headquarters by 12 noon on Zero plus one day.

10. After completing their barrage fire "A" and "D" Coys. will remain in position for 3 hours ready to respond to any S.O.S. call.
    They will then withdraw to their present positions.
    Great care must be exercised in withdrawing to avoid being seen, and the exact route must be carefully reconnoitred beforehand. Empty belt boxes which cannot be carried will be left till Zero plus 1 night.

11. The forward section of "A" Coy. will probably be unable to withdraw till Z/Z plus 1 night.

12. Care must be taken by the batteries -

    (a) That the on-coming tanks do not over-run their positions (a yellow lamp facing to the rear will be placed at each end of the battery positions.).
    (b) That when opening fire the attacking troops have cleared their front sufficiently.

13. Eight filled belts must always be kept on hand for emergencies; all empty belts must be refilled as quickly as possible.

14. Care should be taken to check alignment and elevation after each burst and not to exceed the rate of fire ordered.

15. Rate of fire on final line may be eased down on the right where attacking troops reach their objective early after Zero plus 30 minutes. This also applies to forward section of "A" Coy. who if visibility is good will only fire after Zero plus 30 if they see a target. If visibility is bad they will maintain a slow rate of fire continuously until Zero plus 60 minutes.

Confidential.

W&

War Diary

of

32nd Bn. Machine Gun Corps.

from 1st September 1918 to 30th September 1918.

No. 8

Army Form C. 2118.

WAR DIARY
or
INTELLIGENCE SUMMARY.
(Erase heading not required.)

Instructions regarding War Diaries and Intelligence Summaries are contained in F. S. Regs., Part II. and the Staff Manual respectively. Title pages will be prepared in manuscript.

Place	Date	Hour	Summary of Events and Information	Remarks and references to Appendices
S.a.v.10.20	1/9/18		Situation Normal. Night Quiet. Enemy Artillery Normal. Two Platoons	62° S.W.
Soyecourt			Crossed Canal & Established Themselves on the Right Bank.	
			O.21.c. + O.26.c. Bn. HQ Moved Forward to S.a.a. 10.20 from	
			Quarry X.23.b	MH
S.a.a.10.20	2/9/18		Situation Normal. Night Quiet. Enemy Artillery Active During Day	
Soyecourt			Carriers Corpse Heavily Shelled During Morning. O.8.a. + b.	
			Gas Shells Between 9.30 P.M + 10.30 P.M. Enemy MGs	WH
			Fired Indiscriminate Harassing Fire. Our MGs Fired	
			20,500 Rounds on Centres of Activity	
S.a.a.10.20	3/9/18		Attempts made to Bridge the Somme unsuccessful. Enemy Artillery	
Soyecourt			Very Active. Enemy M.G. Very Active on Somme Crossings, both Day	WH
			and Night. Our M.G. Fired 26,00 Rounds, Harassing Fire. Provisional	(A.P.1)
			Instructions Issued, and Instructions N° IX re Harassing Fire	(A.P.2)
				RSA

Army Form C. 2118.

WAR DIARY
or
INTELLIGENCE SUMMARY.

(Erase heading not required.)

Instructions regarding War Diaries and Intelligence Summaries are contained in F.S. Regs., Part II. and the Staff Manual respectively. Title pages will be prepared in manuscript.

Place	Date	Hour	Summary of Events and Information	Remarks and references to Appendices
V.11.b.7.7	8.9.18		Casualties - 2 O.R killed, 3 O.R injured accidentally. Patrols occupied DEAD WOODS	62.c. S.E.
MONTECOURT			N° 1 and 2. - WOOD at X.2d.8.1. - LEAF WOOD - JOHN DEVAUX WOODS N° 1 and 2.	O/A
			Own M.G. fired 2200 rounds on roads in ATILLY. Enemy bombing planes	
			active during the night. Preliminary Instructions N° 19 issued. (A.P.5) RRRJ	
V.11.b.7.7	9.9.18		Situation quiet. Time spent in consolidating positions. Instructions N° 20 issued. (A.P.6)	O/A
MONTECOURT			Operation Orders N° 42 issued. (A.P.7) RRRJ	
V.11.b.7.7	10.9.18		97th Brigade attacked MARTEVILLE and ATILLY. Enemy artillery active. Own M.G.	O/A
MONTECOURT			fired 2000 rounds at direct targets. Instructions N° 21 issued. (A.P.8) RRRJ	
V.11.b.7.7	11.9.18		Casualties 1 O.R. killed 7 O.R wounded. Situation quiet. Enemy aeroplanes dropped	
MONTECOURT			bombs on forward areas at about 9 p.m. one enemy M.G. was captured (A.P.9)	O/A
and			by 'B' Co. OMO	
V.12.c.5.3.				
MOISY -				
LACACHE.				

Army Form C. 2118.

WAR DIARY
or
INTELLIGENCE SUMMARY.
(Erase heading not required.)

Instructions regarding War Diaries and Intelligence Summaries are contained in F.S. Regs., Part II. and the Staff Manual respectively. Title pages will be prepared in manuscript.

Place	Date	Hour	Summary of Events and Information	Remarks and references to Appendices
S4 a 10.2.0.			From our O.R. onward (5pm)	
SOYECOURT	4/9/18		Patrols pushed forward to trench system in O.21.a-d. Enemy artillery normal.	62° S.W. AMP
			Our M.G. fired 1500 rounds harassing fire. During the afternoon enemy were observed behind R.a line. RRM.	114
S4 a 10.2.0.	5/9/18		Our line advanced to E. of LE-MESNIL-BRUNTEL — CROSS ROADS P.25.c.—	62° S.W. AND 62° S.E.
SOYECOURT			O.4.a.0.2. RRM.	114
S4.a.10.2.0.	6/9/18		Advance continued during day with little opposition. Approximate line at 6pm	
SOYECOURT AND T.22.c.4.7.			E of MANCOURT — E of VRAIGNES — W of TERTRY.— E of MONCHY-LAGACHE. RRM.	62° S.E. 114
MARCHELEPOT.			Battalion H.Q. moved to MARCHELEPOT.	
T.22.c.4.7.	7/9/18		Advance continued. Line over X.19. a.6.3. — VILLEVEQUE — High ground W.6.1.99 62° S.E.	
MARCHELEPOT			Trenches W.6.d.8 — high ground W.6.t.99 — late trench line to Q.35.6.8.0.	
AND			Operations carried out by B Coy. 0042 rounds. (A.P. 3)	
V11.6.77.			a le column 6.89. (A.P.L.)	
MONTECOURT			RRM	114

D. D. & L., London, E.C. (A5853) Wt. W803/M1672 350,000 4/17 Sch. 52a Forms/C/2118/14

Army Form C. 2118.

WAR DIARY
or
INTELLIGENCE SUMMARY.

(Erase heading not required.)

Instructions regarding War Diaries and Intelligence Summaries are contained in F. S. Regs., Part II. and the Staff Manual respectively. Title pages will be prepared in manuscript.

Place	Date	Hour	Summary of Events and Information	Remarks and references to Appendices
V.12.c.5.3	12/9/18		Enemy artillery active. Situation normal.	
MONCHY - LAGACHE				R.R.&y.
				WA
V.12.C.5.3	13/9/18		Hostile artillery fired 200 rounds on ST. QUENTIN WOOD and HOLNON WOOD.	
MONCHY - LAGACHE				R.R.M. WA
V.12.C.5.3 MONCHY - LAGACHE a.n.g. LA NEUVILLE	14/9/18		C Company embussed to VILLERS-BRETONNEUX. The Battalion was relieved by the 6th Battalion M.G.C. and minus 'C' Coy, embussed to LA NEUVILLE (I.34.d.) Sheet 62 b.	R.R.M. R.R.M. 62.D WA
I.34.d. LA NEUVILLE	15/9/18		'C' Coy marched from VILLERS-BRETONNEUX, and joined the battalion at LA NEUVILLE	R.R.M WA
I.34.d. LA NEUVILLE	16/9/18		Day spent in cleaning up	R.R.I. WA

Army Form C. 2118.

WAR DIARY
or
INTELLIGENCE SUMMARY.

(Erase heading not required.)

Instructions regarding War Diaries and Intelligence Summaries are contained in F.S. Regs., Part II. and the Staff Manual respectively. Title pages will be prepared in manuscript.

Place	Date	Hour	Summary of Events and Information	Remarks and references to Appendices
I.34.d LA NEUVILLE	17/9/18		Day spent in training. C Company moved into reserve at WIENCOURT 62 D La EQUIPEE — V.12.b.80.40.	RR&1. M.A
I.34.d LA NEUVILLE	18/9/18		Casualties — 1 O.R. wounded. 2 O.R. wounded at duty by aerial bombs. Forenoon spent in training	RR&1.
I.34.d LA NEUVILLE	19/9/18		Forenoon spent in training	AR&1. M.A
I.34.d LA NEUVILLE	20/9/18		Forenoon spent in training. Capt & adjt A.M. HUMBLE proceeded to ENGLAND on duty. Duties of adjt taken over by Lieut A.H. FRESHWATER RR&1	M.A
I.34.d LA NEUVILLE	21/9/18		Forenoon spent in training. Sports held by A,B and D companies in the afternoon	RR&1. M.A
I.34.d LA NEUVILLE	22/9/18		B Company moved to VALLEY WOOD (Q.2.b.d	RR&1.
I.34.d LA NEUVILLE	23/9/18		Forenoon spent in training	62.c. M.A RR&1.

Army Form C. 2118.

WAR DIARY
or
INTELLIGENCE SUMMARY.
(Erase heading not required.)

Instructions regarding War Diaries and Intelligence Summaries are contained in F. S. Regs., Part II. and the Staff Manual respectively. Title pages will be prepared in manuscript.

Place	Date	Hour	Summary of Events and Information	Remarks and references to Appendices
LANEUVILLE	24/9/18		Battn H.Q, A and D Companies embussed on FOUILLY — VILLERS B.RETONNEUX ROAD,	62c.
			debussed near ESTREES and bivouaced in VALLEY WOODS. (P.32c.)	MA
P.32.C.			RRA.	MA
VALLEY WOODS	25/9/18		training in the forenoon.	62.C.
			RRA.	MA
P.32 C.				MA
VALLEY WOODS	26/9/18		Training in the forenoon.	62C
			RRA.	MA
P.32.C.				MA
VALLEY WOODS	27/9/18		Training in the forenoon.	62.C.
			RRA.	MA
R.15.6.	28/9/18		The battalion marched to LE VERQUIER TRENCH. (R.15.6.)	R.15.6.2 SHT.
LE VERQUIER			O.O N° 43 issued.	MA
TRENCH.				APP. 9.
			RRA.	

Army Form C. 2118.

WAR DIARY
or
INTELLIGENCE SUMMARY.
(Erase heading not required.)

Instructions regarding War Diaries and Intelligence Summaries are contained in F. S. Regs., Part II. and the Staff Manual respectively. Title pages will be prepared in manuscript.

Place	Date	Hour	Summary of Events and Information	Remarks and references to Appendices
R. 15 b. LEVERGUIER TRENCH.	29/9/18		CASUALTIES – 2 O.R. KILLED 4 O.R. WOUNDED. The 32nd Div., as part of the 4th Army, attacked the HINDENBURG LINE, crossing it at BELLINGLISE. D and C Companies co-operated with the 14th Bde. and 97th Bde. respectively. A and B Companies in Divi Reserve.	b2.C. A21
H.25.a.9.2. MAGNY-LA-FOSSE	30/9/18		CASUALTIES – 2 O.R. KILLED 10 O.R. WOUNDED. Bn H.Q. marched to MAGNY-LA-FOSSE.	62.B.N.W. A21

W. Harrison Major
for Lt Col Cmdg 32 Batt M.G.C.

SECRET

Copy No. 121

32ND BATTALION MACHINE GUN CORPS PROVISIONAL INSTRUCTIONS FOR ANTICIPATED ACTIVE OPERATIONS.

1. In view of future operations gun positions will be sited and prepared for an additional 16 guns on the Right Brigade Sector and an additional 16 guns on the Left Brigade Sector, giving a total of 32 barrage positions per Brigade Sector.

2. Ammunition dumps will be made under Company arrangements on a basis of 8 S.A.A. boxes per gun exclusive of belt ammunition.

   It must be kept in mind when arranging dumps that the S.A.A. therein may have to be moved forward at short notice.

3. The rear guns of the forward system will also be moved up into line with the forward guns in the event of active operations taking place. Positions for these therefore should also be sited.

4. Gun positions will be in groups of 8.

5. O.C., "A" Coy. will assist O.C., "D" Coy. in construction of positions and forming ammunition dumps.

   O.C., "B" Coy. will assist O.C., "C" Coy. as above.

6. ACKNOWLEDGE.

3.9.1918.

Lieut. Col.,
Commdg. 32nd Battalion M.G.Corps.

Copies to :-

1. C.O.
2. Adjutant.
3. O.C., "A" Coy.
4. O.C., "B" Coy.
5. O.C., "C" Coy.
6. O.C., "D" Coy.
7. 14th Inf.Bde.
8. 96th Inf.Bde.
9. 97th Inf.Bde.
10. H.Q., 32nd Division.
11/12. War Diary.
13. File.

SECRET.   Copy No. 11

32ND BATTALION MACHINE GUN CORPS INSTRUCTIONS NO. 18.

Harassing Fire.

1. A system of night harassing fire will be carried out.

2. Company Commanders will make arrangements to bring fire to bear every night on some of the targets given in attached appendix "A".

3. Companies in front line will fire at least 8,000 rounds each night. Times of firing and targets will be <u>submitted to Brigades for approval,</u> to avoid our patrols.

4. Guns will traverse 5° each way within safety limits, so as to cover as large an area as possible.

5. Amount of ammunition and targets fired on, to be sent in with morning Intelligence Report.

6. ACKNOWLEDGE.

                                                         Lieut. Col.,
                                   Commdg. 32nd Battalion M.G.Corps.

3.9.1918.

    Copies to :-

        1. C.O.
        2. Adjutant.
        3. O.C., "A" Coy.
        4. O.C., "B" Coy.
        5. O.C., "C" Coy.
        6. O.C., "D" Coy.
        7. 14th Inf.Bde.
        8. 96th Inf.Bde.
        9. 97th Inf.Bde.
      10. H.Q.,32nd Division.
  11/12. War Diary.
      13. File.

APPENDIX "A".

Target.	Location.	Target.	Location.
Trench	O.16.c. & d.	Quarry	U.4.d.
~~Road~~		Tracks	U.3.d.
~~Cemetery~~		Trenches	U.3.b.
~~Road~~		Cemetry	U.9.d.
~~Trench~~		Road	U.9.d. - U.10.b.
Track on N. Edge of RENE WOOD	U.3.b.50.80.-U.4.a.50.70.-U.4.a.70.70. O.34.d.0.0.	CORPORAL COPSE	U.15.d.
South E. of RENE WOOD	U.4.a.		

Report on Operations carried out by "B" Company, 32nd Battalion
M.G. Corps in conjunction with 13th Australian Light Horse 7.9.18.

Major J.B. NEILSON Commanding "B" Coy.

1. No. 1 Section (Lt. HENDRIE))
   No. 2 Section (2/Lt. CHANDLER)) Took part in these Operations.

2. Zero hour was 7.a.m.

3. Starting point was high ground E. of MONCHY LAGACHE.

4. Description of Events.

Covered by a screen of cavalry patrols these 2 sections pushed up the valley in W.13.a. & b. - W.14.a. etc. due eastwards; No. 1 Section in front, with 100 yards between sections. Gun teams rode on rear half of limbers. The initial movement was somewhat slow owing to broken perch poles; but use was then made of a certain number of pack mules, and the advance proceeded more rapidly. The cavalry patrols met no opposition till they reached the ridge S.E. of TREFCON in w.10.d. and W.16.b. where they were held up by machine guns firing from ARGOSY WOODS (No.2) BEAUVOIS WOODS (No.1) and from small thickets in W.11.a. about 7.45.a.m.

No. 1 Section was immediately brought into action just behind road in W.11.c.2.6. and engaged ARGOSY WOODS (No.2) BEAUVOIS WOODS (No.1) with concentrated fire. Hostile fire was silenced after a short time; and small parties of the enemy disappearing eastwards were dispersed with bursts of rapid fire.

No.2 Section simultaneously pushed up to W.11.c.5.6. and engaged the enemy machine guns in the thickets in W.11.a. and w.11.b. and parties of the enemy on the ridge in W.17.central. Enemy Machine Gunners held out more strongly here, and machine gun fire continued heavily on both sides for some time. 2 mules and 1 Officer's charger were wounded here while the sections were getting into action. Enemy Artillery (light) grew more active.

Meanwhile advanced parties of our infantry came up and held the line of the cross roads in W.11.c. - ARGOSY WOOD No.2 - BEAUVOIS WOOD No. 1.

My sections limbered up, and pushed on just in rear of these towards VILLEVEQUE; passing through the infantry when the latter halted in trench system in w.18. There were no cavalry in advance.

Both sections obtained good targets from the ridge w. of VILLEVEQUE in W.12.d. and w.18.b. - engaging parties of the enemy disappearing over the ridge in w.7.b. and w.7.d. Hostile shelling was slight.

About 12 noon, still in front of the infantry, these sections pushed through VILLEVEQUE. No. 1 Section recaptured a 9'2" Damaged British Howitzer at X.7.c.8.4.

Finally No.1 Section took up positions to cover the ground towards ATTILLY, as follows :-
    2 guns at X.7.b.20.18.
    2 guns at X.7.d.50.30.

No.2 Section was withdrawn slightly to form depth, and took up positions in trench system in w.12.d. and w.18.b.

The infantry consolidated on high ground E. of VILLEVEQUE. The sections stayed in position till late afternoon (about 4.30.p.m.) when guns of "C" Company consolidated the line of defence, and the guns withdrew to bivouacs in w.18.b.8.8.

S E C R E T.

Copy No. 12

32ND BATTALION MACHINE GUN CORPS OPERATION ORDER NO. 42.

Reference Sheet :- 62ᶜ.

1. "A" Company will relieve "C" Company in the forward system of the Divisional Front on the evening 8th September. Relief will be carried out as far as possible by daylight.

2. All details will be arranged direct between Company Commanders concerned.

3. After relief, "A" Company will come under the orders of G.O.C. 97th Infantry Brigade and "C" Company will be in Divisional Reserve and will keep in touch with 96th Brigade.

4. Relief complete will be notified to Battalion Headquarters and to Brigades concerned by code word "RUM".

5. ACKNOWLEDGE.

K. Allen
Lieut. Col.,
Commdg. 32nd Battalion M.G.Corps.

7.9.1918.

Copies to :-

1. C.O.
2. Adjutant.
3. O.C., "A" Coy.
4. O.C., "B" Coy.
5. O.C., "C" Coy.
6. O.C., "D" Coy.
7. 14th Inf. Bde.
8. 96th Inf. Bde.
9. 97th Inf. Bde.
10. H.Q., 32nd Division.
11/12. War Diary.
13. File.

SECRET.   Copy No. 12

32ND BATTALION MACHINE GUN CORPS PRELIMINARY INSTRUCTIONS NO.19.

1. In the event of active operations taking place tonight, these will probably consist of capturing and consolidating the ground and copses in X.8.b., X.3.c. - X.3.a. and R.33.c.

2. This operation will probably be carried out by troops of the Australian Light Horse with one section of "D" Coy., 32nd Battalion M.G. Corps, clearing the valley up to MARTEVILLE and the high ground immediately East of this village.

3. The 97th Infantry Brigade with one section of "A" Coy. will capture and consolidate the remainder, including LEAF WOOD and DEAD WOOD.

4. Machine Guns will give covering fire where possible, and in consolidating will be placed so as to cover as far as possible the sunken road in X.9.b. and c., the valley running from X.8.d. to X.15.b., the valley in X.3.d. and the left flank.

5. It should be borne in mind that cavalry is cooperating in this action and every precaution must be taken. The situation must be clear before fire is opened.

6. ACKNOWLEDGE.

8.9.1918.
                                                    Lieut. Col.,
                                    Commanding 32nd Battalion M.G.Corps.

Copies to :-

   1. C.O.
   2. Adjutant.
   3. O.C., "A" Coy.
   4. O.C., "B" Coy.
   5. O.C., "C" Coy.
   6. O.C., "D" Coy.
   7. 14th Inf.Bde.
   8. 96th Inf.Bde.
   9. 97th Inf.Bde.
   10. H.Q., 32nd Division.
11/12. War Diary.
   13. File.

S E C R E T.   Copy No. 12

32ND BATTALION MACHINE GUN CORPS INSTRUCTIONS NO. 20.

Reference Sheet 62^c S.E.

1.   The Machine Gun Defence of the Divisional Front will be arranged as follows, in the event of enemy counter attack.

   "A" Company will hold the front system as at present.

   "B" Company will occupy the area in squares W.9.c. & d., W.10.c. & d., W.15., W.16., W.21., W.22.

   "C" Company will occupy the area Q.33.c. & d., Q.34.c. & d., W.3., W.4., W.9.a. & b., W.10.a. & b.

2.   O's.C. Companies and Section Officers will reconnoitre their respective areas without delay and will select gun positions for the defence of the Divisional Front in depth.

3.   Selected gun positions in the above mentioned area, will not be manned; but sections and gun teams must know their respective battle positions and the routes to them, so that the positions can be occupied immediately after receipt of the order "MAN BATTLE POSITIONS"

4.   ACKNOWLEDGE.

                                                            for Lieut. Col.,
9.9.1918.   Commanding 32nd Battalion M.G.Corps.

Copies to :-

  1. C.O.
  2. Adjutant.
  3. O.C., "A" Coy.
  4. O.C., "B" Coy.
  5. O.C., "C" Coy.
  6. O.C., "D" Coy.
  7. 14th Inf.Bde.
  8. 96th Inf.Bde.
  9. 97th Inf.Bde.
10. H.Q., 32nd Division.
11/12. War Diary.
13. File.

SECRET.   Copy No. 216A

32ND BATTALION MACHINE GUN CORPS OPERATION ORDER NO. 42.

Reference Sheet 62.C. S.E. 1/20,000.

---

1. Information.

The enemy are holding as far as is known, the following line :-
X.20.b.80.75 - X.15.c.8.1. - X.9.central - X.3.b.80.45 - R.34.c.4.6.

His strength is not known but is in all probability a rear guard only which will withdraw if attacked boldly.

2. Intention.

It is intended to attack the HOLNON and ST QUENTIN Woods on both sides of the Railway in X.10. 11. 17. & 18.
The main attack will be South of the Railway.

3. Objective.

The first objective will be -
- (a) South of the Railway
  X.10.central - HILL 135 (X.10.c.5.0.) - HILL 135 (X.16.c.00.25.).

- (b) North of Railway
  Level crossing (X.10.a.65.65.) - X.4.b.45.20.

The second objective will be the line of trenches 300 to 500 yards East of the BROWN Line (R.36.a. & c. X.6.a. & c., X.12.a. & c., X.18.a. & c.).

4. Forming up Position.

96th Infantry Brigade will form up for attack as follows :-

Right Battalion.
Line of track from track junction X.2.c.30.45 - Level crossing (X.3.a.1.5.).

Left Battalion.
From Level crossing at X.3.a.1.5. to track at R.33.c.55.15.

16th Lancs. Fus. (Support Battalion).
Will form up immediately behind No. 1 & 2 Battns. and will follow at about 600 yds. distance.

5. Artillery.

The advance will take place under an artillery barrage.

6. Consolidation.

Both 1st and 2nd Objectives are to be consolidated at once.

7. Machine Guns.

Machine Guns will co-operate as follows :-

(a) "A" Company will remain in their present positions for defence in depth.

(b) /

2.

(b) 8 guns of "B" Company will move forward with the Infantry, take up their positions on the final objective in X.17.c.9.4. (2 guns) X.18.a.5.0. (2 guns) S.7.d.4.9. (2 guns) S.7.a.4.5. (2 guns). These last two guns will be pushed forward and take up position in S.1.d.5.4., in the event of the infantry occupying this part of the line.

4 guns of "B" Company will take up position in the vicinity of X.8.b. and bring fire to bear on the road from X.10.a.4.3. to X.10.b.20.00. These guns will fire from zero to zero plus 20. The remaining section of "B" Company will advance along the ATTILLY - VILLEVEQUE Road and be in Brigade Reserve and be used as the situation demands. Two of these guns will be pushed forward and will engage the strong point at X.15.central to provide covering fire for the attacking infantry. The other two guns of this Section will remain with the limbers in the vicinity of X.8.d. until the limbers of the other sections going forward have passed through them.

The guns of "C" Company will take up a position in X.8.c. Eight of these guns will bring covering fire to bear on the sunken road in X.4.a. & c. These guns will fire from zero to zero plus 10. From zero plus 10 to zero plus 20 they will fire on Sunken Road in X.4.d. The remaining eight guns of "C" Company will fire on the ATTILLY main road from X.9.d.4.6. to X.10.a.4.3. These guns will fire from zero to zero plus 20.

4 guns of "D" Company will push through behind the infantry and will take up position on the high ground in R.34.c.8.3. to form a flank defence. 4 guns of "D" Company will go forward with the infantry and take up position on the high ground in X.10.c.3.0. to protect the right flank. The remaining eight guns of "D" Company will be held in Divisional Reserve.

Rate of fire of all Barrage guns will be rapid for 5 minutes and 120 rounds per minute thereafter.

It should be borne in mind that the French troops are attacking on our immediate right and as the objectives of the 96th Brigade is not directly frontal every care must be taken to prevent loss of direction thereby endangering French troops. It should also be pointed out that the French Uniform being similar in colour to the enemy uniform, fire must not be opened on distant parties of men, unless it is absolutely certain that they are hostile troops. This situation should be explained to all ranks. and guns going forward will in every case be preceeded by an escort. This must be supplied by companies concerned.

O.C., "B" Company will arrange with the 96th Brigade as to carrying parties for the eight guns going forward.

Section Officers of the 8 guns going forward will keep in close touch with the Battalion Commanders of the attacking infantry.

8. Reports.

Advanced Report Centre will be at X.9.b.2.2. and Section Officers will send in their reports immediately after reaching their final objectives.

9. Identifications.

All identifications, documents, etc., will be forwarded at once to Advanced Report Centre by special messenger.

10. Zero day and hour will be notified later.

11. ACKNOWLEDGE.

9.9.1918.

Lieut. Col.,
Commanding 132nd Battalion M.G.Corps.

Distribution of 32nd Battalion Machine Gun Corps Operation Order No. 42.

Copy No. 1. C.O.
2. Adjutant.
3. O.C., "A" Coy.
4. O.C., "B" Coy.
5. O.C., "C" Coy.
6. O.C., "D" Coy.
7. 14th Inf. Bde.
8. 96th Inf. Bde.
9. 97th Inf. Bde.
10. 15th Lancs. Fus.
11. 16th Lancs. Fus.
12. 2nd Manchester Regt.
13. H.Q., 32nd Division.
14. C.R.A.
15. 34th French Div. d'Infc.
16/7. War Diary.
17. File.
18. 5th Austl. Inf. Bde.

SECRET.   Copy No. 12

32ND BATTALION MACHINE GUN CORPS INSTRUCTIONS NO.21.

1.   96th Brigade are relieving 97th Brigade in the advanced line tonight.

2.   "B" Company will be attached to 96th Brigade and will consolidate the new line captured.

3.   "A" Company will occupy defence positions for 16 guns in the line Q.36.c., W.6.b., VILLERVEQUE, X.13.a. & c., X.19.central. Guns in advance of this line will be withdrawn on completion of relief by 96th Brigade.

4.   "C" Company will reconnoitre positions in the line Q.34.d., W.10.b., BEAUVOIS, BEAUVOIS being defended by one section.
        These positions will be occupied at once in case of hostile attack.

5.   "D" Company will be in mobile reserve.
        2 Sections will continue to co-operate with 13th Australian Light Horse.
        2 Sections will co-operate with 96th Brigade in any offensive actions where covering fire is required.

6.   ACKNOWLEDGE.

                                     F.S. Aldous   Lieut. Col.,
                                     Commanding 32nd Battalion M.G.Corps.

10.9.1918.

Copies to :-
    1. C.O.
    2. Adjutant.
    3. O.C., "A" Coy.
    4. O.C., "B" Coy.
    5. O.C., "C" Coy.
    6. O.C., "D" Coy.
    7. 14th Inf.Bde.
    8. 96th Inf.Bde.
    9. 97th Inf.Bde.
    10. R.O.,32nd Division.
    11/12. War Diary.
    13. File.
    14. 13th Aust. Light Horse.

S E C R E T.   Copy No. 13

32ND BATTALION MACHINE GUN CORPS OPERATION ORDER NO. 45.

Reference 1/20,000 62B S.W. & N.W.: 62C S.E. & N.E.

1. On a date to be named later the Fourth Army will attack the HINDENBURG LINE, cross the Canal and exploit its success up to the RED LINE shown on the map issued at Conference at Divl. H.Q. on 25th Sept.

2. The II American Corps and Australian Corps will be on the left of the IX Corps. The former after crossing the Canal tunnel at BELLICOURT will open out the breach made in the HINDENBURG LINE and the latter will pass through and join up with the IX Corps about JONCOURT.

   The 30th American Division and 5th Australian Division will be successively on the left of the IX Corps.

3. The IX Corps will attack as follows :-

   The 46th Division will capture the first objective which includes the villages of BELLENGLISE, LEHAUCOURT and MAGNY LA FOSSE; and the 32nd Division will pass through the 46th Division and push forward at least as far as the RED LINE. If opposition is weak the Divisional Commander intends to capture the ridge running from LE TRONQUOY to SEQUEHART and the trench system running thence to the point of junction with the Australians at R.16.b.9.7.

4. The 1st Division, now on the right of the 46th Division, pivoting on its right may move its centre and left Eastwards South of the Canal to conform with the progress made by the Divisions North of the Canal and both it and the 6th Division on its right may eventually cross the Canal at LE TRONQUOY when the RED LINE has been reached by the 32nd Division.

5. The 32nd Division will be ready to resume the advance on Z plus 2 days.

6. During "Y/Z" night 32nd Battalion M.G.Corps will move to LE VERGUIER Switch R.15.b.0.0.

7. DISPOSITIONS.

   Companies will be disposed as follows :-

   "D" Coy. will co-operate with 14th Infantry Brigade.
   "C" " " " " 97th Infantry Brigade.

   Successive positions have been discussed at Conferences and approved by G.O's.C. the above Brigades.
   Officers Commanding these Coys. will report to their respective Brigade Commanders by 5.p.m. on "Y" day.

   "B" Coy. will be attached to 96th Infantry Brigade, who are in Divisional Reserve, and will cross the Canal with the Brigade later on "Z" day.

   "A" Coy. will be in Divisional Reserve; on receipt of the order to move they will occupy at the earliest possible moment with one Section each, the positions about H.26.b. & d. covering LE VERGIES and the Spurs running through H.26 & 27 and H.26 D into 33 C in order to form a link between the divergent attacks of the 14th and 97th Infantry Brigades.

                                                                       The/

The other 2 sections will move at the same time to the SUNKEN ROAD in
H.32.b. from where they will assist "D" Coy. in covering the advance of
14th Infantry Brigade.

O.C. "A" Coy. will arrange to move forward one Section to LE VERGIES
and one section to SEQUEHART successively as soon as these places are
captured.

In the event of the ground being further exploited on Z plus 1 day the
O.C. "A" Coy. will continue to form a strong link between the divergent
attacks of 14th and 97th Brigades using SEQUEHART as a "point d'appuie."

8. TASKS.

Companies will support the advance of the infantry by opening an
intense fire on the objective and on to areas where hostile troops are
likely to be massing. A proportion of guns will then be pushed boldly
forward in order to bring close range fire to bear upon any points
where the infantry are held up. On the position being captured, guns
detailed for consolidation will be pushed forward at once and will be
disposed so as to command roads and all main approaches to the position.

These guns form the back bone of the defence against hostile attack
and even if the infantry are forced to withdraw at certain points the
positions will be maintained and the guns kept firing in order that the
infantry may re-form and deliver a counter attack. Consolidation in
depth will be secured by the reserve guns of Companies.

9. AMMUNITION.

Battalion Transport Officer will, as early as possible, form a forward
Ammunition dump at about H.25.a.2.5. and later in the Sunken Road about
H.26.d.2.5. A central belt filling depot will be arranged in the latter
place if possible. O.C. "A" Coy. will detail an Officer to take charge
of this and will provide the necessary personnel. Coy. Commanders will
arrange that at each gun position finally occupied there are 16 belt boxes
and 2 boxes S.A.A., the surplus belt boxes will be on the limbers.

10. CROSSING THE CANAL.

As soon as orders to move are received "A" Coy. "C" Coy. and "D"
Coy. will cross the Canal with all possible speed and take up their
positions. The Ammunition Column will follow them with all possible
speed and moving ahead of the infantry. O.C. "B" Coy. will detail 1
Officer and 32 O.R. to assist in getting the other Coys. and the
ammunition across the Canal.

11. COMMUNICATIONS.

It is of utmost importance that communications be maintained
between Companies and Battalion Headquarters and also with their
respective Brigades. O's C. Companies will report every 2 hours in
writing. They will, as far as possible, remain at their Headquarters
while operations are proceeding and will report personally to their
respective Brigades at the end of Z day. Coys. Headquarters and advanced
Battalion Headquarters will all be established as early as possible
in the Sunken Road running North and South through H.26.b. & d.

An advanced Report Centre will be established here, and a system
of D.R's arranged by the Battalion Signal Officer with the Divisional
Signal Officers.

12. RATIONS.

Troops will advance in Battle Order carrying the unexpended
portion/

portion of the day's ration and one other day's ration. Rations for the following day will be carried on the Coy's Transport. O's.Commanding Coys. will arrange to draw their rations from Brigades as follows:- "A" and "D" with 14th Brigade; "B" with 96th Brigade, and "C" with 97th Brigade. Owing to the scarcity of water, the strictest Water discipline must be enforced.

13. GAS.

Hostile areas will be shelled with mustard gas 48 hours before operations. Troops must be warned to take the necessary precautions.

14. MEDICAL ARRANGEMENTS.

A Bearer division will accompany each Infantry Brigade.

A Walking Wounded Dressing Station will be established at VADENCOURT Chateau R.11.c.1.1.

As soon as the 32nd Division crosses the Canal two Advanced Dressing Stations will be established one of them behind each leading Infantry Brigade on the LEVERGIES - BELLENGLISE and JONCOURT - BELLENGLISE Roads respectively.

When the Advanced Dressing Stations have been established a Main Dressing Station will be established at R.11.c.1.1.

15. A.A.GUNS.

At least 2 of the reserve guns of each Coy. will be detailed to engage low flying enemy aircraft.

16. RECONNAISSANCE.

It is of the greatest importance that whenever guns are moved forward either by hand or in limbers that an Officer's patrol should proceed well in advance in order to reconnoitre the route or to select gun positions.

17. BRIDGES.

Bridges will be constructed as soon as possible as follows :-

(a) Light footbridges (pack if possible) over the Canal.
(b) Heavy bridges at about C.34.d.5.5., N.5.b.8.0. and C.22.b.8.0.

18. TANKS.

Tanks will co-operate with the infantry, they will be marked with a large IX in Roman figures and with the Divisional sign.

19. LIGHT SIGNALS.

The following will be used :-

(a) Success signal (we have reached our objective) - White over white over white.

(b) S.O.S. - Red over Red over Red.

20. ACKNOWLEDGE.

28.9.18.

Lieut. Col.,
Commanding 32nd Battalion M.G.Corps.

Distribution of 32nd Battalion M.G.Corps Operation Order No.43.

Copy No. 1. C.O.
       2. Adjutant.
       3. O.C., "A" Coy.
       4. O.C., "B" Coy.
       5. O.C., "C" Coy.
       6. O.C., "D" Coy.
       7. Signal Officer.
       8. Transport Officer.
       9. 14th Inf.Bde.
      10. 96th Inf.Bde.
      11. 97th Inf.Bde.
      12. H.Q., 32nd Division.
   13/14. War Diary.
      15. File.

CONFIDENTIAL.

Vol 9

WAR DIARY

of

32ⁿᵈ Bⁿ Machine Gun Corps

from 1ˢᵗ October 1918 to 31ˢᵗ October 1918.

WAR DIARY
or
INTELLIGENCE SUMMARY.
(Erase heading not required.)

Army Form C. 2118.

Place	Date	Hour	Summary of Events and Information	Remarks and references to Appendices
MAGNY-LA-FOSSE	1/10/18		CASUALTIES Lt. E. BOYD Killed In Action. 2.O.R. Killed 30.O.R. Wounded. The 32nd Division attacked at 0600. The village of LEVERGIES and the greater part of JONCOURT were captured in spite of the enemy's strong opposition in the latter place. In the afternoon, SEQUEHART and part of BEAUREVOIR - FONSOMMES LINE were captured. During these operations, 50 prisoners RREY. were taken. Lt. B. Scott, A Coy. Guns of A. B and D Coys gave covering and neutralising fire.	RREY
MAGNY-LA-FOSSE	2/10/18		CASUALTIES 4.O.R. Killed Lt. J. Roberts. Wounded 22.O.R. Wounded. At 0700, the enemy, having been reinforced, counter-attacked, and entered SEQUEHART. He was driven out leaving 500 prisoners in our hands. A second attack succeeded in taking the village from us, our guns withdrawing to their original positions.	RREY.

Army Form C. 2118.

WAR DIARY
or
INTELLIGENCE SUMMARY.
(Erase heading not required.)

Place	Date	Hour	Summary of Events and Information	Remarks and references to Appendices
MAGNY-LA-FOSSE	3/10/18		CASUALTIES 2/Lt. L.F. WILLEY WOUNDED. 8.O.R. KILLED. 16.O.R. WOUNDED.	62. D
			At 0600, an attack was carried out with the object of taking the high ground about MANNEQUIN HILL. All objectives were gained. At 0900 the enemy massed for a counter-attack. No.1 and 4 sections of A Coy opened fire at 600-700 yards inflicting heavy losses on the enemy who wavered and finally fell back. At 1800, a heavy barrage was put down on our left. The enemy then counter-attacked and succeeded in forcing back our line. For this operation he used fresh troops. Enemy artillery were active on CHATAIGNES WOOD, SEQUEHART, and the valley running from H.22.b to LEVERGIES. Our M.G. fired on enemy movements and low flying planes. REDA.	Ref.
MAGNY-LA-FOSSE	4/10/18		CASUALTIES 3.O.R. KILLED. 12.O.R. WOUNDED.	Ref. Sueet.
			SITUATION NORMAL. NIGHT QUIET. ENEMY ARTILLERY ACTIVE AT INTERVALS ON CHATAIGNES WOOD, WEST OF JONCOURT AND SEQUEHART. OUR MGS FIRED ON ENEMY MOVEMENT & LOW FLYING PLANES.	62. B

WAR DIARY
or
INTELLIGENCE SUMMARY.

Army Form C. 2118.

Place	Date	Hour	Summary of Events and Information	Remarks and references to Appendices
Magny-la-Fosse	5/10/18		CASUALTIES 2 O.R. KILLED, 2 O.R. WOUNDED. SITUATION NORMAL. NIGHT QUIET. ENEMY ARTILLERY NORMAL. BN. RELIEVED BY 2ND LIFE GUARDS MGBn. O.O. 44. ISSUED.	62.B. A.P.1.
Magny-la-Fosse + Vendeuee	6/10/18		BN. MOVED TO VENDEUES.	62.C.
Vendeuee + Bouvincourt	7/10/18		BN. MOVED TO BOUVINCOURT. Q.19.a.8.8.	62.C.
Bouvincourt	8/10/18		BN. SPENT DAY IN CLEANING UP BILLETS	62.C.
Bouvincourt	9/10/18		COYS. CARRIED OUT TRAINING	62.C.

Army Form C. 2118.

WAR DIARY
or
INTELLIGENCE SUMMARY.
(Erase heading not required.)

Instructions regarding War Diaries and Intelligence Summaries are contained in F. S. Regs., Part II. and the Staff Manual respectively. Title pages will be prepared in manuscript.

Place	Date	Hour	Summary of Events and Information	Remarks and references to Appendices
Bouvincourt	10/2/18		Coys. Carried Out Training	App. 62ᶜ ffr
Bouvincourt	11/2/18		Coys. Carried Out Training	App. 62ᶜ ffr
Bouvincourt	12/10/18		Coys carried out training	RR21. 62ᶜ ffr
Bouvincourt	13/10/18		Coys attended church parade.	RR21. 62ᶜ ffr
Bouvincourt	14/10/18		Coys carried out training	RR21. 62ᶜ ffr
Bouvincourt	15/10/18		Following officers joined Battn:- 2/Lt. J.A.S.ROBERTS, 2/Lt. H.O.SKITT, 2/Lt. I.MASON, 2/Lt. D.H.SHEWARD, Lieut C.S.GRUNDY & U.K. for 6months substitution. 2/Lieut C.W.MAYOW. Coys. carried out training.	RR21. 62ᶜ ffr

WAR DIARY or INTELLIGENCE SUMMARY.

Army Form C. 2118.

Place	Date	Hour	Summary of Events and Information	Remarks and references to Appendices
BOUVINCOURT	16/10/18	Forenoon	2/Lt. L. PARSONS joined for duty.	62c.
			Coys. carried out training.	
BOUVINCOURT	17/10/18	Forenoon	Coys. carried out training.	62c.
BOUVINCOURT & BELLENGLISE	18/10/18		Lieut. A. de F. MACMIN joined for duty. H.Q., "A" & "D" Coys. moved to BELLENGLISE; "B" Coy moved with 96th Inf. Bde. to LEHAUCOURT; "C" Coy. moved with 97th Inf. Bde to PONTRUET.	62c.T THORIGNY 1/50,000
BELLENGLISE	19/10/18	Afternoon	Coys. carried out training.	THORIGNY 1/20,000
BELLENGLISE & BOHAIN	20/10/18		Battn. moved to BOHAIN.	THORIGNY 1/50,000 WASSIGNY 1/40,000
BOHAIN (D.15 & D.27)	21/10/18	Forenoon	Lieut. C.L. O'SHAUGHNESSY & 2/Lieut. W.T. EVANS joined for duty.	WASSIGNY 1/40,000
			Spent in improving billets & cleaning up	
		Afternoon	Battn. paraded with 14th Inf. Bde. for presentation of Medal Ribands by Divisional Commander.	

Army Form C. 2118.

WAR DIARY
or
INTELLIGENCE SUMMARY.

(Erase heading not required.)

Place	Date	Hour	Summary of Events and Information	Remarks and references to Appendices
BOHAIN (D15 + D27)	22/10/18		"A" + "C" Coys. moved forward to St. SOUPLET to assist 6th Division by firing a barrage.	WASSIGNY. 1/10,000.
			"B" + "D" Coys. carried out training.	
BOHAIN (D15 + D27)	23/10/18		CASUALTIES. 2/Lt. F. MINTER Killed in action. 1 O.R. wounded.	WASSIGNY 1/40,000.
			"A" + "C" Coys. fired barrage. Supply of ammunition poor, barely 200,000 rounds were fired.	
			"B" + "D" Coys. carried out small tactical schemes.	
BOHAIN (D15 + D27)	24/10/18		Lieut. W.G. Elias went to U.K. on business.	WASSIGNY. 1/40,000.
			"A" + "C" Coys. withdrew from barrage positions to Billets at St. SOUPLET	
		afternoon	"B" + "D" Coys. carried out emplacement building, Immediate Action & Gun Drill.	
			Recreational Training.	
BOHAIN. (A15 + D27)	25/10/18		Lieut. W.E. Sandom & Lieut. H.C. Hendrie evacuated sick.	WASSIGNY. 1/40,000.
		forenoon	Coys. carried out Emplacement making, Gun Drill, Immediate Action, Arms Drill.	
		afternoon	Coys. carried out Recreational Training.	
			Lieut. L.H. SMITH assumed duties of Intelligence Officer and Assistant Adjutant	

Army Form C. 2118.

WAR DIARY
or
INTELLIGENCE SUMMARY.

(Erase heading not required.)

Instructions regarding War Diaries and Intelligence Summaries are contained in F. S. Regs., Part II. and the Staff Manual respectively. Title pages will be prepared in manuscript.

Place	Date	Hour	Summary of Events and Information	Remarks and references to Appendices
BOHAIN (DIST-D27)	26/4/18		All Coys. carried out Emplacement Building, Gun Drill & Arms Drill.	WASSIGNY 1/20,000.
		afternoon	Coys. carried out Recreational Training.	
BOHAIN (DIST-D27)	27/4/18	forenoon	Coys. carried out Training.	WASSIGNY 1/20,000.
		afternoon	Recreational Training.	
BOHAIN (DIST-D27)	28/4/18		Coys. carried out Training. Lt. B.R. WOODWARD joined for duty.	WASSIGNY 1/20,000.
BOHAIN (DIST-D27)	29/4/18	forenoon	Coys. carried out Training. Inspection by Divisional Commander of H.Q. WASSIGNY 1/20,000. "B" and "D" Coys. with Transport.	
		afternoon	Recreational Training. O.O. no. 441/2 ISSUED	APPENDIX 2.
BOHAIN (DIST-D27)	30/4/18		"D" Coy. moved forward to St. SOUPLET. "A" Coy. relieved "A" Coy. 6th B.M.G.C. in the line. Major BLOOR joined for duty.	WASSIGNY 1/20,000.

Army Form C. 2118.

WAR DIARY
or
INTELLIGENCE SUMMARY.

(Erase heading not required.)

Instructions regarding War Diaries and Intelligence Summaries are contained in F. S. Regs., Part II. and the Staff Manual respectively. Title pages will be prepared in manuscript.

Place	Date	Hour	Summary of Events and Information	Remarks and references to Appendices
BOHAIN and BAZUEL (Sqs 2.5)	31/10/18		Bn. H.Q. moved to BAZUEL. 'B' Coy. moved to St. SOUPLET. "C" Coy. relieved "D" Coy. 6th Bn. M.G.C. in the line.	WASSIGNY 1/40,000. Yes

H. Oldens Clout
Lieut. Col.
32nd Bn. M.G.C.

Engs: 8
37.10.18

W.D.

A.P.1

SECRET.

Copy No. 14

32ND BATTALION MACHINE GUN CORPS ORDER NO.44.

1. The 32nd Battalion M.G. Corps will be relieved in the line by the 2nd Life Guards M.G. Battalion on 5th inst. All details to be arranged by Commanders of Companies concerned.

2. Completion of relief to be reported to Battalion Headquarters as follows :-

   Relief complete ... SKY

   Much Shelling ... CLOUDY

   Little Shelling ... CLEAR.

3. The Battalion will move in "Action not expected" formation by route march to BOUVINCOURT on 6th and 7th inst. staging at VENDELLE on night 6/7th.
   Starting point - Western end of Bridge over Canal at G.34.d.5.5., heads of Coys. to pass starting point as follows :-

H.Q.	...	15.05.
"A" Coy.	...	15.15.
"B" Coy.		15.30.
"C" Coy.	...	15.40.
"D" Coy.		15.50.

   500 yards interval between Companies.

4. Each Coy. will detail a billeting party of 1 Officer or N.C.O. and 4 O.R. to report to Lieut. TITCHENER at Battalion Headquarters MAGNY-LA-FOSSE at 08.45 tomorrow. They should take rations for 6th and 7th with them. Lieut. TITCHENER will detail guides to meet Coys. at road junction at VADENCOURT R.10.d.5.1. on 6th inst.
   Extra billeting parties may be sent on if desired by Coys. in order to prepare accommodation.

5. The Battalion Transport Officer will arrange direct with Coy. Transport Officers as to Transport lines etc.

6. The strictest march discipline will be maintained throughout the move.

7. ACKNOWLEDGE.

Lieut. Col.,
5.10.1918.   Commanding 32nd Battalion M.G.Corps.

Copies to :-

1. C.O.
2. Adjutant.
3. O.C., "A" Coy.
4. O.C., "B" Coy.
5. O.C., "C" Coy.
6. O.C., "D" Coy.
7. Quartermaster.
8. Transport Officer.
9. Signal Officer.
10. 14th Inf.Bde.
11. 96th Inf.Bde.
12. 97th Inf.Bde.
13. H.Q.,32nd Division.
14/ 15. War Diary.
16. File.

SECRET.

Copy No. 11

APPENDIX

32ND BATTALION MACHINE GUN CORPS OPERATION ORDER NO. 44.

Reference Maps - Sheets 57B. and 57A. 1/20,000.

1. The 32nd Battalion Machine Gun Corps will relieve 6th Battalion Machine Gun Corps in the Line on the 30th and 31st inst. as follows:-

   "A" Coy. relieves "A" Coy. 6th Battn. M.G. Corps in the Right Sector on 30th inst.
   Coy. Headquarters BAZUEL R.8.d.8.5.

   "D" Coy. moves with 14th Brigade Group on 30th inst. to ST. SOUPLET and takes over from "A" Coy. 32nd Battn. M.G. Corps on 31st inst. These billets will be taken over by Battn. H.Q. and fresh ones allotted to the Coy.

   "C" Coy. relieves "D" Coy. 6th Battn. M.G. Corps in the Left Sector on 31st inst.
   Coy. Headquarters BAZUEL R.8.a.8.5.

   "B" Coy. moves with 97th Brigade Group on 31st inst. to ST. SOUPLET and takes over from "C" Coy. 32nd Battn. M.G. Corps.

   Headquarters moves with 97th Brigade Group on 31st inst. to ST. SOUPLET and takes over billets from "D" Coy.

2. The usual billeting parties will be sent on in advance by "O.C." "D" Coy. on 30th inst. and by Headquarters and "B" Coy. on 31st inst.

3. Billeting Certificates to be handed in to the Quartermaster before leaving present billets in BOHAIN.

4. As much of the relief as possible will be carried out by day, but there will be no movement of formed bodies of troops East of a grid line R.3.central - R.9.central - R.15.central in daylight.

5. 1/20,000 maps of the Line and aeroplane photographs will be taken over from 6th Battn. M.G. Corps.

6. All other details of the reliefs will be made direct by the Os.C. Companies concerned.

7. Completion of relief will be wired to Battn. H.Q. using the code -

   Relief complete ... ON
   Much shelling ... LES
   Little shelling ... AURA.

8. Battalion Headquarters will close at BOHAIN at 12.00 hours on 31st inst. and open at ST. SOUPLET Q.33.d.6.5. on arrival.

9. ACKNOWLEDGE.

Capt. & Adjt.,
32nd Battalion M. G. Corps.

29.10.1918.

Issued to :-
1. C.O.
2. 2nd-in-Command.
3. Quartermaster.
4. Signal Officer.
5. O.C., "A" Coy.
6. O.C., "B" Coy.
7. O.C., "C" Coy.
8. O.C., "D" Coy.
9-11. 6th Battn. M.G. Corps. (3)
12. H.Q., 32nd Div. "G".
13. H.Q., 14th Inf. Bde.
14. H.Q., 96th Inf. Bde.
15. H.Q., 97th Inf. Bde.
16. 32nd Div. Train.
17-18. War Diary.
19. File.

CONFIDENTIAL.

Vol 10

War Diary

of

32nd Bn Machine Gun Corps

1st November 1918 to 30th November 1918.

Nº 10.

WAR DIARY
or
INTELLIGENCE SUMMARY.
(Erase heading not required.)

Army Form C. 2118.   1918

Place	Date	Hour	Summary of Events and Information	Remarks and references to Appendices
BAZUEL (R&A 2.5)	1/11		Situation normal. "B" Coy. prepared & reinforced Barrage Positions.	
	2/11		Casualties. 2/Lt. H.D. SKITT wounded. 2.O.R. Killed. 19.O.R. wounded. 96th Inf. Bde. attacked the high ground in HAPPEGARBE. "B" Coy. putting down barrage in support. One Section of "C" Coy. advanced with the attacking Infantry, the situation first direct along the railway cutting in G 26. On advance pushing forwards, all objectives were taken except one. A second one shown in greater force preceded by Jerry H.E. bombardment — troops retained to original position.	APPENDIX I 57 A + 57 B 1/10 ○○○ ○/I.
	3/11		Casualties. 3. O.R. wounded. Yesterday Operation reported, all objectives taken, but repeated counter attacks compelled withdrawal to original line. Six guns of "Y" Coy. 6th M.G. Bn. retired 6 guns of "C" Coy. 32nd Bn.	APPENDIX II ○/I.
	4/11		Casualties. 2/Lt. T.W. VINE wounded. 1 O.R. Killed. 4 O.R. wounded. 1st 96th Inf. Bdn. attacked SAMBRE Canal, 4 Coys. 32nd Bn. M.G.C., 3 Coys. 6th M.G. Bn. one Coy. R.H.G. M.G. Bn. + 5th Cavalry C.Bde. M.G.Squadron co-operating with them. The attack progressed well on the right, but was held up on its left by enfilade fire from hostile field guns which destroyed the bridges constructed. "Z".2 Barrage was repeated from Z+225 to Z+210 the advance continued.	APPENDIX III ○/I.

Army Form C. 2118.

WAR DIARY
or
INTELLIGENCE SUMMARY.

(Erase heading not required.)

1918

Place	Date	Hour	Summary of Events and Information	Remarks and references to Appendices
BAZUEL (R8a.8.5)	4/11		Four guns of "Y" by 6th Bn M.G.C. were pushed forward to high ground S. of the Railway in G.27 & engaged hostile M.Gs who were shelling up the advance, with divisional fire with good effect. Patrols & opposition on the left- the final objective (RED line) was almost opposition reached. M.Gs consolidated in depth & fresh were established with flank defences. In all 250,000 rounds were expended. Pack animals were much used early in the day to carry forward ammunition, but later during the day the MGs were brought up across the canal.	Sheet 57A + 57B. 1/40,000 [signature]
SAMBRETON G.35.b.cg.	5/11		Bn. HQ. moved to SAMBRETON. Advance was resumed by 97th Inf. Bde & its Coys. Little opposition was encountered. Support MG Bns & posts were left. After the enemy, but unsupported action's M.G. fire, although they were neutralised by our M.Gs which were pushed well forward. Cavalry patrols entered FAVRIL early in the morning. Very little hostile shelling was experienced following the day. The enemy were found back on a E. of a line 6d BEART - CROIX-HAINAULT which was held for the night. M.Gs consolidating in depth. Transport was difficult during the day owing to the large number of the extra but limbers were brought forward & all cases when required.	APPENDIX IV & V Sheet 57A 1/40,000 [signature]

WAR DIARY or INTELLIGENCE SUMMARY

Army Form C. 2118.

1918.

Place	Date	Hour	Summary of Events and Information	Remarks and references to Appendices
GRAND FAYT (I 31 b 3.9)	6/11		Bn. H.Q. moved to GRAND FAYT. The advance was continued at an early hour. Opposition was only encountered from M.G. posts. Bridges at GRAND FAYT and PETIT FAYT were destroyed, but the Lft. M.G. Coy. with infantry escorts pushed across the river at MAROILLES where its bridge was intact. Guns of the right Coy. were manhandled across the improvised foot bridges at GRAND FAYT & transport crossed by MAROILLES and joined them later. The M.G.s. then went forward in close touch with the infantry and good work was done in engaging hostile M.Gs., its enemy being pushed beyond DOMPIERRE – CARTIGNY road before nightfale.	57A 1/40,000 B.M.
LES ARDENNES (I.9.a.4.8)	7/11		Bn. H.Q. moved to LES ARDENNES. Casualties - 12 O.R. wounded. 97th Bde. with B.13 Coy. continues its advance to a line WEST of AVESNES where enemy had a strong offensive M.Gs. held up our troops for some considerable time. Our M.Gs. successfully engaged several hostile posts lui-tre (advance)	57A 1/40,000 B.M.

WAR DIARY
or
INTELLIGENCE SUMMARY.
(Erase heading not required.)

Army Form C. 2118.

1918

Place	Date	Hour	Summary of Events and Information	Remarks and references to Appendices
LES ARDENNES (I. 19 d 4.8)	7/11 continued		advance continued. We carried through AVESNES before dawn a line W. of the town was consolidated for the night. The 25th Divn. which had on the left, his its left flank was exposed until late in the night when touch was gained with the 148th Divn. Meanwhile flank guards of M.Gs. suitably posted were formed. The remainder of the guns disposed in depth. Stores transport was not greatly hindered by the mine craters blown and bridges destroyed as alternative routes were found for the same destinations by making detours. Casualties: 1 O.R. killed 2 O.R. wounded. Bn. H.Q. moved to AVESNELLES.	57 A. 1/200,000 @M.
AVESNELLES (K25a.1.6)	8/11		Little progress was made until about 1300 hours, the advance being held up by Snipers +M.Gs. at this item. Its resistance was overcome +Bn. by moved forward through AVESNES +AVESNELLES. During the day 3 hostile M.Gs. were put out of action by our M.G. fire then movement to continue. Adve was taken up 1000 yards East of AVESNELLES. M.Gs. consolidating in depth + guarding flanks	@M.

WAR DIARY
INTELLIGENCE SUMMARY

Army Form C. 2118.

1918

Place	Date	Hour	Summary of Events and Information	Remarks and references to Appendices
AVESNELLES 8/11 (K25 A.1,6)		continued	Both flanks were exposed, but little was established with 16th Div divisions during the night. Orders were again shown in the road, but stow shelters were every by our transport.	O.1.
AVESNELLES 9/11 (K25 A.1,6)			Casualties - 21 O.R. killed. 17 O.R. wounded. 2 O.R. missing. 2/Lt. L. PARSONS Killed outright. The cavalry were covered by the explosion of hostile ammunition dumps along the Railway in K30 & K30a. The enemy had lit many railway action trains in these, which exploded dumps when the time up. It was known in the morning that the enemy had commenced his retirement, having only M.G.s in rear as a guard. Practically no opposition was encountered, the advance continued fairly rapidly to about 1000 yds East of RANZOUSIES. Shortly was occupied at nightfall. Cavalry Patrols were working well East of the line.	57 A 1/40.000 O.1.

Army Form C. 2118.

WAR DIARY
or
INTELLIGENCE SUMMARY.

(Erase heading not required.)

Instructions regarding War Diaries and Intelligence Summaries are contained in F. S. Regs., Part II. and the Staff Manual respectively. Title pages will be prepared in manuscript.

1918

Place	Date	Hour	Summary of Events and Information	Remarks and references to Appendices
AVESNELLES (R25a 1.6)	10/11		The reorganisation was continued by 32nd Divn. Inc. touch was maintained with the enemy by cavalry patrols, reports. all defensive measures were observed, all precautions taken. Lt. G.B.M. REED joined for duty from M.G. Base.	57 A 1/40,000 Q.M.
AVESNELLES (R25a 1.6)	11/11		Hostilities ceased 11.00 hours. Defensive measures were not relaxed. "A" Coy with 14 Inf. Bde., holding the line. "B" & "D" Coys were billeted in AVESNES & AVESNELLES "C" Coy with 96th Bde. in SAMBRETON area.	57 A 1/40,000 Q.M.
AVESNELLES (R25a 1.6)	12/11		"A" Coy with 14th Inf. Bde. continued to hold the line, all other Coys continued reorganisation, cleaning up.	57 A 1/40,000 Q.M.
SAINS-DU-NORD (R12a 0.1)	13/11		Bn. H.Q. moved to SAINS-DU-NORD. "A","B" & "D" Coys moved to SAINS-DU-NORD "C" Coy to AVESNELLES.	57 A 1/40,000 Q.M.
SAINS-DU-NORD (R12a 0.1)	14/11		"C" Coy moved to SAINS-DU-NORD. Coys continued reorganisation relieving of personnel, Kit, Transport etc. 2/Lt. T.O. WILLIAMS joined for duty from M.G.T.C. GRANTHAM.	57 A 1/40,000 Q.M.

Army Form C. 2118.

WAR DIARY
or
INTELLIGENCE SUMMARY.
(Erase heading not required.)

1918

Instructions regarding War Diaries and Intelligence Summaries are contained in F. S. Regs., Part II. and the Staff Manual respectively. Title pages will be prepared in manuscript.

Place	Date	Hour	Summary of Events and Information	Remarks and references to Appendices
SAINS-DU NORD (Q12a.0.0.)	15/11 16/11 17/11 18/11		Bn. spent three days in expectation of an order releasing up. also in preparing for the march to the RHINE. Following Officers joined for duty from M.G. base. Lt. C.M. DELF, Lt. T. ROBERTS, Lt. C.H. SMITH, 2Lt. J.S. LEE, 2Lt. C.T. HARDWICK on 15/11. Lt. D. GARDNER went to MAJOR C.T. DENROCHE on 17/11. U.K. (6 months) Lt. C.R. MOSELEY on 18/11	57 A 1/40,000 [initials]
SIVRY	19/11		March into GERMANY commenced. Bn. marches with 'B' Group 32nd Div. under C.R.A. Bn. moved to SIVRY.	NAMUR 1/100,000 [initials]
FOURBECHIES	20/11		Bn. marches to FOURBECHIES.	NAMUR 1/100,000 [initials]
FOURBECHIES	21/11 22/11 23/11		Coys. were employed on clearing the roads in the neighbourhood of FOURBECHIES and FROIDCHAPPELLE, also in clearing the ground round above fields, which was in an extremely bad and unsanitary condition. Ceremonial training was also carried out. Capt. F.A. LOTT left for U.K. (6 months) 22/11. Major P. MATHISEN reported for duty from 18th M.G. Bn. 23/11	NAMUR 1/100,000 [initials]

Army Form C. 2118.

WAR DIARY
or
INTELLIGENCE SUMMARY.
(Erase heading not required.)

1918.

Place	Date	Hour	Summary of Events and Information	Remarks and references to Appendices
CERFONTAINE	24/11		Batn. moved to CERFONTAINE	NAMUR 1/100,000
CERFONTAINE	25/11 26/11 27/11 28/11 29/11 30/11	forenoon afternoon	Coys. carried at- training & were also employed in clearing the roads in the neighbourhood of CERFONTAINE in clearing the vicinity of shells. Recreational training was carried out.	NAMUR 1/100,000

Mathieson
Major

W.D. APPENDIX

Report on Operations commencing 06.00 hours
on 2.11.1918.

"B" and "C" Companies, 32nd Battalion Machine Gun Corps co-operated with 96th Infantry Brigade as follows :-

"B" Coy. formed two batteries of 8 guns at L.30.c.8.7. (right battery) and L.24.c.8.8. (left battery).

Right Battery put down two barrages simultaneously from Zero to Zero plus 45 minutes on areas enclosed by points -
(1) G.32.b.9.1., G.33.a.2.7., G.33.b.1.5., G.33.c.8.7.
(2) G.33.a.9.0., G.33.b.3.8., G.33.b.9.6., G.33.d.8.8.

Left Battery put down a barrage from Zero to Zero plus 45 mins. on area enclosed by points - G.26.b.9.3., G.21.c.1.1., G.27.b.9.8., G.27.d.6.7.

"B" Coy's guns were withdrawn after the barrage.

"C" Coy. 2 guns at L.30.c.4.0. barraged area enclosed by points G.32.a.9.6., G.26.d.1.0., G.32.b.9.6., G.32.b.7.2. from Zero to Zero plus 45.

2 guns in L.30.c. fired direct along the Railway cutting in G.26 from Zero to Zero plus 2 and then moved along the cutting and took up positions at G.27.a.0.6.

4 other guns moved forward with the attacking infantry and occupied positions as follows :-
2 at G.26.c.4.8. and 2 at G.20.d.5.8.

Rounds fired.

95,000 rounds in all were expended.

During the action battery positions were fairly heavily shelled with Gas and H.E. which apparently was area shooting and not aimed fire on the positions. Gun teams were well dug in and very few casualties occurred whilst in position.

Casualties, which were fairly heavy were mainly suffered in going forward to take up barrage positions and also whilst withdrawal was in progress.

A counter attack developed at 10.30 hours coming from direction of LANDRECIES and up the gulley in G.21.c. This was repulsed. A further counter attack developed in great force about 16.00 hours preceded by heavy Gas and H.E. bombardment. Great execution was done by Machine Guns who were finally compelled to withdraw to their original positions after covering the withdrawal of the infantry. Two teams and guns are missing up to the present.

2.11.1918.   Lieut. Colonel,
                                     Commanding 32nd Battalion M.G.Corps.

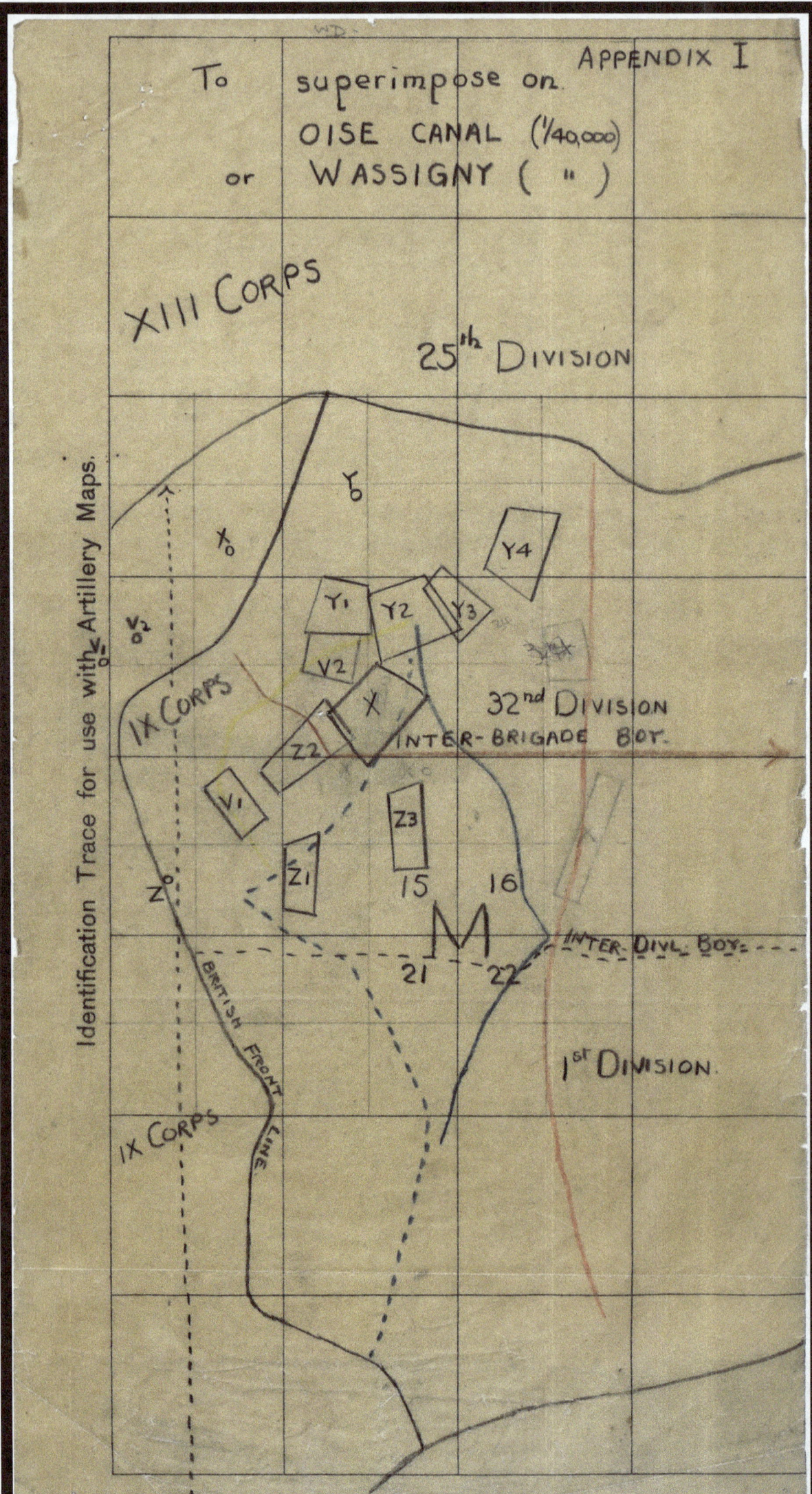

To be superimposed on MESSAGE MAP 1/20,000

G.S.G.S. 3023.

NOTE.—(1). These traces are intended to facilitate the communication of information as to the position of targets, which have [...]
(2). The squares on this trace are 500 yards in length on the 1/10,000 scale, 1,000 yards in length on the 1/20,000 [...] on the 1/40,000 scale.
(3). The squares on the trace are fitted to the squares of the map showing the targets, which are then dr[...] letters and numbers must also be added to enable the recipient to place the trace in the correct position on [...] may also be traced, but this is not essential. The name and scale of the map to which the trace refers mus[...] can be used for the 1/10,000, 1/20,000, or 1/40,000 scale.

				Y4
	31	32 Y1	33 Y2	Y3 34
L	G			
R	M			
	1	2	3	4

APPENDIX II.

TIME AND RATES OF BARRAGE.

COMPANY.	TARGET.	TIME.
Y. (8 guns).	Y1.	Zero to Z plus 35.
	Y3.	Zero plus 35 to Z plus 130.
Y. (8 guns).	Y2.	Z. to Z. plus 90.
Y. (16 guns).	Y4.	Z plus 180 to Z. plus 210 or as ordered by G.O.C. 96th Inf.Bde.
X. (16 guns).	X.	Z. plus 30 to Z. plus 90.
V. (V1 battery, 8 guns)	V1.	Z. to Z. plus 30.
V. (V2 battery, 8 guns)	V2.	Z. to Z. plus 30.
Z. (8 guns).	Z1.	Z.plus 20 to Z. plus 130.
Z. (8 guns).	Z2.	Z. to Z. plus 130.
Z. (16 guns).	Z.3.	Z. plus 180 to Z. plus 200.

RATE OF FIRE.

In cases where batteries are firing for long periods, guns will fire in turn at rate of about 200 rounds per minute, so as to make a total of 5,000 to 6,000 rounds per gun.

All batteries will commence with 2 to 5 minutes rapid fire.

V Company will fire fairly rapidly during its whole barrage.

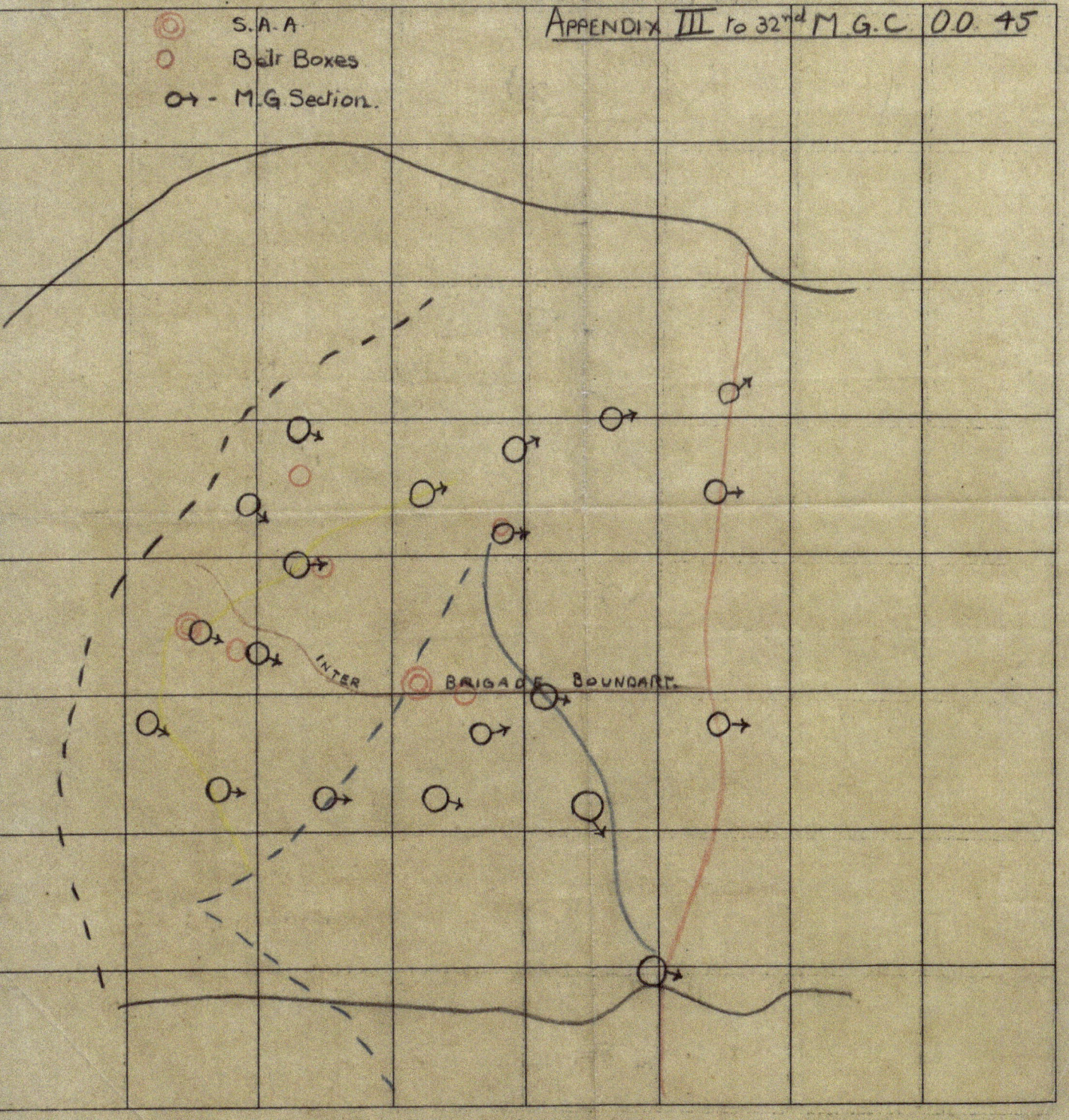

SECRET.

AMENDMENT No.1 to APPENDICES I and II to 32nd BATTALION MACHINE GUN
CORPS OPERATION ORDER NO.45.

Barrages and times have been revised as follows in order to cope
with the requirements of the present situation and also to comply with
Artillery Barrage and request of 1st Division.

New location of Y Battery - G.25.a.9.0.

Y1, Y2, Y3, and Y4 barrages have been revised as shown on the attached
map (issued to those concerned).

Times :-

Y1	Z. to Z. plus 35.
Y2	Z. plus 35 to Z. plus 70.
Y3	Z. plus 70 to Z. plus 100.
Y4	Z. plus 180 to Z. plus 210.

Time change.

X Barrage. For Z. plus 30 to Z. plus 90 read:- Z. plus 30 to
Z. plus 75.

ACKNOWLEDGE.

Capt. & Adjt.,
32nd Battalion M. G. Corps.

3.11.1918.

Issued to all recipients of 32nd Battalion M.G. Corps Operation
Order No.45, concerned.

SECRET.   *War Diary*   *Appendix II*

Copy No. 4

32ND BATTALION MACHINE GUN CORPS OPERATION ORDER NO. 45/1.

1. Y Company, 6th Battalion Machine Gun Corps will detach 6 guns to act as flank defence to their battery. These will take over positions from "C" Company, 32nd Battalion Machine Gun Corps.

2. Guides at Infantry Battalion Headquarters G.20.c.4.2. at 1830.

3. O.C., Y Company will also place 2 guns about G.26.c.5.8. on the Railway or on the Canal bank from where they can enfilade hedges (see air photo) and will engage hostile machine guns direct.

4. The barrage will be fired with 8 guns only.

Capt. & Adjt.,
3.11.1918.   32nd Battalion Machine Gun Corps.

Issued to :-

1. O.C., "Y" Coy. 6th Battn. M.G. Corps.
2. Adjutant.
3- 4. War Diary.
5. H.Q., 32nd Div. "G".
6. C.M.G.O.
7. File.

SECRET.   Copy No. 19.
APPENDIX III

2ND BATTALION MACHINE GUN CORPS OPERATION ORDER NO.45.

In connection with 32nd Division Order No.212.

Reference Map - OISE CANAL - 1/40,000.

1. **Designation of attached M.G. Coys.**

    Three Companies of the 6th Battalion M.G.Corps, the Royal Horse Guards Machine Gun Coy. and the 5th Cavalry Brigade Machine Gun Squadron will be attached to the 32nd Division for these operations. In this Order the three Coys. of the 6th Battalion M.G.Corps will be referred to as X Y and Z Coys. and the Royal Horse Guards Coy. as V Coy.

2. **Disposition of Companies.**

    (a) "A" Company will co-operate with Right Brigade.
        "C"   "   "   "   " Left   "
        "B" and "D"   "   "   " Reserve "   .

    (b) V, X, Y and Z Companies will take up barrage positions before the attack.

3. **Companies with Brigades.**

    These Coys. will co-operate with attacking Brigades on the following general lines which have been approved by G.O's.C. Brigades :-

    (a) Two Sections of each Coy. will push up close to the Canal previous to the crossing and will dig in or take up positions in houses. They will open an intense fire on any hostile Machine Guns that fire.
    After the Canal is completely cleared they will overhaul their guns and move forward to predetermined positions and consolidate in depth using pack transport or limbers if possible (see Appendix III).

    (b) The other two Sections will go forward in close support and will move closely behind the infantry. An Officer with escort will be in touch with leading infantry. The guns will be close behind and ready to come into action at once, they will move into positions for consolidation when objective is gained. Houses to be used where possible.

    (c) In future advances neutralizing fire must always be put on an area before the infantry go forward, especially if opposition is expected there.

    The 2 forward Sections will be largely responsible for this as no barrage guns will be available beyond the Blue dotted line. The other two Sections will assist if this can be arranged.

4. **Companies taking up barrage positions before the attack.**

    These Companies will occupy positions as follows :-

    X Coy. in L.30.c.
    Y Coy. in G.26.b. keeping in touch with the Left Brigade.
    Z Coy. in R.17.b. as far forward as possible and keeping in touch with the Right Brigade.
    V Coy. with their guns arranged in 2 batteries of 8 will take up positions, one battery in L.35.c. and one in L.34.d.

5. Machine Gun Squadron 5th Cavalry Brigade will co-operate with the Cavalry.

6. **Ammunition.**

    Companies are responsible for their own belt filling and will at the earliest possible moment form dumps of belt boxes.

Battalion Headquarters is responsible for forming successive dumps of S.A.A. The first of these has been formed at BAZUEL R.1.d.6.0. The Battalion Transport Officer will be responsible for forming the succeeding ones.

Coys. when moving forward as a column will arrange to carry as much S.A.A. as possible.

7. **Barrages.**

V, X, Y, and Z Coys. will put down barrages as shown in Appendices I and II.

NOTE. (a) Y Coy. will fire with 8 guns on to area Y1, then on to Y2, and 8 guns on to Y3; then whole 16 guns will later fire on to Y4.
(b) Z Coy. 8 guns fire on Z1 and 8 on Z2 then all 16 on Z3.

8. The Battalion Signal Officer will arrange for communications to be maintained between all Companies and Battalion Headquarters throughout the battle. Coys. co-operating with Brigades will report gun positions to their Brigades and to Machine Gun Battalion Headquarters.

9. Z day and Zero hour will be notified later.

0. ACKNOWLEDGE.

Capt. & Adjt.,
32nd Battalion Machine Gun Corps.

2.11.1918.

Issued to :-

1. C.O.
2. ~~2nd-in-Command.~~ CMGO.
3. Adjutant.
4. Quartermaster.
5. Transport Officer.
6. Signal Officer.
7. O.C., "A" Coy.
8. O.C., "B" Coy.
9. O.C., "C" Coy.
10. O.C., "D" Coy.
11. H.Q.,32nd Div."G".
12. 6th Battn.M.G.Corps.
13. Royal Horse Gds. M.G.Coy.
14. M.G.Squadron, 5th Cav.Bde.
15. H.Q.,14th Inf.Bde.
16. H.Q.,96th Inf.Bde.
17. H.Q.,97th Inf.Bde.
18/19. War Diary.
20. File.

W.D.

APPENDIX IV

SECRET.

Copy No. 7

32ND BATTALION MACHINE GUN CORPS ORDER NO. 68.

1. As soon as 97th Brigade go through on November 5th, "A" and "C" Companies will bring up all their limbers and will assemble their Companies (Transport and G.B. Stores included) in Billets in a convenient place in or near Square G.33, near a forward route and will make all preparations for a forward move.

2. M.G. Battalion Headquarters and S.A.A. dump will probably move to this square in the afternoon.

3. Report position of Company Headquarters to present Battalion Headquarters, BAZUEL.

4. As soon as 97th Brigade have gone forward, O.C., "C" Company will provide limbers and will move the section Royal Horse Guards M.G. Coy. at present attached to him to T Roads L.19.d.central, (North of POMMEREUIL). This is to be carried out as early as possible tomorrow morning.

5. ACKNOWLEDGE.

Capt. & Adjt.,
32nd Battalion Machine Gun Corps.

4.11.1918.

SECRET. Copy No. 6

32ND BATTALION MACHINE GUN CORPS ORDER NO. 47.

1. The Red line has been approximately reached on the whole of the IX Corps front and on the front of the 25th Division. The enemy is reported to be in full retreat on the whole front.

2. The 32nd Division will pursue the enemy vigorously and it is hoped to reach the line L.24, 30, 36 tomorrow. The infantry will cross the Red line in G.29 and 35 and M.5, at 0800.

    THE RIGHT DIVISIONAL BOUNDARY WILL RUN FROM H.11.b.1.9 – GRAND BEART (EXCL) – ROAD JUNCTION N.5.c.0.3 – GRAND FAYT (INCL) – ROAD JUNCTION L.35.a.5.5. – THENCE DUE EAST.
    LEFT DIVISIONAL BOUNDARY AS BEFORE.

    The 139th Infantry Brigade, 46th Division will be on our right.

    The 66th Division will be on our left.

3. "B" and "D" Companies will co-operate with two Battalions of the 97th Brigade.

4. Each Company will move forward in depth on a two section front.

    Limbers will be used as much as possible and when not possible, pack transport.

    Successive positions will be consolidated as far as possible. Depth will be maintained during the move forward. Positions will be sited so as to cover all roads and approaches from the front, from the flanks and the country on either side of the roads. This can often be done by placing the machine guns in houses. When moving along roads which have not been cleared by the infantry an infantry escort will be arranged for between Company Commanders and the nearest Infantry unit. Owing to the change in the Southern boundary, new objectives will be arranged by O.C. Companies in accordance with above principles.

5. Battalion Headquarters will open at G.33.central tomorrow at 12.00 hours.

6. ACKNOWLEDGE.   B & D Coys only.

                                                Capt. & Adjt.,
4.11.1918.   32nd Battalion M. G. Corps.

Issued to :-

   1. O.C., "B" Coy.
   2. O.C., "D" Coy.
   3. H.Q., 32nd Div. "G".
   4. Adjutant.
   5/6. War Diary.
   7. File.

Army Form C. 2118.

WAR DIARY
or
INTELLIGENCE SUMMARY.
(Erase heading not required.)

1912

Instructions regarding War Diaries and Intelligence Summaries are contained in F. S. Regs., Part II. and the Staff Manual respectively. Title pages will be prepared in manuscript.

Place	Date	Hour	Summary of Events and Information	Remarks and references to Appendices
CERFONTAINE	1/12		Batt. in rest. Coys. carried out training and recreation.	NAMUR 1/100,000
	2/12			
	3/12			do
	4/12			
	5/12			
	6/12		Educational classes commenced.	
	7/12			
	8/12			
	9/12		Lt. F.H Broom to U.K. 6/12/18 (6 months).	
	10/12			
	11/12			
FLORENNES	12/12		Batt. moved to FLORENNES.	NAMUR 1/100,000
RIVIERE	13/12		Batt. moved to RIVIERE.	do
DURNAL	14/12		Batt. moved A+D Coys to CRUPET, H.Q. B+C Coys to DURNAL. B.-C. M.T. DELF to M.T. School (Reg. A.S.C. Offrs)	NAMUR 1/100,000
DURNAL	15/12 to 31/12		Batt. in rest. Training Educational recreational canned out. Capt. O.C. NORMAN joined for duty 23/12/18.	do

Confidential

WAR DIARY

of

32nd Bn. Machine Gun Corps.

from 1st Jan. 1919 to 31st Jan 1919

No 12.

Army Form C. 2118.

WAR DIARY
or
INTELLIGENCE SUMMARY. 1919.
(Erase heading not required.)

Place	Date	Hour	Summary of Events and Information	Remarks and references to Appendices
DURNAL	Jan 1st to Jan 28th		Coys carried out Training, Education & Recreational Training.	NAMUR 1/100,000
			Officers joined Lt. H.G. HENDRIE, M.C. from leave 8.1.19.	
			Lt. F.E. SLADE, " " 16.1.19.	
			2/Lt. E.E. SHORTHOUSE " " 16.1.19.	
			Capt. A.H. LEWIS, C.F. attached posted 18.1.19.	
			Major F. BLOOR to 30th M.G. Bn. 6.1.19	
			Major P. MATHISEN to Senior Officers' School, Aldershot. 6.1.19	
			Officers quitted	
			Lt. T. ROBERTS, M.C. Dispersal Draft. 10.1.19.	
			2/Lt. A.H. COLLINS, M.C. " " 10.1.19.	
			Lt. V. St C. HILL " " 10.1.19.	
			Major F.W. GORDON, M.C. " " 17.1.19.	
			2/Lt. W.T. EVANS " " 17.1.19.	
			Lt. C.H. SMITH, DCM. " " 21.1.19	
			Lt. A. d.F. MACMIN " " 21.1.19.	
			2/Lt. W.H. HAMMOND " " 19.1.19.	
			2/Lt. P.H. TYLER, M.C. " " 19.1.19.	
			Lt. H.S. JONES, M.C. " " 27.1.19.	
			Major J.B. NEILSON, M.C.	

Army Form C. 2118.

WAR DIARY
or
INTELLIGENCE SUMMARY.
(Erase heading not required.)

1919

Instructions regarding War Diaries and Intelligence Summaries are contained in F. S. Regs., Part II. and the Staff Manual respectively. Title pages will be prepared in manuscript.

Place	Date	Hour	Summary of Events and Information	Remarks and references to Appendices
DURNAL	29/11		C to B Sqn. marched to NAMECHE staying for night.	NAMUR 1/100,000
	30/11		C & B Sqn. entrained at NAMECHE for GERMANY.	
	31/11		C & B Sqn. arrived at BEVEL & detrained, afterwards marching into GERMANY Sector of the Defence line E. of the RHINE	GERMANY Sheet 22

Confidential

No 13

WAR DIARY

of

32ⁿᵈ Bⁿ Machine Gun Corps

from 1st February 1919 to 28th February 1919

No. 13

Army Form C. 2118.

WAR DIARY
or
INTELLIGENCE SUMMARY
(Erase heading not required.)

Instructions regarding War Diaries and Intelligence Summaries are contained in F. S. Regs., Part II. and the Staff Manual respectively. Title Pages will be prepared in manuscript.

Place	Date	Hour	Summary of Events and Information	Remarks and references to Appendices
DURNAL.	1/2/19 to 5/2/19		C. Coy in GEISTINGEN. D. Coy in OBERCASSEL. Coys carried out Training, Education and Recreational training	S.P.
			Capt & Q.M. BARKER. M.C. D.C.M. granted leave to U.K. 31/1/19.	S.P.
FAULX.	6/2/19		H.Q. A & B. Coys. moved to FAULX.	S.P.
NAMECHE.	7/2/19		H.Q. A & B. Coys moved to NAMECHE & THOM SAMSON.	S.P.
	8/2/19.		H.Q. A & B. Coys entrained for GERMANY.	S.P.
HERSEL.	9/2/19 to 11/2/19		H.Q. A & B. Coys. arrived at BEUEL detrained and marched to HERSEL. Coys. carried out training. Education & Recreational training	S.P.
	12/2/19		LIEUT. COL. P.E. ALDOUS. granted leave to NICE & U.K. Coys carried out Training, Education & Recreational training.	S.P.
	15/2/19		LIEUT. J.W. HANN. R.A.M.C. attached granted leave to U.K. 18.2.19. A boxing contest was held in the Gymnasium HERSEL	S.P.

Army Form C. 2118.

WAR DIARY
or
INTELLIGENCE SUMMARY

(Erase heading not required.)

Instructions regarding War Diaries and Intelligence Summaries are contained in F. S. Regs., Part II. and the Staff Manual respectively. Title Pages will be prepared in manuscript.

Place	Date	Hour	Summary of Events and Information	Remarks and references to Appendices
HERSEL.	20/2/19.		A dance was held in the Convent Hall HERSEL.	SR
	23.2.19		A whist drive was held in the evening Here HERSEL. Coys carried out Training, Education & Recreational Training.	SR
	25.2.19		LIEUT. O.B. SWAIN granted leave to U.K. 25.2.1919. Coys carried out Training, & Recreational Training.	SR
	26.2.19.		A lantern lecture was held in the Y.M............ HERSEL. Coys carried out Training, Education & Recreational Training.	SR
	27.2.19		Coys carried out Training, Education & Recreational Training.	SR
	28.2.19		2LT D.H. SHEWARD granted leave to U.K. 27.2.1919. Coys carried out Training, Education & Recreational Training.	SR

Confidential.

MD 14

WAR DIARY

of

32nd Bn Machine Gun Corps.

from 1st March 1919 to 31st March 1919.

No. 14

Army Form C. 2118.

WAR DIARY
or
INTELLIGENCE SUMMARY
(Erase heading not required.)

Instructions regarding War Diaries and Intelligence Summaries are contained in F. S. Regs., Part II. and the Staff Manual respectively. Title Pages will be prepared in manuscript.

Place	Date	Hour	Summary of Events and Information	Remarks and references to Appendices
HERSEL	1.3.19 to 3.3.19		Coys carried out Training, Education & Recreational Training.	S.P.
	3.3.19		LIEUT. W.M SLADE. granted leave to U.K. 3-3-1919. A Boxing Contest was held in the Gymnasium BONN.	
	4.3.19		Coys carried out Training, Education & Recreational Training. A Divisional Boxing Contest was held in the BEETHOVEN HALLE. BONN.	S.P.
	5.3.19		Coys carried out Training, Education & Recreational Training.	S.P.
	6.3.19		LIEUT. B.R WOODWARD. granted leave to U.K. 6-3-1919. A Lantern Lecture was held in the Gymnasium HERSEL. A Football match between H.Q. & 'C' Coy. was played at HERSEL.	S.P.
	7.3.19		Coys carried out Training, Education & Recreational Training.	S.P.

Army Form C. 2118.

WAR DIARY
or
INTELLIGENCE SUMMARY

(Erase heading not required.)

Instructions regarding War Diaries and Intelligence Summaries are contained in F.S. Regs., Part II and the Staff Manual respectively. Title Pages will be prepared in manuscript.

Place	Date	Hour	Summary of Events and Information	Remarks and references to Appendices
HERSEL.	9.3.19		Coys carried out Training, Education & Recreational Training.	S.F.
	9.3.19 to 12.3.19		A football match was played between A & B coys at HERSEL. Coys carried out Training, Education & Recreational Training.	
	13.3.19		A football match was played between 1st Division & 32nd M.G.B. at FLERZHEIM. Coys carried out Training, Education & Recreational Training.	S.F.
	14.3.19 to 17.3.19		A concert was held in B Coys dining hall HERSEL. Coy carried out Training, Education & Recreational Training.	S.F.
	18.3.19 to 22.3.19		A football match was played between 32nd B" & R.A.M.C. BONN. Coys carried out Training, Education & Recreational Training.	S.F.

Army Form C. 2118.

WAR DIARY
or
INTELLIGENCE SUMMARY

(Erase heading not required.)

Instructions regarding War Diaries and Intelligence Summaries are contained in F. S. Regs., Part II and the Staff Manual respectively. Title Pages will be prepared in manuscript.

Place	Date	Hour	Summary of Events and Information	Remarks and references to Appendices
HERSEL.	24.3.19. to 26.3.19		Coys carried out Training, Education & Recreational Training.	SP
	27.3.19.		A Lantern Lecture was held in "B" Coys dining hall HERSEL. A football match was played between H.Q. & A Coy. at HERSEL. Coys carried out Training, Education & Recreational Training.	SP
	28.3.19.		A & B Coys moved to RHEINDORF. H.Q. to BUSCHDORF.	SP
BUSCHDORF.	29.3.19. to 31.3.19		Coys carried out Training, Education & Recreational Training.	SP

H Callous Lieut Col.
C.mdg. 32nd (B). In. Bn.

Confidential.

WAR DIARY
of
32nd Bn. Machine Gun Corps
from 1st April 1919 to 30th April 1919.

No 15

32ND BATTALION.
MACHINE GUN
CORPS.
2 - MAY 1919

Army Form C. 2118

WAR DIARY
or
INTELLIGENCE SUMMARY
(Erase heading not required.)

Instructions regarding War Diaries and Intelligence Summaries are contained in F.S. Regs., Part II. and the Staff Manual respectively. Title Pages will be prepared in manuscript.

Place	Date	Hour	Summary of Events and Information	Remarks and references to Appendices
BUSCHDORF.	1.4.19.		A football match was played between "A" + "B" Coys at HERSEL. Lieut. J.A.J. ROBERTS. Lieut. RAYSON. H.G. Lieut. MICHELL.D.D. 2 Lieut. GUY.W.E. and 2 Lieut. McEWAN. granted leave to U.K. reported for duty with the battalion.	/a
"	2.4.19.		Coys carried out training, Education and Recreational training.	/a
"	3.4.19.		2 Lieut. WARD. J.J. reported for duty with the battalion.	/a
DRANSDORF.	4/4/19.		Headquarters moved to DRANSDORF.	/a
"	5.4.19.		A football match was played between "H.Q." and "A" Coy at DRANSDORF. Coys carried out training, Education and Recreational training. 2 Lieut. OXLEY.E. and Lieut. BOULTON.T.E. granted leave to U.K.	/a
"	6.4.19		CAPT + Q.M. W. McKINLAY and REV. HOPE. J.W.C.F. reported for duty with the battalion.	/a
"	7.4.19		Coys carried out training, Education and Recreational training. Capt. G. MASTERS. granted leave to U.K. REV. H.F. LEWIS. C.F. proceeded to Base depot.	/a

WAR DIARY.

PLACE.	DATE.	SUMMARY of EVENTS and INFORMATION.	REMARKS
DRANSDORF.	8.4.19.	A football match was played between 12th Loyal North Lancs and 32 Bn H.Q.C. at BONN. Lieut. C.T. HARDWICK granted leave to U.K.	/for
"	9.4.19.	Bt. Col. Temp. Brig. Gen-rl J. HARRINGTON. D.S.O. assumed Command of the Battalion.	/for
"	to 12.4.19.	Coys carried out training, Education and Recreational training. 〈 Lieut. H.W. LEES. 〈 2Lieut. J.T. LEE. granted leave to U.K.	/for
"	13.4.19.	〈 Lieut. T.C. MILLER proceeded to U.K. on duty. 〈 2 Lieut. C.T. JOSLIN. reported for duty with the Battalion.	/for
"	14.4.19.	A/Major. J.F. ALLIN. M.C. granted leave to U.K. Coys carried out training, education and recreational training Lieut. RAYSON. M.C. Admitted to Hospital. 2Lieut. A.L.R. HARRIS. granted leave to U.K.	/for
"	15.4.19.		/for
"	16.4.19.	〈 A/Major. HOOPER. M.C. 〈 T/Major. C.T. DENROCHE. disposal draft for U.K. 〈 Lieut. LOVETT. Coys carried out training, Education and Recreational training	/for

WAR DIARY
or
INTELLIGENCE SUMMARY

(Erase heading not required.)

Army Form C. 2118

Place	Date	Hour	Summary of Events and Information	Remarks and references to Appendices
DRANSDORF.	19/4/19		Lieut. J. YULE granted leave to U.K.	for
"	19/4/19		2Lieut. F. FLATTLEY. D.C.M. Lieut. A. ELLIOT. 2Lieut. W. BENTHAM. Lieut. J. DARNELEY. 2Lieut. L. SEARCHFIELD. reported for duty with the battalion.	for
"	20/4/19		"B" Coy held a Sports meeting at RHEINDORF.	for
"	21/4/19		"C" Coy held a Sports meeting at NIEDERPLEIS. Lieut. W.H. CLARK granted leave to U.K.	for
"	22/4/19		Lieut. A. ROME and Lieut. S. ROWE granted leave to U.K. Coys carried out training, recreational training and Education. The Divisional Commander inspected "A" & "B" Coys at RHEINDORF.	for
"	23/4/19 to 25/4/19		Lieut. E.T.J. TAPP granted leave to U.K. A football match was played against the 1/5th Border Regt. at BONN. Coys carried out training, Education and Recreational training.	for

WAR DIARY
or
INTELLIGENCE SUMMARY
(Erase heading not required.)

Army Form C. 2118

Place	Date	Hour	Summary of Events and Information	Remarks and references to Appendices
DRANSDORF	25/4/19		Lieut. Col. J. HARRINGTON. DSO. Granted leave to U.K.	&c
"	28/4/19		2 Lieut. J. MASON. Granted leave to U.K. Coys carried out training. Education & Recreational training. Divisional Commander inspected a composite Company of the Battalion at HANGELAR. Lieut. A. J. DALE. Granted leave to U.K. Lieut. G.B.M. REED. Granted leave to U.K.	&c
"	29/4/19		The Divisional Commander gave a lecture to the Officers of the Battalion at DRANSDORF.	&c
"	30/4/19		Capt. H.G. HENDRIE. M.C. Granted leave to U.K. Lieut. G.R. WILSON. M.C. reported for duty as Signals Officer. Coys carried out Education, training & Recreational training. Lieut. F.G. BEARD. M.C. Granted leave to U.K. A/Major J.F. ALLIN. M.C. Returned from leave.	&c

H. Aldous
Major M.G.
Cmdg. 32nd Bn.

Confidential.

WAR DIARY

of

32nd. Bn. Machine Gun Corps.

from 1st May 1919 to 31st May 1919.

No. 16

Army Form C. 2118

WAR DIARY
or
INTELLIGENCE SUMMARY
(Erase heading not required.)

Place	Date	Hour	Summary of Events and Information	Remarks and references to Appendices
DRANSDORF	1.5.19		Coys carried out training, education and recreational training. Major J.F. ALLIN M.C. returned from leave.	JH.
"	2.5.19		Lieut D.S. LINDSAY. Granted leave to U.K. Lieut A.L.R. HARRIS. returned from leave. Coys carried out training, education and recreational training.	JH.
"	3.5.19		Lieut A.O. THOMPSON. Granted leave to U.K. Coys carried out training, education and recreational training.	JH.
"	4.5.19		Lieut D.D. MICHELL. Granted leave to U.K. Lieut J. YULE returned from leave.	JH.
"	5.5.19		Capt & Q.M. W. McKINLAY. granted leave to U.K. Coys carried out training, education and recreational training.	JH.
"	6.5.19		Lieut C.K. MOSELEY. and Lieut W.E. GUY. granted leave to U.K.	JH.

WAR DIARY
or
INTELLIGENCE SUMMARY

(Erase heading not required.)

Army Form C. 2118

Place	Date	Hour	Summary of Events and Information	Remarks and references to Appendices
DRANSDORF	7.5.19.		Coys carried out training, education and recreational training.	J.H.
"	8.5.19.		Lieut. W.H. CLARKE. returned from leave	J.H.
"	9.5.19.		Lieut. S. ROWE and Lieut. H.W. LEES. returned from leave.	J.H.
"	10.5.19.		Lieut. Col. J. HARTINGTON.D.S.O.returned from leave.	J.H.
"	11.5.19.		"A" Coy relieved "C" Coy. "A" Coy from RHEINDORF. "C" Coy from NIEDERPLEIS. "B" Coy relieved "D" Coy. "B" Coy from RHEINDORF. "D" Coy from OBERCASSEL.	J.H.
"	12.5.19		Capt. A.J.C. FRESHWATER. M.C. granted leave to U.K.	J.H.

WAR DIARY or INTELLIGENCE SUMMARY

Army Form C. 2118

Place	Date	Hour	Summary of Events and Information	Remarks and references to Appendices
DRANSDORF	13.5.19.		The Commander in Chief inspected a composite Company of the Battalion at HANGELAR.	J.H.
"	14.5.19 to 16.5.19		Coys carried out training, education and Recreational training.	J.H.
"	16.5.19		Lieut. D.S. LINDSAY returned from leave.	J.H.
"	17.5.19 to		Lieut. A.O. THOMPSON returned from leave.	J.H.
"	21.5.19		Coys carried out training, education and recreational training. 2/Lieut. J. GOODWILL granted leave to U.K. Lieut. D.D. MICHELL returned from leave.	J.H.
"	22.5.19		Capt + Q.M. W. McKINLAY returned from leave. Lieut. C.K. MOSELEY and Lieut. W.E. GUY returned from leave.	J.H.
"	23.5.19 to 24.5.19		Coys carried out training, education and recreational training.	J.H.
"	25.5.19		2Lieut. J.P. CARBERY, 2Lieut. THOMAS and 2Lieut. PELLUET reported for duty with the Battalion.	J.H.

WAR DIARY
or
INTELLIGENCE SUMMARY
(Erase heading not required.)

Army Form C. 2118

Instructions regarding War Diaries and Intelligence Summaries are contained in F.S. Regs, Part II. and the Staff Manual respectively. Title Pages will be prepared in manuscript.

Place	Date	Hour	Summary of Events and Information	Remarks and references to Appendices
DRANSDORF	26.5.19 to 27.5.19		Coys carried out training, education and recreational training.	JH.
"	28.5.19		The Divisional Commander inspected "B" Company at O.B.R. HOLTORF. Capt A.J.C. FRESHWATER returned from leave.	JH.
VILLICH	29.5.19		Headquarters moved to VILLICH. "D" Coy moved to MONDORF. "C" Coy moved to SIEGLAR.	JH.
	30.5.19		Coys carried out training, education and recreational training.	JH.
	31.5.19		LIEUT. E.J. TAPP. LIEUT. H.W. LEES. to dispersal draft for U.K. 2 LIEUT. D.H. SHEWARD)	JH.

J. Harrington Lt. Col.
Comg. 32nd Bn. M.G.C.

Confidential:

WAR DIARY

of

32nd. Bn. Machine Gun Corps.

from 1st June 1919 to 30th June 1919.

No. 17. N

Army Form C. 2118

WAR DIARY
or
INTELLIGENCE SUMMARY
(Erase heading not required.)

Place	Date	Hour	Summary of Events and Information	Remarks and references to Appendices
VILLICH (GERMANY).	1.6.19		Coys carried out training, Education and Recreational training. 2 Lt. T.F. TROWER returned from leave to U.K.	
"	2.6.19		2/Lieut. MASON. J. returned from Educational Course at OXFORD. Major. PETRE. W.H. Lieut. HITCHCOCK. W.E.R. Lieut. STEWART. C.H. Lieut. BULLIVANT. W. } reported to the Battalion for duty. Lieut. WILDERS. H.F. Lieut. DUGGAN. C.E. M.C. Lieut. SLACK. J.D.G. Lieut. ALSTON. F.J. Lieut. GRESHAM. H.	
"	3.6.19		Coys carried out Training, Education and Recreational training.	

Harrington Lt/Col
Cmd. 32nd Bn. M.G.C.

WAR DIARY or INTELLIGENCE SUMMARY

Army Form C. 2118

Place	Date	Hour	Summary of Events and Information	Remarks and references to Appendices
VILLICH (GERMANY)	4.6.19. to 5.6.19		MAJOR W.E. ROBERTON. M.C. Granted leave to U.K. Coys carried out training, Education and Recreational training.	
"	6.6.19.		LIEUT. COLVERWELL. R.E. reported to the Battalion for duty.	
"	7.6.19.		LIEUT. WILDER. H.F. Granted leave to U.K. The Divisional Commander inspected "C" Company at SIEGLAR. MAJOR W.E. SMALLMAN returned from leave to U.K. Coys carried out training, Education and Recreational training.	
"	8.6.19.		CAPT. A. ROME proceeded to R.F.A Course at WAHN. 2 LIEUT. E.E. SHORTHOUSE. granted leave to U.K.	
"	9.6.19.		2 LIEUT. E.E. SHORTHOUSE Granted leave to U.K. LIEUT. GOODWELL. J. returned from leave to U.K. LIEUT. GRIFFIN. J. reported from Hospital. MAJOR. W.E. SMALLMAN to disperbal draft for U.K.	
"	10.6.19.		The Divisional Commander inspected "D" company at MONDORF.	

J. Harrington M/C
Cmdg. 32nd Bn. M.G.C.

Army Form C. 2118

WAR DIARY
or
INTELLIGENCE SUMMARY
(Erase heading not required.)

Instructions regarding War Diaries and Intelligence Summaries are contained in F. S. Regs., Part II. and the Staff Manual respectively. Title Pages will be prepared in manuscript.

Place	Date	Hour	Summary of Events and Information	Remarks and references to Appendices
VILLICH	11.6.19.			
	12.6.19.		Lieut. D.D. Michell. 2 Lieut. J.A.S. Roberts. and Lieut. F.E. Slade disposal draft to U.K.	
	13.6.19.		Lieut. W.E.A. Hitchcock. granted leave to U.K.	
	14.6.19.		Lieut. W.M. Slade. granted leave to U.K. Companies carried out Training, Education & Recreational Training.	
	16.6.19.		Lieut Napier-Hemy granted leave to U.K.	
	17.6.19.		" McEwan H.H. granted leave to U.K. Boys carried out Training, Education & Recreational Training	
	18.6.19.		Lieut O.B. Swain. granted leave to U.K.	
SIEGBURG.	19.6.19		H.Q. & C Coy moved to SIEGBURG. A Coy " " SCHINNEREI. B " " " GEILGEN & HOHOLZ. D " " " MENDEN.	

Anningham ....
Comdg. 32nd Bn. M.G.C.

Army Form C. 2118.

WAR DIARY
or
INTELLIGENCE SUMMARY.
(Erase heading not required.)

Instructions regarding War Diaries and Intelligence Summaries are contained in F. S. Regs., Part II. and the Staff Manual respectively. Title pages will be prepared in manuscript.

Place	Date	Hour	Summary of Events and Information	Remarks and references to Appendices
SIEGBURG	20-6-19		Coys carried out Training, Education & Recreational Training.	
	21-6-19 to 24-6-19		Coys carried out Training, Education + Recreational Training.	
	25-6-19 to 27-6-19		Major W. HARRISON. M.C. granted leave to U.K. Coys carried out Training, Education + Recreational Training.	
	28-6-19		PEACE Signed.	
VILICH	29-6-19		H.Q. moved to VILICH. C Coy – SIEGLAR.	
	30-6-19		B Coy – OBERCASSEL.	

J. Stronghtn ?.?.?.
Comdg. 32nd Bgr. M.G.C.

WAR DIARY
INTELLIGENCE SUMMARY.

33rd Br. M.G. Corps

Army Form C. 2118.

Place	Date	Hour	Summary of Events and Information	Remarks and references to Appendices
VILICH	1-7-19		Boys carried out Training, Education + Recreational Training.	
	2-7-19		A boy moved to NIEDER PLEIS.	
	3-7-19		Boys carried out Training, Education + Recreation Training.	
			LIEUT. J. GRIFFIN. granted leave to U.K.	
	4-7-19 to 6-7-19		Boys carried out Training, Education + Recreation Training.	
	7-7-19		LIEUT. G.T. JOSLIN granted leave to U.K.	
			LIEUT. L. RICHARDS to U.K.	
			LIEUT. R.E. CULVERWELL to U.K. } On Duty	
			LIEUT. E.R. ELPHICK to U.K. } Auth. Lanc. Div. A451.	

Army Form C. 2118.

WAR DIARY
or
INTELLIGENCE SUMMARY.
(Erase heading not required.)

Instructions regarding War Diaries and Intelligence Summaries are contained in F. S. Regs., Part II. and the Staff Manual respectively. Title pages will be prepared in manuscript.

Place	Date	Hour	Summary of Events and Information	Remarks and references to Appendices
VILICH	7-7-1919		LIEUT. N.C. FOUNTAIN. to U.K. } FOR DUTY. AUTH. LANCS. DIV. A.451.	
			" H.H. McEWAN " "	
			" W.E. GUY " "	
			" J.F. ALSTON " "	
			" J. DARNELEY " "	
			" L.G.W. SEARCHFIELD " "	
	8-7-1919		Boys carried out Training, Education & Recreational Training.	
	10-7-1919		LIEUT. A.V. ELLIOTT. granted leave to U.K.	
	11-7-1919		Boys carried out Training Education & Recreational Training	
	12-7-1919		LIEUT. P.J. CARBERY. returned from U.K.	
	13-7-1919		LIEUT. G.P. BURDETT. granted leave to U.K.	
	14-7-1919		Boys carried out Training, Education & Recreational Training.	

Army Form C. 2118.

WAR DIARY
or
INTELLIGENCE SUMMARY.
(Erase heading not required.)

Place	Date	Hour	Summary of Events and Information	Remarks and references to Appendices
VILIC.H.	15-7-1919.		Boys carried out Training Education & Recreational Training. 2 Lieut. P.J. CARBERY. to U.K. Auth. Lancs. Div. N.4.51. Lieut. Colonel. J. HARINGTON. C.M.G. D.S.O. to U.K. Auth. W.A.N.P.T/690/M.P.G.2(o)	
	16-7-1919.		Boys carried out Training Education & Recreational Training. 2 Lieut. W. BENTHAM. granted Leave to U.K.	
	17-7-1919		Major F.C. ALDOUS D.S.O. returned from Leave (PARIS). Boys carried out Training, Education.	
	18-7-1919.		Lieut. Colonel. T.R. McCREADY. D.S.O. M.C. returned & assumed command of the Battalion.	

Army Form C. 2118.

WAR DIARY
or
INTELLIGENCE SUMMARY.
(Erase heading not required.)

Place	Date	Hour	Summary of Events and Information	Remarks and references to Appendices
VILICH	19-7-1919		Battalion Sports were held at VILICH.	
	20-7-1919		LIEUT. C.E. DUGGAN M.C. granted leave U.K. Boys carried out training, Education & Recreational	
	22-7-1919		training.	
	22-7-1919		LIEUT. H. GRESHAM granted leave to U.K.	
	23-7-1919		Boys carried out Training, Education etc.	
	24-7-1919		LIEUT. C.T. HARDWICK granted leave to U.K.	
	25-7-1919		Boys carried out Training, Education & Recreational Training.	
	27-7-1919		LIEUT. E. OXLEY granted leave to U.K.	
	28-7-1919		LIEUT. C.H. STEWART to U.K. AUTH LANCS DIV. 316.A.G.9(0). Boys carried out Training, Education, & Recreational Training.	

Army Form C. 2118.

WAR DIARY
or
INTELLIGENCE SUMMARY.
(Erase heading not required.)

Place	Date	Hour	Summary of Events and Information	Remarks and references to Appendices
VILICH	29-7-19		LIEUT. H.F. WILDERS granted leave to U.K.	
	30-7-19 to 31-7-19		Boys carried out Training, Education & Recreational Training.	
	31-7-19		LIEUT. J.S. LEE granted leave to U.K.	
	31-7-19		LIEUT. GOODWILL granted leave to U.K.	

E. W. Kearny
Lt. Col.
O.C. 39nd Bn. made alterable

Lancashire Division "A".

   Herewith copy of War Diary for August sent to you please for transmission to Xth Corps as per C.R.O. 4208. The duplicate copy has been sent to O. i. c Records as per C.R.O. 4086.

                 Lieut.Colonel,
3.9.19.   Commanding 32nd Battn. Machine Gun Corps.

CONFIDENTIAL

WAR DIARY

of

32ND BN MACHINE GUN CORPS

from 1st August 1919 to 31st August 1919.

No. 19.

Army Form C. 2118.

WAR DIARY
or
INTELLIGENCE SUMMARY.
(Erase heading not required.)

Instructions regarding War Diaries and Intelligence Summaries are contained in F. S. Regs., Part II. and the Staff Manual respectively. Title pages will be prepared in manuscript.

Place	Date	Hour	Summary of Events and Information	Remarks and references to Appendices
VILICH	1-8-19		Boys carried out Training, Education & Recreational Training.	
	2-8-19		H.Q. moved from GIESLAR to VILICH.	
	4-8-19		B Coy moved from OBERCASSEL to GIESLAR.	
	"	"	Boys carried out Training, Education & Recreational Training.	
	"	"	LIEUT. P.P. STEVENS attended leave to U.K.	
	5-8-19		Boys carried out Training, Education & Recreational Training.	
	7-8-19			
	8-8-19		Boys carried out Training, Education & Recreational Training.	
	"		MAJOR E.H. PETRE to U.K. West Lancs Div. A841.	
	9-8-19		Boys carried out Training, Education & Recreational Training.	

Army Form C. 2118.

WAR DIARY
or
INTELLIGENCE SUMMARY.
(Erase heading not required.)

Instructions regarding War Diaries and Intelligence Summaries are contained in F. S. Regs., Part II. and the Staff Manual respectively. Title pages will be prepared in manuscript.

Place	Date	Hour	Summary of Events and Information	Remarks and references to Appendices
VILICH	11-8-19		Boys carried out Training Education & Recreational Training.	
	12-8-19		LIEUT. C.L. O'SHAUGHNESSEY. D.S.O. granted leave to U.K. Major T.F. ALLIN M.C. granted leave to U.K. Boys carried out Training Education & Recreational Training.	
	13-8-19		Boys carried out Training Education & Recreational Training. LIEUT. M. CLIFFORD granted leave to U.K.	
	14-8-19		Boys carried out Training Education & Recreational Training.	
	15-8-19		LIEUT. A.L. HARRIS granted leave to U.K. Boys carried out Training Education & Recreational Training.	
	16-8-19			

WAR DIARY
or
INTELLIGENCE SUMMARY.

Army Form C. 2118.

Place	Date	Hour	Summary of Events and Information	Remarks and references to Appendices
VILICH	17-8-19		Church Parade for H.Q and B Coy. of Seinelow	
	18-8-19		Training Suspended on account of Rhine Army Horse Show. Won 3rd Prize for 4 Mule Team. G.S. Limbered wagon. Lieut J. JULE proceeds leave to UK.	
	19.8/19		Training & Education carried out. Lieut S. Rowe leave to UK	
	20/8/19		Training & Education Carried out	
	21/8/19		Training & Education continued. Lieut A.J. Thomas proceeds leave to UK. Majors C.B.A. Jackson and W. Harrison M.C. proceed to England. Rejoins O'Brien	
	6/8/10		One section of 2nd Coy moves to Troisdorf and took over guarding in the Powder Factory. Captain G. Mateo (grants) leave to UK	

WAR DIARY
INTELLIGENCE SUMMARY.
(Erase heading not required.)

Army Form C. 2118.

Place	Date	Hour	Summary of Events and Information	Remarks and references to Appendices
Wich	23/8/19		Inspection of Kit & billets	
	24/8/19		Church Parade for H.Q. and B Coys in morning. Captain W. McKinley M.C. to hospital, newcastle, Lt CHT PELLVET granted leave to UK	
	25/8/19		Training suspended owing to D Coy Horse Show. 12 mouth of Battalion won prizes. C Coy won eighth competition. Lieut A.G. BERESFORD granted leave to UK	
	26/8/19		Training and Education as usual. 2/Lt A. DUDDIN granted leave to UK	
TROISDORF	27/8/19		Battalion moved to Barracks at TROISDORF, move completed by 1400 hours.	
	28/8/19		Day devoted to cleaning & straightening up	
	29/8/19 30/8/19		Training & Education Carried out. Lieut D.S. LINDSAY M.C. granted leave to UK. 29/8/19. Capt. H.G. HENDRIE M.C. on 30/8.	

WAR DIARY

INTELLIGENCE SUMMARY.

Army Form C. 2118.

Place	Date	Hour	Summary of Events and Information	Remarks and references to Appendices
TROISDORF	31/8/19		Battalion Church Parade 1000 hours. Lieut. E. BREEN granted leave to U.K. F. FLATTLEY	

W. Moresby
Lt. Col.
Commanding 3/5 Bn. M.G.C.

Confidential.

WAR DIARY

of

32nd Bn. M.G.C. Corps.

from 1st Sept. 1919 to 30th Sept. 1919.

Nº 20.

Army Form C. 2118.

WAR DIARY
or
INTELLIGENCE SUMMARY.
(Erase heading not required.)

Instructions regarding War Diaries and Intelligence Summaries are contained in F. S. Regs., Part II. and the Staff Manual respectively. Title pages will be prepared in manuscript.

Place	Date	Hour	Summary of Events and Information	Remarks and references to Appendices
TROISDORF	1/9/19 to 5/9/19		Training and Education in mornings, bathing in afternoons. Lieut. F.G. BEARD M.C. granted leave to U.K. 1/9/19. " " G. MASON " " " " 2/9/19. " " C.K. MOSELEY " " " " 3/9/19. " " J.S. STOREY " " " " 5/9/19.	
	6-9-19		Inspection of Barracks by C.O.	
	7-9-19		Battalion Church Parade 10.00 hours.	
	8-9-19		Capt. A.J.C. FRESHWATER M.C. granted leave to U.K. 8.9.19.	
	9-9-19		Lieut. G.P. BURDETT to Concent. Camp for dispersal. Lieut. SLADE } to Concent. Camp for " ELLIOTT } dispersal. " O'SHAUGHNESSEY D.S.O. } " YULE }	
	10-9-19		Coys. carried out Training, Education & Recreational Training. Lieut. MARTIN granted leave to U.K.	

D. D. & L., London, E.C.
(A8001) Wt. W2774/M2031 750000 5/17 Sch 52 Forms/C2118/14

Army Form C. 2118.

WAR DIARY
or
INTELLIGENCE SUMMARY.
(Erase heading not required.)

Instructions regarding War Diaries and Intelligence Summaries are contained in F. S. Regs., Part II. and the Staff Manual respectively. Title pages will be prepared in manuscript.

Place	Date	Hour	Summary of Events and Information	Remarks and references to Appendices
Troisdorf	11-9-19		Coys. carried out Training, Education, etc.	
	12-9-19 to		Coys. carried out Training, Education, etc.	
	13-9-19		Inspection of Barracks by C.O. MAJOR O.C. NORMAN granted leave to U.K.	
	14-9-19		Battalion Church Parade 10.00 hrs.	
	15-9-19		Inspection of Barracks by Commander-in-Chief.	
	16-9-19 to		Coys. carried out Training, Education, etc.	
	17-9-19.		Capt. A. ROME granted leave to U.K. RHINE ARMY BOXING Semi-finals COLOGNE.	
	18-9-19		Coys. carried out Training, Education, & Recreational Training.	

Army Form C. 2118.

WAR DIARY
or
INTELLIGENCE SUMMARY.
(Erase heading not required.)

Instructions regarding War Diaries and Intelligence Summaries are contained in F. S. Regs., Part II. and the Staff Manual respectively. Title pages will be prepared in manuscript.

Place	Date	Hour	Summary of Events and Information	Remarks and references to Appendices
Troisdorf	18-9-19.		Boxing Finals in Cologne.	
	19-9-19		Coys. carried out Training, etc.	
	20-9-19 to		Lieut. SLACK granted leave to U.K.	
			Battalion Church Parade 10.00 hrs.	
	22-9-19		Coy. carried out Training, etc.	
	23-9-19		MAJOR ROBERTON M.C. granted leave to U.K.	
			CAPT. DOSSITTOR (A.E.D) " " "	
	24-9-19 to		Coys. carried out Training, Education & Recreational Training.	
	26-9-19		Lieut. E.E. SHORTHOUSE granted leave to U.K. 27-8-19-19.
			Lieut. C.H. ANDERSON to Concentration Camp 16-9-1919.
			Capt. F.W.E. HOOD " " 16-9-1919.
			Capt. J.S. RUSSELL " "
	27-9-19		Inspection of Barracks by C.O.	

Army Form C. 2118.

WAR DIARY
or
INTELLIGENCE SUMMARY.
(Erase heading not required.)

Instructions regarding War Diaries and Intelligence Summaries are contained in F. S. Regs., Part II. and the Staff Manual respectively. Title pages will be prepared in manuscript.

Place	Date	Hour	Summary of Events and Information	Remarks and references to Appendices
Troisdorf	28-9-19		Battalion Church Parade 10.00 hrs.	
	29-9-19 to 30-9-19		Coys carried out Training, Education, & Recreational Training.	

[Signature]
Lt. Col.
Commanding 3rd Bn. A.G.R.

32 Bn M.T.C.

Army Form C. 2118.

WAR DIARY
or
INTELLIGENCE SUMMARY.

(Erase heading not required.)

Instructions regarding War Diaries and Intelligence Summaries are contained in F. S. Regs., Part II. and the Staff Manual respectively. Title pages will be prepared in manuscript.

Place	Date	Hour	Summary of Events and Information	Remarks and references to Appendices
TROISDORF	1-10-19		Boys carried out Training Education + Recreational Training.	
	3-10-19		Inspection of Barracks by C.O.	
	4-10-19			
	5-10-19		Church Parade (Bn) at 10.30 hrs	
	6-10-19		Boys carried out Training Education + Recreational Training.	
	7-10-19		Boys carried out Training, Education + Recreational Training	
			Inspection of Barracks by Corps Commander	
	8-10-19		Boys carried out Training Education	
	9-10-19		Boys carried out Training Education + Recreational	
	10-10-19		Training	
	11-10-19		Inspection of Barracks by C.O.	
	12-10-19		Battalion Church Parade 10.30 hrs.	

Army Form C. 2118.

WAR DIARY
or
INTELLIGENCE SUMMARY.
(Erase heading not required.)

Instructions regarding War Diaries and Intelligence Summaries are contained in F. S. Regs., Part II. and the Staff Manual respectively. Title pages will be prepared in manuscript.

Place	Date	Hour	Summary of Events and Information	Remarks and references to Appendices
TROISDORF	13-10-19.		Boys carried out Training, Education & Recreational Training.	
"	14-10-19.		Lieut Col. H.S. Crady. D.S.O. M.C. granted 14 days leave to U.K. Boys carried out Training Education &c. Major F.C. ALDOUS, assumes command of the Battalion from this date.	
"	15-10-19.		Boys carried out Training, Education & Recreational Training.	
"	16-10-19.		Boys carried out Training, Education & Recreational Training.	
"	17-10-19			
	18-10-19.		Inspection of Barracks by C.O. Lieut. Col. H.S. Crady D.S.O. M.C. from leave & resumes command of Battalion from this date.	

Army Form C. 2118.

WAR DIARY
or
INTELLIGENCE SUMMARY.
(Erase heading not required.)

Instructions regarding War Diaries and Intelligence Summaries are contained in F. S. Regs., Part II. and the Staff Manual respectively. Title pages will be prepared in manuscript.

Place	Date	Hour	Summary of Events and Information	Remarks and references to Appendices
TROISDORF	19-10-19		Bn exercise & minute parade at 10.00 hrs.	
	20-10-19		Packing & Checking Stores	
	22-10-19			
	23-10-19		Handing in Stores	
	"			
	26-10-19			
	27-10-19		Checking Stores & handing in	
	"			
	29-10-19			
	30-10-19		Checking Stores & handing in	
	"			
	31-10-19		Checking Stores & handing in	

T. W. Tweedy.
Lieut. Col.
C. M. O. G., 32nd Bn Machine Gun Corps.